Selected Titles in ABC-CLIO's
CONTEMPORARY
WORLD ISSUES
Series

For a complete list of titles in this series, please visit
www.abc-clio.com.

Books in the Contemporary World Issues series address vital issues in today's society, such as genetic engineering, pollution, and biodiversity. Written by professional writers, scholars, and nonacademic experts, these books are authoritative, clearly written, up-to-date, and objective. They provide a good starting point for research by high school and college students, scholars, and general readers as well as by legislators, businesspeople, activists, and others.

Each book, carefully organized and easy to use, contains an overview of the subject, a detailed chronology, biographical sketches, facts and data and/or documents and other primary-source material, a directory of organizations and agencies, annotated lists of print and nonprint resources, and an index.

Readers of books in the Contemporary World Issues series will find the information they need to have a better understanding of the social, political, environmental, and economic issues facing the world today.

VIRTUAL LIVES

A Reference Handbook

James D. Ivory

**CONTEMPORARY
WORLD ISSUES**

 ABC-CLIO

Santa Barbara, California • Denver, Colorado • Oxford, England

3/27/13
Ln
#58 –

Copyright 2012 by ABC-CLIO, LLC

Library of Congress Cataloging-in-Publication Data

Ivory, James.
    Virtual lives : a reference handbook / James D. Ivory.
        p. cm. — (Contemporary world issues)
    Includes index.
    ISBN 978-1-59884-585-3 (hardback) — ISBN 978-1-59884-586-0 (ebook)
1. Information technology—Social aspects.   2. Virtual reality.   I. Title.
    HM851.I96   2012
    303.48'33—dc23   2011036431

ISBN: 978-1-59884-585-3
EISBN: 978-1-59884-586-0

16 15 14 13 12   1 2 3 4 5

This book is also available on the World Wide Web as an eBook.
Visit www.abc-clio.com for details.

ABC-CLIO, LLC
130 Cremona Drive, P.O. Box 1911
Santa Barbara, California 93116-1911

Contents

Preface

In a way, virtual worlds filled with imaginary places, people, and events have existed throughout the history of humankind in the form of the stories we have created and told to one another through speech, writing, print, film, and television. Although these stories have been fictional, they have had social, cultural, and economic impact by influencing the way people have thought, felt, and behaved in their real lives.

Today, the fictional settings we create can impact our society in a way that is arguably unprecedented in human history because of the technologies we can now use to represent our virtual worlds. We have long been able to pick up a book and travel to a faraway place in our minds or visit a theater to look through the eyes of a film character, but new computer applications now allow us to enter virtual worlds vicariously through the Internet using avatar characters that we control. In these virtual worlds, we can interact with one another and with the virtual environment. Our actions in virtual worlds influence the virtual environment and the people in it, and they in turn influence us.

What do people do in virtual worlds? Many of them do fantastic things they cannot do in the real world. They fight heroic battles against fantastic creatures. They wander beloved places from literature and film. They take great risks and reap legendary rewards. But many others do the same things that people do every day in the real world. They go shopping for clothes. They do routine chores. They dance in night clubs. They visit with friends. They fall in love.

Whether people in virtual worlds are engaged in fantastic quests or mundane tasks, their actions have powerful implications for the real world. Millions of people use virtual worlds, and what they do in virtual worlds has a significant impact on them as individuals and on all of us as a society. It may be tempting to dismiss virtual worlds as mere games or silly hobbies, but to do so would be to turn a blind eye to a growing body of knowledge that tells us virtual worlds are having profound effects. Virtual worlds are influencing the lives of their users, and they are influencing the economies, social institutions, and cultures of our real world. Some of the implications of the growth of virtual worlds are troubling, and others are promising.

When Mim Vasan at ABC-CLIO contacted me about writing this book, I was quick to commit to the project because I believe it is important for us to understand the prominent and growing role that virtual worlds have in our real world today. It is also important for us to be aware of the technological and cultural history that led to their development. You don't need to use virtual worlds to benefit from learning about them, because they are affecting all of us whether we use them or not. I wrote this book for anyone seeking to learn more about virtual worlds, including virtual world users, students, parents, educators, policy makers, programmers, hopeful entrepreneurs, researchers, and many others.

This book describes the history, development, function, and societal impact of virtual worlds based on information gathered from an extensive body of academic and industry research, news items, and professional commentary and criticism related to virtual worlds and related technologies. This book is meant to serve as a useful research and reference tool for students in high schools and universities, as well as for researchers and anyone else interested in learning more about virtual worlds, by consolidating and summarizing a broad range of information about virtual worlds here in an easily accessible format.

The first three chapters of this book provide a narrative overview about the history, function, audience, and social impact of virtual worlds. Chapter 1 defines describes concepts and definitions related to virtual worlds, including the definition for the term "virtual world" that is used in this book, and gives a history of virtual worlds from the first virtual world to the latest developments and research on virtual worlds and related applications at the time this book was completed. Chapter 1 also discusses virtual worlds' early technological precursors and cultural inspirations, some of which date back many decades before the advent of virtual worlds.

Chapter 2 describes the global audience of virtual worlds, as well as virtual world users' individual characteristics, motivations for using virtual worlds, and activities within virtual worlds. It also describes how virtual worlds function and how they are developed.

Chapter 3 focuses on issues related to the individual and societal impact of virtual worlds. Issues of concern covered in chapter 3 include virtual worlds' potential for excessive use, effects of violent content in virtual worlds, effects of virtual worlds on users' perceptions of the real world, and misbehavior by users within virtual worlds. Chapter 3 also covers potential benefits that virtual worlds present, including opportunities for social interaction within virtual worlds, educational applications of virtual worlds, virtual worlds' utility to behavioral researchers, and commercial opportunities within virtual worlds.

Chapters 4 through 6 of this book provide additional information about events, people, and organizations related to virtual worlds in an accessible reference format. Chapter 4 is a chronology of events related to virtual worlds that gives a timeline of relevant developments over a period of more than a century. Chapter 5 is a series of brief biographical sketches describing some notable people related to virtual worlds, including computer programmers, game designers, business entrepreneurs, and academic researchers. Chapter 6 presents facts, figures, and data related to virtual worlds in a series of tables, charts, and images.

Chapters 7 and 8 of this book point to other resources that may be useful to anyone interested in virtual worlds. Chapter 7 lists a number of commercial and nonprofit organizations related to virtual worlds, providing contact information and some information about each organization listed. Chapter 8 is a bibliography of many relevant print and online resources, including books, book chapters, articles, and websites. A reference entry for each of these sources is accompanied by a brief annotation describing it.

Finally, a glossary provides definitions for technical terms and jargon related to virtual worlds to help explain any terms that some readers may encounter and find unfamiliar, both when reading this book and when exploring other resources related to virtual worlds.

In sum, this book is meant to be a comprehensive resource about virtual worlds and their place in our real world. I hope that you find it useful. I learned a lot about virtual worlds while writing this book, and I hope you will be able to learn some useful and interesting information about virtual worlds by reading it.

Acknowledgments

I want to thank a number of people who contributed to this book. Mim Vasan, Robin Tutt, Jessica Ramsay, and Jane Messah at ABC-CLIO were very helpful and patient throughout the preparation of this book. As my employer, the Department of Communication at Virginia Tech has provided generous financial support and access to high-quality resources ever since the department first hired me and gave me the chance to pursue an academic career in research and teaching at a top institution. Dr. Jarrod Williams, a skilled emergency physician by trade, also has tremendous insight about the function and social role of virtual worlds and related technologies, and he has been generous in sharing his knowledge and perspectives with me. Finally, my wife Adrienne and my two daughters have provided endless support, inspiration, and motivation, for which I am always grateful.

1

Definitions, Background, and History

When science-fiction authors such as Vernor Vinge (1981), William Gibson (1984), and Neal Stephenson (1992) wrote of people interacting online in three-dimensional virtual spaces, their stories were just that: science fiction. Now, though, virtual worlds are very much a reality. Hundreds of millions go online to socialize, play games, and even work via electronic avatars they use to represent themselves in electronic virtual environments, and the number of people using virtual worlds is continually increasing.

By October 2010, more than 12 million subscribers were paying a monthly fee (usually $14.99, with some discounts for purchasing long-term subscriptions) to fight for fame and fortune in *World of Warcraft*, one of the most popular examples of the massively multiplayer online role-playing game (MMORPG) virtual world genre (Blizzard Entertainment 2010). By April 2011, as many as 18,000 users were creating new accounts each day in the popular virtual world *Second Life*, a free-to-access virtual world that allows users to customize avatars, buy virtual land, create virtual objects, and buy and sell virtual goods and services to each other online. In 2010, *Second Life* users spent a total of more than 400 million hours in the virtual world. These are just two of the many virtual worlds available to users, with more virtual worlds available for more purposes each year. With all of those users comes economic impact. During the first quarter of 2011, *Second Life* users held $29.3 million worth of the virtual world's "Linden Dollars" currency to spend on goods and services in the virtual world.

Given the substantial and growing popularity of virtual worlds and their significant commercial importance, virtual

1

worlds are becoming an everyday part of the media landscape for more and more of us, but they are still a new enough phenomenon that their eventual role in society is uncertain. In the years to come, we may see virtual worlds become the default way that we interact, shop, and learn online, or we may see virtual worlds remain something of a niche media format compared to other more established online interfaces such as the World Wide Web. In any case, virtual worlds have become a prominent part of the online landscape. This chapter reviews some concepts and definitions associated with virtual worlds, shares a brief history of virtual worlds, and describes some technological predecessors and cultural inspirations for virtual worlds.

Characteristics of Virtual Worlds

What Are Virtual Worlds?

The term "virtual world" is one of many used to describe three-dimensional graphical environments that allow users to interact with each other and the environment online by using digital avatars to represent themselves in the environment's virtual space. Alternate terms exist, including "virtual environment," "immersive virtual environment," "multi-user virtual environment," "massively multiplayer persistent universe," and "persistent online world." Although there is no formal terminological consensus, "virtual worlds" appears to be the most widely used and most generally inclusive term to describe the broad existing range of such environments (Bartle 2003; Malaby 2006) despite arguments that other terms such as "synthetic world" (Castronova 2005; Malaby 2006) might be more appropriate. One reason for the popularity of the term "virtual world" is that it is a relatively short descriptive term, compared to some of the alternatives, that lends itself to the similarly brief acronym VW (Castronova 2001). Other popular terms, such as "massively multiplayer online role-playing game" (MMORPG), are also widely used to describe environments that often also fit the more general virtual world category (i.e., MMORPGs are a specific type of virtual world).

Although there are many different types of virtual worlds with many different characteristics, all virtual worlds share a few common features. Castronova (2001) identifies three key traits that all virtual worlds share: interactivity, physicality, and persistence (5–6).

Interactivity

To possess interactivity, a virtual world must allow users to interact with it and with other users in ways that influence the world and the experiences of its other users. For example, a virtual museum tour that allows a user to tour an electronic version of a museum using a digital avatar representing the user is not interactive if the user is not able to perceive and interact with other users' avatars and with the museum environment. If the tour user is able to see and talk with other users on the tour via avatars representing each user, though, the environment is interactive. Similarly, an online game where one player's decisions influence the environment for other players is interactive, but a game where players' decisions have no implications for the game experience of other players is not interactive.

Physicality

One aspect of the physicality criterion for virtual worlds is that a virtual world must provide a graphical, three-dimensional simulation of an environment that can be generally perceived from a first-person perspective, though the "first-person" description of a virtual world's perspective is applied loosely in terms of the actual point of view provided to a virtual world's users. Rather than providing a field of vision that actually represents the character avatar's field of vision (i.e., a viewpoint that approximates "looking through the avatar's eyes"), the point of view provided in a virtual world is typically from slightly behind and above the avatar so that the virtual world's user is better able to observe and control the avatar's location in the virtual environment. For example, the typical virtual world's point of view from just behind an avatar would be more helpful for a virtual world's user than a true first-person perspective when the user is trying to control an avatar's steps through a precarious virtual environment (e.g., a thin bridge) or guiding an avatar who is surrounded by antagonists in a virtual combat setting. Further, virtual world users can often manipulate their point of view slightly when convenient (e.g., zooming in or out or moving the field of vision up or down).

Although this conventional point of view used in virtual worlds is not strictly first-person because it does not simulate the avatar's actual field of vision, it provides an effective viewpoint from which a user can control an avatar while still maintaining a generally first-person point of view because it is unique to the avatar's position (i.e., the user in generally able to see what is in front of the avatar in the virtual environment), and limited by the constraints of the avatar's viewpoint (i.e., the user cannot see parts of the virtual environment that are far removed from the avatar's field of vision or obscured by other elements of the environment that are near the avatar). An online application that provides users with a broad view of the environment that is not tailored to the viewpoint of the users' avatars, such as an online game that provides all of its players with a broad view of the game environment from a sideline position, would not provide the general first-person perspective that is a necessary condition of the physicality of a virtual world.

To possess physicality, a virtual world must also follow some general natural laws (such as the presence of gravity, physical limitations such as avatars' inability to walk through solid walls, limited supplies of certain resources, etc.). For example, an online application that allows users to browse through static images of various cities and landmarks is not a virtual world, but an application that allows the user to virtually approximate traveling through the online representations of such locations in natural ways (for example, by allowing the user's avatar to walk and turn along paths, but not allowing the user to walk through the walls of buildings) would exhibit physicality.

Persistence

To possess persistence, a virtual world must continue to exist online and maintain its characteristics, and be affected by other users whether a user is present or not. For example, an online auto racing game that generates a track for users to race on when they access the game is not persistent if the track is only created temporarily for the race and racers' prizes and cars are not kept in their possession after the game is over. A similar game where racing tracks endure in the environment after a user finishes a session of the game and where a user's prize money and collection of cars is "remembered" when the user starts and finishes game sessions, however, exhibits persistence.

Although a number of online applications possess one or two of these three key elements of virtual worlds, only environments that feature interactivity, physicality, *and* persistence are characterized as virtual worlds. For example, a message board on the World Wide Web is often both interactive and persistent in that users can post information to it that other users can see and those posts remain even when users not connected to the Internet. Nonetheless, it is not physical because it does not simulate a first-person environment with natural laws. Similarly, some online video games that are not virtual worlds are both interactive and physical because they allow users to play the games with one another in a realistic virtual space, but they are not persistent because the game environments are only generated for the duration of one multiplayer game session. The three characteristics of interactivity, physicality, and persistence are therefore useful for delineating the boundaries between virtual worlds and other similar applications. Environments that possess all three characteristics are virtual worlds, while those possessing two or fewer of these characteristics are something else.

Just as there is some lack of consensus as to what we should call virtual worlds, there is some difference of opinion about the traits that define virtual words. Although Castronova's (2001) criteria of interactivity, physicality, and persistence are widely accepted, some typologies use alternate (but roughly synonymous) terms for these criteria or divide these three characteristics into more specific subcategories (e.g., Book 2006; Jakobsson 2006). There is also some disagreement as to whether a three-dimensional graphical interface, or any graphical interface at all, is a necessary element of a virtual world (e.g., Bartle 2003; 2010), though typical definitions of virtual worlds limit the term's use to those environments that present their users with a three-dimensional graphical representation of their environment that can be encountered from a first-person perspective (Castronova 2001; Dickey 2005; Schroeder, Heather, and Lee 1998). In the absence of a universal and formal definition, then, virtual worlds can generally be understood to be defined as online three-dimensional graphical environments that feature interactivity, physicality, and persistence.

The History of Virtual Worlds

The First Virtual World

Because there is some disagreement as to what precise criteria define what is a virtual world and what is not, there is consequently some disagreement as to when the first virtual world was created and released. In 1985, LucasFilm employees Chip Morningstar and F. Randall Farmer led the creation of *Habitat*, an online community environment that was released online from 1986 to 1988 (Morningstar and Farmer 1991). *Habitat* was reworked and re-released as *Club Caribe* in 1988, and other renamed versions would follow in subsequent years. *Habitat* boasted many of the characteristics of a virtual world. *Habitat* users connected to the game's persistent environment online and were able to talk (via typed text) with other users, trade resources, and even "kill" other users' avatars (though the slain avatars were returned to a home location without possessions rather than being removed from the game). Despite rudimentary graphics and controls, the range of involvement that *Habitat* provided its users allowed them to play a substantial role in the function of the game's online community (Biocca 1992).

Given the interactive and persistent characteristics of *Habitat*, some consider it to be the first virtual world, but others maintain that *Habitat* was not a true virtual world because its graphical representation of the users' environment was two-dimensional rather than three-dimensional and because users' avatars were portrayed from a third-person point of view rather than a first-person point of view (Castronova 2002; Robinett 1994). Of the three commonly agreed-upon virtual world characteristics of interactivity, physicality, and persistence, then, *Habitat* could be interpreted as having possessed only interactivity and persistence; *Habitat*'s limited technical capabilities presented it from exhibiting the physicality that is now characteristic of virtual worlds.

There is little doubt that *Habitat* was an important landmark in the history and development of virtual worlds. For example, *Habitat* is often credited with originating the practice of using avatars to represent users in online environments (Castronova 2002, 2003; Dickey 1999; Morningstar and Farmer 1991). Because *Habitat* lacked three-dimensional graphical interface and first-person perspective, however, an online role-playing computer game titled *Meridian 59* is often credited as having been the first true virtual world (Castronova 2001, 2002; Copier, 2005).

Meridian 59 was released in an incomplete form in 1995 by Archetype Interactive and received a full commercial launch by The 3DO Company in 1996. *Meridian 59* subscribers paid a monthly fee to access the game; this format remains the most common payment structure used by most virtual worlds that charge players usage fees. *Meridian 59* was also the first of many virtual worlds to employ a medieval fantasy theme, which would become a dominant setting for virtual world games in years to come.

Like *Habitat, Meridian 59* allowed users to interact with each other in a persistent game environment, but *Meridian 59* also employed a three-dimensional, first-person representation of its game environment. Therefore, *Meridian 59* was the first virtual world because it possessed all three of the characteristics associated with virtual worlds: interactivity, persistence, and physicality. Although *Meridian 59* is now recognized as the first of the virtual worlds, it was not nearly as commercially successful as some of its followers. *Meridian 59* was shut down in 2000, though another studio rereleased it in 2002 and it remains in use by a small group of players today after being turned over to original developers Andrew and Chris Kirmse in 2010. According to some estimates, *Meridian 59* never amassed more than about 12,000 active subscribers at any time during its availability.

The Early Growth of Virtual Worlds

The next popular virtual world to be released would dwarf the popularity of *Meridian 59*. Origin Systems and Electronic Arts released *Ultima Online*, another online role-playing computer game, in 1997. *Ultima Online*, which has a medieval fantasy theme, eventually developed a subscriber base of more than 200,000 players, making it arguably the first virtual world to be commercially successful on a large scale (Castronova 2001, 2002). In addition to exhibiting the potential of the virtual world format as a commercially viable large-scale online application, *Ultima Online*'s creators are also believed to have popularized the term "virtual world" itself (Castronova 2001). The game is still in operation.

A year after *Ultima Online* opened, the South Korea–based company NCSoft released *Lineage*, another virtual world in the form of an online role-playing computer game with a medieval fantasy setting. A creator of *Lineage*, designer Jake Song, had previously designed a popular online multiplayer game titled *Nexus: The Kingdom of the Winds*, which attracted more than one million players after its 1996 release in South Korea by Nexon (a North American release would come two years later) and boasted many similar features to virtual worlds. (*Nexus: The Kingdom of the Winds* isn't considered a virtual world, though, because its graphical presentation was two-dimensional rather than three-dimensional.) *Lineage* became extremely popular in its home nation, with some estimating at one point that as many as one in four South Korean teenagers played the game (Balkin 2004). The game peaked in popularity with more than four million subscribers worldwide, most of them from Asia, and is still in operation in Asia even though its North American servers were shut down in 2011 (Castronova 2002; Kent 2003).

While *Lineage* amassed a massive subscriber base in Korea, it was a virtual world called *EverQuest* that arrived in 1999 to eclipse the subscription numbers of *Ultima Online* in the United States. *EverQuest*, an online role-playing computer game released by Sony's Verant Interactive brand, was technologically superior to previous virtual worlds like *Ultima Online* and *Lineage* because it offered true three-dimensional graphical representation of its environment. *Ultima Online* and *Lineage* had approximated a three-dimensional representation with two-dimensional graphics by using axonometric projection to give the two-dimensional graphics a three-dimensional appearance (Bradley and Froomkin 2004; Kent 2003; Lastowka and Hunter 2004). *EverQuest* was not, however, the first virtual world to provide true three-dimensional graphical representation; *Meridian 59,* though inferior technologically to *EverQuest,* had also provided fully three-dimensional graphics (Wolf 2008).

This technical superiority and Sony Online Entertainment's prominence in the entertainment industry netted *EverQuest* a large player pool that grew to more than 400,000 subscribers (Castronova 2001; 2002). The intense commitment to *EverQuest* that many of these players displayed was well-documented, with typical players devoting as much as 20 hours a week or more to the game (Castronova 2001, 2002; Yee 2001) and some anecdotes describing users who spent nearly all of their waking hours playing the game (Chappell, Eatough, Davies, and Griffiths 2006). *EverQuest* also spawned a large market for sales of in-game items (e.g., player accounts, weapons) for actual money via online auction sites such as eBay (Castronova 2001; 2003)—a market that endured in underground form after Sony banned the sale of in-game items by players and declared in its user agreement that all property created by players in the game was the property of Sony (Castronova 2003; Grimes 2006). *EverQuest* remains currently active.

The year 1999 also saw the release of another fully three-dimensional virtual world, *Asheron's Call,* from Turbine and Microsoft. Like *Ultima Online* and *EverQuest, Asheron's Call* was another online role-playing computer game that employed a medieval fantasy theme. *Asheron's Call* drew fewer subscribers than *EverQuest,* but still managed to attract as many as 200,000 subscribers (Castronova 2002) and is still operational. Together,

Ultima Online, EverQuest, and *Asheron's Call* are often referred to as the "big three" MMORPGs of the late 1990s in light of their unprecedented commercial success in the United States (Axelsson and Regan 2002).

Following on the success of these games, the pace at which new virtual worlds were released quickened dramatically beginning in the 21st century. The year 2001 saw the release of at least four significant virtual worlds: *Dark Age of Camelot, Anarchy Online, RuneScape,* and *Phantasy Star Online.* Mythic Entertainment's *Dark Age of Camelot,* yet another online role-playing computer game with a medieval fantasy setting, popularized the realm-versus-realm player competition format wherein players' avatars belonging to one allied group could attack players' avatars from another allied group (Bartle 2003). Although prior games had either allowed indiscriminate combat between players' avatars, encouraged cooperation between players' avatars against computer-controlled foes, or featured a mix of both formats, the realm-versus-realm format used in *Dark Age of Camelot* (the game featured three such realms) would be used by several virtual world offerings. *Dark Age of Camelot* is still online.

Funcom's 2001 release *Anarchy Online* broke the trend of virtual worlds with medieval fantasy themes by employing a science fiction theme (Cornett 2004). The online role-playing computer game, which is still active, also popularized the use of "instancing" in virtual worlds, wherein a private iteration of a virtual setting within the vastly populated virtual world is temporarily created or spawned (Aarseth, Smedstad, and Sunnanå 2003) for one or more players while they complete a task or event (e.g., a separate version of a small area in which a mission is completed only by one player while other versions of the area would be created for other players in the virtual world completing the same mission).

Jagex Game Studio's online role-playing computer game *RuneScape,* released in 2001, followed the common trend of using a medieval fantasy theme, but provided a novel method for its users to access its virtual world environment. While most online role-playing games required users to install the game's software from a purchased disc (or later, by downloading software from the Internet and installing it), *RuneScape* allowed its players to access the game using their Web browsers. *RuneScape* was also novel among popular virtual worlds at the time in that it charged players no subscription fee, though some additional game features were available to players who chose to pay a fee. Instead of charging all subscribers a fee, *RuneScape* generated revenue through advertisements displayed at the top of the game user's screen. These unique features earned *RuneScape* an ongoing following of millions of players and recognition from *Guinness World Records* as the most popular free MMORPG in the world (Drain 2010; Hindman 2010).

Sega's Sonic Team also broke new ground in presentation formats for virtual worlds with *Phantasy Star Online*. Unlike previous virtual worlds that were played on personal computers, the science-fiction game was played online using Sega's Dreamcast console. This novel format did not prove advantageous, however, when the unsuccessful Dreamcast console stopped being promoted and the Internet servers for *Phantasy Star Online* were shut down (Guttenbrunner, Becker, and Rauber 2010; Kirriemuir 2006). More successful implementation of a virtual world on a game console in the United States would wait until *EverQuest Online Adventures,* a spin-off of the popular *EverQuest* computer game that is still online, was released by Sony Online Entertainment in 2003 for the PlayStation 2 console. *Final Fantasy XI,* the first online incarnation of the popular *Final Fantasy* video game franchise, was released by Square Enix for the PlayStation 2 in 2004 (the year after it was released for personal computers in the United States and two years after it was released for both formats in Japan) and is still in operation.

Phantasy Star Online was not the only virtual world released on a large scale that failed to succeed. In 2002, Westwood Studios and Electronic Arts launched *Earth and Beyond,* an online role-playing computer game with a science fiction theme, but the game was closed two years later. The same year, Maxis and Electronic Arts released *The Sims Online,* an online incarnation of the popular *The Sims* computer game series in which players simulated daily activities such as building and decorating homes, maintaining friendships and romantic relationships, and working at a job. Despite an initially positive critical response, *The Sims Online* did not sustain the success of its offline predecessor (Steen, Greenfield, Davies, and Tynes 2006). *The Sims Online* was shut down in 2008. Turbine followed up the success of *Asheron's Call* with *Asheron's Call 2* in 2002, but the game did not emulate the success of its predecessor and was shut down in 2005.

These occasional commercial letdowns did little to halt the continued commercial release of more virtual worlds. Offerings in 2003 included *Shadowbane,* an online role-playing computer game from Wolfpack Studios and Ubisoft, with a medieval fantasy theme that allowed players to alter the game environment substantially and placed emphasis on combat between players' avatars; *EVE Online,* an online role-playing computer game from Crowd Control Productions with a science fiction theme that has drawn the attention of economists and legal scholars interested in the function and implications of its open and player-driven economic system (Casey 2010; Glushko 2007); and *Star Wars Galaxies,* an online role-playing computer game from Sony and LucasArts based on the popular *Star Wars* movie franchise and related media properties. *Star Wars Galaxies* represented one of the first virtual worlds developed to capitalize on a popular film franchise, but it would not be the last. *Shadowbane* closed in 2009 and *Star Wars Galaxies* closed in 2011, but *EVE Online* is still active.

Another occasional strategy used to draw traffic to new virtual worlds was to capitalize on the success of existing offerings. After releasing the console-based *EverQuest Online Adventures* in 2003, Sony Online Entertainment also released *EverQuest II* in 2004, and NCSoft launched *Lineage II* in the United States in 2004 after releasing the game in South Korea during the previous year. Both *EverQuest II and Lineage II,* like their predecessors, had a medieval fantasy theme and were online role-playing computer games, and both were released even while their predecessors maintained large subscription bases. Even so, both games mirrored the success of the titles that had come before them, with *EverQuest II* garnering as many as half a million players and *Lineage II* drawing well more than a million players (Schiesel 2005; Steinkuehler 2007). As with the first *Lineage* offering, most subscribers to *Lineage II* hailed from the game's home nation of South Korea. NCSoft also staked another claim in the North American market in 2004 by releasing *City of Heroes,* a superhero-themed online role-playing computer game, in cooperation with Cryptic Studios. (A companion game, *City of Villains,* was released in 2005.) *EverQuest II, Lineage II,* and *City of Heroes* all remain active.

Not a Game Anymore: *Second Life* and Social Virtual Worlds

In a crowded virtual world market dominated by online role-playing games with fantasy and science-fiction themes, one virtual world made public in 2003 was distinguished by its different theme and purpose. In fact, it might be said that Linden Lab's *Second Life* had neither. Like many virtual worlds, *Second Life* was accessed online by users who downloaded and installed its software on their personal computers, then logged in to the virtual world to interact with each other and the virtual world's environment using customizable avatar characters. In many ways, though, the similarities between *Second Life* and other popular virtual worlds ended there.

While most virtual worlds previously provided game environments with clear play mechanics, general plotlines, and overarching objectives, the environment provided by *Second Life* included very little content and infrastructure and instead allowed its users to interact with each other and the environment with whatever objective they choose. The vast majority of content in the *Second Life* world was designed and created by its users rather than by Linden Lab, and Linden Lab assured its users that they would retain intellectual property rights to content they created in the virtual world (Horowitz 2007). The genre-free nature of *Second Life* also reached out to a broad demographic base beyond those who had typically been interested in the computer game genres represented by most virtual worlds.

Initially, Linden Lab charged *Second Life* users a monthly subscription fee like many other virtual worlds, but this fee was later changed to a one-time fee before being waived altogether when users were provided free game accounts in 2005. Instead, *Second Life* generated revenue for Linden Lab by charging fees to subscribers who wished to purchase premium property and services in the virtual world and by selling "Linden Dollars" (L$). Users who bought L$ exchanged the virtual currency by buying and selling virtual goods and services in exchanges with other users in the virtual world. Linden Lab also provided users with the opportunity to exchange Linden Dollars back to legal tender for a small fee.

Although users were not required to purchase Linden Dollars or buy or sell virtual goods and services, many users spent Linden Dollars to better enjoy their virtual world experience and others made real profits by earning Linden Dollars in the virtual world and exchanging them with Linden Lab for legal currency. For example, it was a common practice for *Second Life* users to purchase advanced representations of their skin, clothing, and hair that had been designed by other users and were aesthetically superior to the customizable avatar appearance options provided to players free of charge by Linden Lab (Heider 2009). More diverse and dramatic avatar embellishments, such as customizations that give an avatar the appearance of a vampire, animal, or almost whatever else might suit a user's fancy, are also available from talented and entrepreneurial *Second Life* users.

This bustling economy ensured that *Second Life* would continue to be full of new content created by users. It also ensured a revenue stream for Linden Lab, as players paid to exchange Linden Dollars for currency and leased virtual land from Linden Lab from which they could run their virtual businesses. The open, customizable, entrepreneur-friendly nature of *Second Life* drew broad interest from the private and public sectors, with motion picture companies, recording labels, clothing manufacturers, automobile manufacturers, politicians, news agencies, and universities creating presences in *Second Life* (Chin 2007; Foster 2007; Harp 2009: Huang 2009). The virtual world's rich social environment also attracted researchers who examined the virtual world and the social behavior of its users (Bainbridge 2007; Malaby 2009; Miller 2007; Yee et al., 2007). In 2006, *Second Life* registered its millionth user. More than 20 million *Second Life* user accounts had been created by 2011 (Shepherd 2011), with as many as 18,000 new accounts registered each day and between 700 and 800 million active users logging in more than once a month (Linden Lab 2011).

Second Life was not the first virtual world designed to provide an open community with most content created by users. As early as 1997, *Active Worlds* was developed by Worlds, Inc., (later renamed Active Worlds, Inc.) to provide an early virtual world with similar elements to those of *Second Life*, and Blaxxun Interactive introduced the *ColonyCity* (later called *Cybertown*) virtual environment during the same year to demonstrate its Virtual Reality Modeling Language (VRML). Other virtual worlds with similar schemes as *Second Life* included *There*, which was developed by There, Inc. (later operated by Makena Technologies) and also saw a public launch in 2003; *The Virtual World of Kaneva*, released in 2006 by its namesake company; and *SmallWorlds*, released in 2008 by Outsmart. In 2003, MindArk launched *Entropia Universe*, a virtual world with a science-fiction theme but which also resembled *Second Life* in that it featured a large-scale economy whose currency could be exchanged for real money. *Second Life* has eclipsed these competitors in terms of prominence (Kumar et al., 2008), though most of them remain active. *There*, however, was shut down in 2010.

World of Warcraft Changes the Game

Despite the advent of *Second Life* and similar virtual worlds, the dominant virtual world format continued to be that of combat-oriented online computer games (Hemp 2006). In fact, it was yet another online role-playing computer game with a medieval fantasy theme, Blizzard Entertainment's *World of Warcraft*, that completely redefined expectations regarding the popularity of a virtual world when it was released in 2004.

World of Warcraft was a continuation of Blizzard Entertainment's successful *Warcraft* game series, which had begun in 1994 with the personal computer game *Warcraft: Orcs and Humans*. *World of Warcraft* featured similar plot elements, characters, and themes as the previous *Warcraft* games, but while previous games in the series allowed players to compete against each other in online games, *World of Warcraft* was the first game in the series to use a virtual world format.

After years of development, *World of Warcraft* was released, to critical acclaim. The game was praised for maintaining popular elements common to previous virtual world games while introducing innovative new features that served to improve the game experience for experienced virtual world users while also making the game very accessible to users who were unfamiliar with virtual worlds and computer role-playing games in general (Kasavin 2004; McNamara 2004; Rausch 2004). Many of the features added by *World of Warcraft* would become standard among competing virtual world games in future years.

World of Warcraft's impact was immediate. The game drew more than 200,000 subscribers within 24 hours of its release in November 2004, and more than a million were playing the game by March 2005 (Ducheneaut, Yee, Nickell, and Moore 2006). By 2011, *World of Warcraft* boasted more than 12 million subscribers globally. The game is estimated to hold a majority of the subscription market for massively multiplayer online role-playing games, and is recognized as the most popular MMORPG in the world by *Guinness World Records*. *World of Warcraft* also released expansion packages in 2007, 2008, and 2010 that provided players who purchased them with additional content and game features.

As with *Second Life*, researchers were also drawn to study *World of Warcraft*. Although the medieval fantasy setting that the trend-setting virtual world provided was not as realistic thematically as the setting of *Second Life*, researchers saw great value in exploring the very real social dynamics of the *World of Warcraft* community despite the fact that users' avatars represented such fantastic species as orcs, trolls, and night elves, and such supernatural professions as mages, warlocks, and death knights (Bainbridge 2007). Shortly after the game's release, academic studies explored such elements of *World of Warcraft* as its social dynamics (Ducheneaut, Yee, Nickell, and Moore 2006; Nardi 2010; Williams, Caplan, and Xiong 2007; Williams et al., 2006), players' exploration of self-identity when creating and customizing avatars (Bessière, Seay, and Kiesler 2007), and the implications of a virtual outbreak of an infectious corrupted blood disease among avatar characters in the game for the study of real-world disease epidemiology (Balicer 2007).

Other Virtual Worlds Look to Keep Up

While *World of Warcraft* set the standard for commercial success in virtual worlds, there have been plenty of other competing offerings since its release. Like *World of Warcraft,* most of the more prominent virtual worlds have continued to be online role-playing computer games. While existing virtual world titles worked to maintain a share of the online role-playing computer game market in the face of *World of Warcraft*'s popularity, NCSoft added another competing virtual world in 2005. *Guild Wars,* a product of ArenaNet and NCSoft that was released to users in countries across the globe (Kosak and Lopez 2005), added to the slew of existing medieval fantasy online role-playing computer games in the virtual world market. Although *Guild Wars* shared a common theme with many previous virtual worlds, it differed from most of them in that it charged users no subscription fee beyond the initial software price.

Additionally, *Guild Wars* featured limited use of virtual regions where all of the game's players could interact; in most game regions other than major hubs (e.g., key cities in the game environment), separate "instances" of each region were created for the user and the user's companions to use privately (Gillen 2005). While it was not uncommon for other virtual worlds to use instances at some points, *Guild Wars* made more extensive use of the instance feature to provide a less crowded environment to its users in some virtual areas while still providing interaction with a larger population of users in other virtual areas. While never threatening to surpass *World of Warcraft*'s subscription base,

Guild Wars' unique format and lack of subscription fees attracted enough interest to support the release of a two additional campaign sequels in 2006 plus an expansion update in 2007. The game remains active.

In 2006, another challenge to the commercial dominance of *World of Warcraft* came from a brand that had arguably been providing virtual worlds of one kind or another to its followers since long before personal computers or the Internet were common in any household. *Dungeons and Dragons,* a famous medieval fantasy role-playing game since its first publication in the form of three booklets containing its rules in 1974 (Gygax and Arneson 1974), was adapted by Turbine and Atari from its roots in rulebooks and dice to the virtual world format as the online role-playing computer game *Dungeons and Dragons Online: Stormreach.*

Like *Guild Wars* before it, *Dungeons and Dragons Online: Stormreach* did not draw a group of subscribers to rival the popularity of *World of Warcraft,* but its generally close adherence to the conventions of the popular gaming franchise on which it was based (McNamara 2006) made for a successful game. In September 2009, the virtual world was made accessible to a broader audience when monthly subscription fees were waived for users and the newly free-to-play game was renamed *Dungeons and Dragons Online: Eberron Unlimited* (Peters 2009). Although users could access the virtual world at no cost, *Dungeons and Dragons Online: Eberron Unlimited* continued to generate income because paid subscribers were afforded VIP status, and some virtual items were available for purchase in an optional game store. The change in cost structure netted *Dungeons and Dragons Online: Eberron Unlimited* more than 2 million new users in 2009, and both the game's market share and number of VIP subscribers also doubled in 2009 (Murdoch 2010).

After successfully adapting the *Dungeons and Dragons* media franchise for the virtual world environment, Turbine cooperated with Midway Games in 2007 to bring a much bigger name in the fantasy genre to virtual worlds with the online role-playing computer game *The Lord of the Rings Online: Shadows of Angmar.* The game's setting was contemporaneous with J. R. R. Tolkien's best-selling fantasy epic *The Lord of the Rings* (Tolkien 1954a, 1954b, 1955) and placed the user in a storyline loosely associated with the plot of Tolkien's famed tale. Adaption of a legendary fantasy franchise suited *The Lord of the Rings Online: Shadows of Angmar* well, as the virtual world earned praise immediately after its release for its plot (both the elements related to the Tolkien novel and the storylines unique to the game), adherence to Tolkien's themes and work, and beautiful settings as much as its actual features as a virtual world game (Onyett 2007; Rausch 2007). The successful transfer of a familiar tale to the virtual world setting brought enough attention to *The Lord of the Rings Online: Shadows of Angmar* to support the release of frequent content updates and three expansion modules: *Mines of Moria* in 2008, *Siege of Mirkwood* in 2009, and *Rise of Isengard* in 2011. As with the *Dungeons and Dragons Online* game, *The Lord of the Rings Online* was changed from a subscription-based virtual world to a free-to-play one in 2010, with items and features available from an in-game store and monthly VIP subscriptions also available (Murdoch 2010; Peckham 2010). Revenues for *The Lord of the Rings Online* tripled after the free-to-play format was introduced (Orland 2011).

Although virtual worlds like *The Lord of the Rings Online* and *Star Wars Galaxies* were successful in bringing popular media franchises into virtual worlds, other attempts to capitalize on well-known media properties enjoyed mixed success. *The Matrix Online*, an online role-playing computer game based on the film *The Matrix* and its sequels, was launched by Sega and Monolith Productions in 2005 (and later acquired by Sony Online Entertainment) but met a poor critical reception (Sjöberg 2005) and was shut down in 2009 due to a low number of subscribers (Mastrapa 2009). *Age of Conan: Hyborian Adventures*, an online role-playing computer game based on Robert E. Howard's popular fantasy stories featuring the character Conan the Barbarian, was released in 2008 by Funcom and Eidos Interactive. *Age of Conan: Hyborian Adventures* was reviewed positively, but reviewers also noted that the virtual world's features and game story could have been more developed (Saltzman 2008; Schiesel 2008a). Despite these flaws noted by critics, the game is still active.

The year 2008 also saw Mythic Entertainment and Electronic Arts release *Warhammer Online: Age of Reckoning*, an online role-playing computer game based on the popular *Warhammer Fantasy* tabletop and pen-and-paper role-playing game series with a focus on combat between players of the realm-versus-realm variety previously used in Mythic Entertainment's *Dark Age of Camelot* (Scheisel 2008b). Also in 2008, Sony Online Entertainment and Flying Lab Software explored a new online role-playing game setting—the open seas—with their pirate-themed game *Pirates of the Burning Sea*. While these and other games focus primarily—though not exclusively—on a North American virtual world audience, NCSoft scored another hit in South Korea with *Aion: The Tower of Eternity,* an online role-playing computer game with a fantasy theme. *Aion: The Tower of Eternity* was released in South Korea in 2008 and garnered millions of subscribers across Asia even before it was introduced in the United States, Europe, and Australia as *Aion* in 2009 (Fahey 2009).

Although virtual worlds with original themes and content continue to emerge and draw audiences to their novel online environments, many other new virtual worlds continue to adapt themes and settings from existing media franchises in an attempt to stand out in an increasingly crowded field. In 2010, the famed *Star Trek* science-fiction franchise took virtual world form with the online role-playing computer game *Star Trek Online* from Cryptic Studios, which opened to mixed reviews (VanOrd 2010; Yolan 2010). In 2011, Sony Online Entertainment brought the popular DC Comics series to a virtual world with *DC Universe Online,* an online role-playing computer game playable on personal computers and the PlayStation 3 console, featuring locations such as Gotham City and Metropolis, and including characters such as Superman, Batman, and Wonder Woman. Despite its famed content, *DC Universe Online* also received mediocre reviews (Kolan 2011; VanOrd 2011a). The *Star Wars* media franchise, first adapted to a virtual world in 2003 with the online role-playing computer game *Star Wars* Galaxies, became the source material for a second major virtual world when development of the online role-playing computer game *Star Wars: The Old Republic* was announced in 2008 (Butts 2008). The virtual world was eagerly anticipated by audiences, so much so that comic book series and best-selling novels based on the game were published before the game's release, and it was highly lauded as a ground-breaking game even before its 2011 release by BioWare and LucasArts (Park 2011; Tanner 2011).

Other recent virtual world releases are familiar to users not because they adapt popular media franchises, but because they come from already-popular providers. Jagex Game Studio followed up on its massively popular title *RuneScape* with the 2011 release of a new online role-playing game called *Stellar Dawn.* Although *Stellar Dawn* featured a science-fiction theme instead of *RuneScape's* medieval fantasy theme, it employed the same browser-based format that helped make *RuneScape* a global hit. Prior success by virtual world developers does not guarantee a hit, though. For example, 2007 saw Sony Online Entertainment and Sigil Games Online, Inc., release the online role-playing game *Vanguard: Saga of Heroes*, which was designed by the same person who led the design of the popular online role-playing game *EverQuest*. The similarities seem to have ended there, as *Vanguard: Saga of Heroes* has struggled to maintain a substantial user population. In a similar move with similar results, NCSoft and Destination Games released *Tabula Rasa*, a game designed by the original producer of *Ultima Online*, in 2007 and the game was closed by 2009. There is still room in the virtual worlds market for newcomers as well. In 2001, Trion Worlds released the online role-playing game *Rift* to generally positive reviews (VanOrd 2011b).

Other Related Online Games, Communities, and Environments

The partial overview and history of virtual worlds presented above focuses on popular online environments that fit the aforementioned criteria for virtual worlds: interactivity, persistence, and physicality (Castronova 2001). These criteria are useful in defining what online applications provide a true virtual world environment where users can interact with each other via the general perspective of their avatars in a persistent simulation of a physical environment. There are, however, many popular online environments that lack all of the characteristics of a virtual world (Castronova 2001) but still merit mention as popular online social environments. Although these environments may lack some technological richness because they do not exhibit interactivity, persistence, or physicality, they nonetheless function to some degree as virtual social spaces where users interact using graphical representations of themselves.

Graphical Chat Applications

One such type of online environment is the graphical chat application that allows users to customize visual avatars that represent themselves, then engage in text-based chat with other users from their personal computers. With these applications, the users do not tend to control their characters' movement through a three-dimensional virtual space. Instead, the chat participants' avatars, which are typically two-dimensional, are simply displayed together in a graphical space to add a visual element to their text-based instant messages. These applications therefore function more or less as graphically enhanced versions of text-based chat room and instant messaging applications rather than as immersive virtual environments (Spence 2008). Examples of such environments are Instant Messaging Virtual Universe (IMVU), available since 2004 from IMVU, Inc., and Zwinky, released in 2006 by IAC Search and Media. Both of these graphical chat applications, have attracted millions of users—many of them adolescents and teens—who are invited by the applications to spend money on a vast array of virtual goods such as clothing and accessories for their avatars and those of their friends (Lee 2007; McCarthy 2007; Michaels 2010).

Social Network Games

Also notable for their online social interaction elements are social network games, which lack many elements of virtual worlds but involve online social interaction through online social networking websites such as Facebook and MySpace (Albaneseus 2010). Prominent among these games are popular offerings from Zynga such as *Mafia Wars,* released in 2009, *FarmVille,* also released in 2009, and *CityVille* and *FrontierVille,* released in 2010. Zynga's Web-based social network games have drawn more than 200 million users and are accessed by tens of millions of users each day (Gannes 2010). Zynga's games generated more than $90 million in profits for the company in 2010 (Blackden 2011). Because social network games are often simple to use and allow users to access them from sites they already use, the number of users a popular social network game can attract is often many times that of a popular virtual world (Chiang 2010).

These social network games provide no real immersive virtual environment. Instead, they function something like online board games, with players completing tasks via their Web browser and "leveling up" (increasing their game scores, enhancing their game account attributes, or advancing to more difficult game content) by making progress in the game. Users are encouraged to interact with friends via social networking sites, however, to recruit assistance in the games. In some cases, they also have the opportunity to compete against others using the games. While the social interaction involved in these games is somewhat tangential to the actual game environment, which is far from any virtual world atmosphere, they are a notable presence in the online social sphere by virtue of their sheer popularity and the fact that they generate millions of dollars via the sale of virtual goods and through in-game advertising promotions (Levy 2010; Miller and Stone 2009; Shields 2010).

Looking Back: Virtual Worlds' Ancestry and Inspirations

The overview provided thus far in this chapter gives a fairly thorough overview of the defining characteristics of virtual worlds and the history of virtual worlds from the arrival of *Meridian 59* to the latest developments at the time this book was published. The real history of virtual worlds, though, extends much further into the past. A true understanding of the history, culture, and technological context behind virtual worlds lies in three elements of virtual worlds' background: the graphical online role-playing computer games that served as direct precursors of virtual worlds, the text-based online game environments that were developed before those graphical online games, and finally, their inspiration from paper-and-pencil games and classic literature that came along even earlier.

Direct Precursors to Virtual Worlds

Given that many popular and commercially successful virtual worlds have been online role-playing computer games with medieval fantasy themes, it is fitting that their most direct predecessors were online computer games with similar themes. During the early 1990s, a number of online role-playing computer games set the stage for virtual worlds by offering a persistent setting in which large numbers of users could interact, though they were not virtual worlds because they didn't provide a three-dimensional physical environment that the user encountered from a generally first-person perspective. The National Science Foundation Network (NSFNET) limited commercial applications' access to the Internet during the early years of these games, so until NSFNET's restrictions were relaxed beginning in the early 1990s these commercial games were usually distributed through online services such as CompuServe and America Online. These services typically charged users a few dollars per hour to connect until the mid-1990s, so playing the early online role-playing computer games could be an expensive endeavor.

An early ancestor of today's virtual world was *Neverwinter Nights,* an online role-playing computer game from Stormfront Studios and Strategic Simulations, Inc., that was available to users of the America Online Internet service from 1991 to 1997. *Neverwinter Nights* is recognized as the first online role-playing computer game to feature graphics. (Although the online graphical community environment *Habitat* predates *Neverwinter Nights,* some do not consider *Habitat* to be an online role-playing game in the traditional sense just as many do not consider virtual worlds such as *Second Life* to be online role-playing games because both *Habitat* and *Second Life* lack the overtly structured goals and competitive tasks typical to role-playing games.) Another online role-playing computer game called *Islands of Kesmai* debuted on the CompuServe Internet service in 1985, but *Islands of Kesmai* approximated graphics using text characters (e.g., a pair of brackets to represent a segment of a wall: "[]") instead of providing actual graphics (Bartle 2010). Other popular early online role-playing computer games with two-dimensional graphics included *The Realm,* released by Sierra Online in 1996, *Tibia,* released by CipSoft in 1997, and the aforementioned *Nexus: The Kingdom of the Winds,* which was developed by the designer who would later contribute to the virtual world *Lineage.*

Earlier Online Ancestors of Virtual Worlds

Although *Meridian 59* was the first virtual world, at least as defined by some (e.g., Castronova 2001), and *Neverwinter Nights* was the first online role-playing computer game with graphical representation, computer users were interacting online in persistent virtual spaces decades earlier. The earliest virtual spaces, however, differed from virtual worlds in that all aspects of their environments and participants were represented completely through text descriptions. From 1978 to 1980, a pair of English computer science students at the University of Essex called Roy Trubshaw and Richard Bartle developed *MUD* (Multi-User Dungeon), a text-based online role-playing game whose users interacted with the environment and with each other on the Internet via text commands and automatically generated responses (Bartle 2010; Bruckman and Resnick 1995; Castronova 2002; Kelly and

Rheingold 1993; Mortensen 2006). *MUD* was inspired to some extent by *Zork,* a text-based computer game developed by researchers at the Massachusetts Institute of Technology that first surfaced in 1977 (Bartle 2010; Lebling, Blank, and Anderson 1979).

The *MUD* system, which could be accessed for no charge by Internet users, could also be freely adapted by users to create and host their own online game environments. So many of these games sprang up over the next decade that the genre of games based on *MUD* became known as MUDs—the original *MUD* game began to be referred to as *MUD1* to reduce confusion with the eponymous genre it spawned (Bartle 2010). By the 1990s, there were hundreds of text-based game environments based on *MUD1* online (Kelly and Rheingold 1993; Turkle 1994). Finer distinctions also began to emerge between these games based on *MUD,* with novel acronyms used to describe various categories of MUD-type games. Games focusing extensively on role-playing through typed poses were described with the acronym MUSH (Multi-User Shared Hallucination), while games whose users tended to be granted extensive ability to redefine the environment by creating virtual objects and rooms were dubbed MOOs (MUD, Object-Oriented) (Andreatos 2007; McKenna and Bargh 2000; Turkle 1994). Many more such acronyms existed, though "MUD" was often used as a general term to describe the myriad varieties of text-based environments based on the *MUD1* application and concept (Turkle 1994). Most MUDs were adventure games like the original *MUD,* with many of them based on popular fantasy and science-fiction novels, films, and television series such as *The Lord of the Rings, Star Wars,* and *Star Trek.* Some of the text-based environments, though, were designed to serve as social communities or environments for research and education (Bruckman and Resnick 1995; Schiano 1999).

In the absence of graphical representations, users of MUDs and MUD-type applications created a simulated environment through the detail of their environments' text descriptions and the typed poses they used to describe their characters' appearance and actions. The actual commands used to interact with the environments were rudimentary (e.g., LOOK, WEST, UP, ATTACK), but many MUDs encouraged their users to supplement these basic commands with rich descriptions to provide a narrative role-playing environment and a collaborative story (Ivory 2009; Kelly and Rheingold 1993; Jacobson 1996; Mortensen 2006; Turkle 1994). These text-based environments would not fit the definitions many provide for virtual worlds (e.g., Book 2006; Castronova 2001; Jakobsson 2006; Schroeder, Heather, and Lee 1998), though some have considered their persistent social environments rich enough to be described by the term (e.g., Bartle 2010; Schiano 1999).

Nevertheless, MUDs were a clear ancestor of virtual worlds. For example, a pair of brothers called Andrew and Chris Kirmse used their years playing a MUD called *Scepter of Goth* as inspiration when they became the original developers of the first virtual world, *Meridian 59,* while Andrew was a junior at the Massachusetts Institute of Technology and Chris was a sophomore at Virginia Tech (Ludlow and Wallace 2007). Although MUDs were in many ways prototypes for the more technologically advanced virtual worlds to come, scores of popular MUDs also continue to exist long after the advent of more technologically advanced virtual worlds.

Offline Inspirations for Virtual Worlds

Although there were a number of online predecessors to virtual worlds, both graphical and text-based, the history of virtual worlds can be understood in many ways to extend beyond even the most basic computer technologies associated with virtual worlds. Several science-fiction novels are widely credited as inspirations for virtual worlds and other immersive online environments. Vernor Vinge's (1981) *True Names* presented an early vision of an online virtual world called the "Other Plane." William Gibson's (1984) *Neuromancer* popularized the term "cyberspace" when he used it to describe the worldwide virtual world used by his characters, though Gibson had first used the term in the short story *Burning Chrome* in 1982 (Shapiro 1998). Neal Stephenson (1992) imagined the "Metaverse," a virtual world accessed via avatars of varying quality depending on users' wealth and technological sophistication. Stephenson is also typically credited with adapting the Hindu term "avatar" to describe a virtual world users' online self-representation (Bailenson and Blascovich 2004).

While these and other science-fiction authors' visions influenced the conceptualization and development of virtual worlds, so did tales of a less technological nature. The *Dungeons and Dragons* role-playing game franchise (Gygax and Arneson 1974) and related role-playing games are widely acknowledged as inspirations for virtual worlds, as well as of the MUDs that preceded them (Castronova 2002; Morales 2002; Steinkuehler 2007; Svensson 2008). In turn, *Dungeons and Dragons* was heavily influenced by the beloved works of J.R.R. Tolkien (e.g., 1937; 1954a; 1954b; 1955), whose fantastic settings and characters are also credited as inspirations for the settings of many MUDs and virtual worlds (Castronova 2002; Lastowka and Hunter 2004; Ng and Wiemer-Hastings 2005; Steinkuehler 2007; Turkle 1994; Turnau 2004; Williams 2006). In fact, Tolkien's works directly provided the themes and settings for MUDs and similar text-based online role-playing games; one example is *Elendor MUSH,* which was founded in 1991 as a noncommercial text-based online role-playing game set in Tolkien's literary world (Davis 2001).

Dungeons and Dragons and Tolkien's *Lord of the Rings* have, of course, contributed the setting for popular virtual worlds on which they are directly based—*Dungeons and Dragons Online* and *Lord of the Rings Online,* respectively. Their influence on virtual worlds, though, has been much greater than that; these works provided inspiration for the entire universe of virtual worlds.

It is perhaps fitting that Tolkien was an indirect inspiration for many virtual worlds. He referred to the imaginary setting created by a storyteller as "a secondary world which your mind can enter" (Rogers, 1999, p. 139), and in many ways virtual worlds strive to create just that. Tolkien died in 1973, so he was never able to comment on today's virtual worlds, and it is difficult to say whether he would have approved of them. Although virtual worlds can create a fantastic setting somewhat akin to his "secondary world" concept, Tolkien was critical of much of the technology that existed even during his lifetime—a view that was reflected in the relegation of most mechanical technology to villains in his works (Carpenter 1977).

The Future of Virtual Worlds

After a long history of development based on a broad range of predecessors and inspirations, virtual worlds are proliferating on the Internet. Virtual worlds for both gaming and social purposes continue to spring up, and billions of dollars in virtual goods are now sold each year worldwide. Despite the large number of virtual worlds on the market, there are more scheduled to be released in the immediate future. Some of these new releases will be familiar to virtual world users because they will be new versions of popular games. ArenaNet and NCSoft are expected to release the online role-playing computer game *Guild Wars 2*, a sequel to the popular *Guild Wars* games, in 2012 (Senior 2011). Others will be new virtual worlds from familiar providers, such as the much-anticipated online role-playing computer game *Titan*, which was announced in 2010 and is expected to be released by Blizzard Entertainment in 2012 or 2013 (Magrino 2010, 2011).

Although it is difficult to say what else the future holds for the development of virtual worlds, it is likely that we can expect to see more of them in the years to come. It is perhaps just as likely, though, that they will continue to draw guidance and inspiration from sources that we have known for generations.

References

Aarseth, Espen, Solveig Marie Smedstad, and Lise Sunnanå. 2005. A multi-dimensional typology of games. In *Proceedings of Level Up Digital Games Research Conference*, 48–53. Utrecht: Utrecht University Press. http://www.digra.org/dl/db/05163.52481.pdf.

Albanesius, Chloe. 2010. Facebook, FarmVille creator Zynga sign five-year game deal. *PCMag*. http://www.pcmag.com/article2/0,2817,2363910,00.asp.

Andreatos, Antonios. 2007. Virtual communities and their importance for informal learning. *International Journal of Computers, Communications and Control* 2(1): 39–47.

Axelsson, Ann-Sofie, and Tim Regan. 2002. How belonging in an online group affects social behavior—A case study of Asheron's Call. http://research.microsoft.com/pubs/69910/tr-2002–07.pdf.

Bailenson, Jeremy N., and Jim Blascovich. 2004. Avatars. In *Encyclopedia of human-computer interaction*, ed. W. S. Bainbridge, 64–68. Great Barrington, MA: Berkshire.

Bainbridge, William Sims. 2007. The scientific research potential of virtual worlds. *Science* 317: 472–476.

Balicer, Ran D. 2007. Modeling infectious diseases dissemination through online role-playing games. *Epidemiology* 18: 260–261.

Balkin, Jack M. 2004. Virtual liberty: Freedom to design and freedom to play in virtual worlds. *Virginia Law Review* 90: 2043–2098.

Bartle, Richard A. 2003. *Designing virtual worlds*. Indianapolis, IN: New Riders.

Bartle, Richard A. 2010. From MUDs to MMORPGs: The history of virtual worlds. In *International handbook of Internet research*, ed. Jeremy

Hunsinger, Lisbeth Klastrup, and Matthew Allen, 23–39. Dordrecht: Springer.

Bessière, Katherine, A. Fleming Seay, and Sara Kiesler. 2007. The ideal elf: Identity exploration in *World of Warcraft*. *CyberPsychology and Behavior* 10: 530–535.

Biocca, Frank. 1992. Communication within virtual reality: Creating a space for research. *Journal of Communication* 42: 5–22.

Blackden, Richard. 2011. Zynga warns of the dangers of getting rich. *The Telegraph*. http://www.telegraph.co.uk/finance/newsbysector/ mediatechnologyandtelecoms/digital-media/8614522/Zynga-warns-of-the-dangers-of-getting-rich.html.

Blizzard Entertainment. 2011. *World of Warcraft subscriber base reaches 12 million worldwide*. http://us.blizzard.com/en-us/company/press/ pressreleases.html?id=2847881.

Book, B. 2006. Virtual worlds: Today and in the future. *ITNOW* 48(2): 32–33.

Bradley, Caroline, and A. Michael Froomkin. 2004. Virtual worlds, real rules. *New York Law School Review* 49: 103–146.

Bruckman, Amy, and Mitchel Resnick. 1995. The MediaMOO project: Constructionism and professional community. *Convergence* 1(1): 94–109.

Butts, Steve. 2008. Star Wars: The Old Republic first details. *IGN*. http://pc.ign.com/articles/922/922115p1.html.

Carpenter, Humphrey. 1977. *J. R. R. Tolkien: A biography*. Boston: Houghton Mifflin.

Casey, Michael. 2010. Real economist learns from virtual world. *Wall Street Journal Real Time Economics Blog*. http://blogs.wsj.com/ economics/2010/06/21/real-economist-takes-lessons-from-virtual-world/.

Castronova, Edward. 2001. *Virtual worlds: A first-hand account of market and society on the cyberian frontier*. CESifo Working Paper No. 618, December. http://ssrn.com/abstract=294828.

Castronova, Edward. 2002. *On virtual economies*. CESifo Working Paper No. 752, July. http://ssrn.com/abstract=338500.

Castronova, Edward. 2003. *Theory of the avatar*. CESifo Working Paper No. 863, February. http://papers.ssrn.com/abstract=385103.

Castronova, Edward. 2005. *Synthetic worlds: The business and culture of online games*. Chicago: University of Chicago Press.

Chappell, Darren, Virginia Eatough, Mark N. O. Davies, and Mark Griffiths. 2006. *EverQuest*—It's just a computer game right? An interpretive phenomenological analysis of online gaming addiction. *International Journal of Mental Health and Addiction* 4: 205–216.

Chiang, Oliver J. 2010. The world's most expensive island—online. *Forbes.* http://www.forbes.com/2010/02/17/farmville-facebook-zynga-technology-business-intelligence-virtual-goods.html.

Chin, Bettina M. 2007. Regulating your Second Life: Defamation in virtual worlds. *Brooklyn Law Review* 72: 1303–1349.

Copier, Marinka. 2005. Connecting worlds: Fantasy role-playing games, ritual acts, and the magic circle. In *Proceedings of DiGRA 2005 conference: Changing views—Worlds in play.* http://www.digra.org/dl/db/06278.50594.pdf.

Cornett, Steve. 2004. The usability of massively multiplayer online roleplaying games: Designing for new users. In *Proceedings of CHI 2004,* 703–710. New York: ACM Press.

Davis, Erik. 2001. The Fellowship of the Ring. *Wired.* http://www.wired.com/wired/archive/9.10/lotr.html.

Dickey, Michele D. 1999. 3D worlds and learning: An analysis of the impact of design affordances and limitations in active worlds, Blaxxun Interactive,and OnLive! Traveler; and a study of the implementation of active worlds for formal and informal education. Unpublished doctoral dissertation, Ohio State University. http://mchel.com/Papers/Dickey-Dissertation.pdf.

Dickey, Michele D. 2005. Three-dimensional virtual worlds and distance learning: Two case studies of active worlds as a medium for distance education. *British Journal of Educational Technology* 36: 439–451.

Drain, Brendan. 2010. RuneScape wishes members a merry Christmas with its December update. *Massively.* http://massively.joystiq.com/2010/12/01/runescape-wishes-members-a-merry-christmas-with-its-december-upd/.

Ducheneaut, Nicolas, Nicholas Yee, Eric Nickell, and Robert J. Moore. 2006. Alone together? Exploring the social dynamics of massively multiplayer online games. In *Proceedings of the SIGCHI conference on human factors in computing systems,* 407–416. New York: ACM Press.

Fahey, Rob. 2009. Angelic pretender Aion threatens to knock king of fantasy games off its throne. *The Times.* http://technology.timesonline.co.uk/tol/news/tech_and_web/gadgets_and_gaming/virtual_worlds/article6850276.ece.

Foster, Andrea L. 2007. Professor Avatar. *Chronicle of Higher Education.* http://chronicle.com/article/Professor-Avatar/30018/.

Gannes, Liz. 2010. How Zynga survived FarmVille. *Salon.* http://www.salon.com/technology/the_gigaom_network/ tech_insider/2010/06/08/how_zynga_survived_farmville.

Gibson, William. 1984. *Neuromancer.* New York: Ace Books.

Gillen, Kieron. 2005. Guild Wars—Review. *Eurogamer.* http://www. eurogamer.net/articles/r_guildwars_pc

Glushko, Bobby. 2007. Tales of the (virtual) city: Governing property disputes in virtual worlds. *Berkeley Technology Law Journal* 22: 507–532.

Grimes, Sara M. 2006. Online multiplayer games: A virtual space for intellectual property debates? *New Media and Society* 8: 969–990.

Guttenbrunner, Mark, Christoph Becker, and Andreas Rauber. 2010. Keeping the game alive: Evaluating strategies for the preservation of console video games. *The International Journal of Digital Curation* 5: 64–90.

Gygax, Gary, and Dave Arneson. 1974. *Dungeons and dragons.* Lake Geneva, WI: Tactical Studies Rules.

Harp, Dustin. 2009. Virtual journalism and Second Life. In *Living virtually: Researching new worlds,* ed. Don Heider, 271–289. New York: Peter Lang.

Heider, Don. 2009. Identity and reality: What does it mean to live virtually? In *Living virtually: Researching new worlds,* ed. Don Heider, 131–143. New York: Peter Lang.

Hemp, Paul. 2006. Avatar-based marketing. *Harvard Business Review* 84(6): 48–57.

Hindman, Beau. 2010. Rise and shiny recap: RuneScape. *Massively.* http://massively.joystiq.com/2010/12/19/rise-and-shiny-recap-runescape/

Horowitz, Steven J. 2007. Competing Lockean claims to virtual property. *Harvard Journal of Law and Technology* 20: 443–458.

Huang, J. Sonia. 2009. Real business and real competition in the unreal world. In *Living virtually: Researching new worlds,* ed. Don Heider, 191–207. New York: Peter Lang.

Ivory, James D. 2009. Technological developments and transitions in virtual worlds. In *Living virtually: Researching new worlds,* ed. Don Heider, 1–22. New York: Peter Lang.

Jacobson, David. 1996. Contexts and cues in cyberspace: The pragmatics of naming in text-based virtual realities. *Journal of Anthropological Research* 52: 461–479.

Jakobsson, Mikael. 2006. Virtual worlds and social interaction design. Unpublished doctoral dissertation, Umeå University, May 4. http://www.diva-portal.org/umu/theses/abstract.xsql?dbid=750.

Kasavin, Greg. 2004. World of Warcraft review. *GameSpot.* http://www.gamespot.com/pc/rpg/worldofwarcraft/review.html.

Kelly, Kevin, and Howard Rheingold. 1993. The dragon ate my homework. *Wired.* http://www.wired.com/wired/archive/1.03/muds.html.

Kent, Steven L. 2003. Alternate reality: A history of massively multiplayer online games. *GameSpy.Com.* http://archive.gamespy.com/amdmmog/week1/index.shtml.

Kirriemuir, J. 2006. A history of digital games. In *Understanding digital games,* ed. Jason Rutter and Jo Bryce, 21–35. London: SAGE.

Kolan, Nick. 2011. DC Universe Online review: It's not exactly super, man. *IGN.* http://ps3.ign.com/articles/114/1143430p1.html.

Kosak, D., and Miguel Lopez. 2005. Reviews: Guild Wars. *GameSpy.* http://pc.gamespy.com/pc/guild-wars/613203p1.html.

Kumar, Sanjeev, Jatin Chugani, Changkyu Kim, Daehyun Kim, Anthony Nguyen, Pradeep Dubey, Christian Bienia, and Youngmin Kim. 2008. *Second Life* and the new generation of virtual worlds. *Computer* 41(9): 56–63.

Lastowka, F. Gregory, and Dan Hunter. 2004. The laws of virtual worlds. *California Law Review* 92: 1–73.

Lebling, P. David, Marc S. Blank, and Timothy A. Anderson. 1979. Zork: A computerized fantasy simulation game. *IEEE Computers Magazine* 12(4): 51–59.

Lee, Ellen. 2007. More Internet users getting a virtual life. *The San Francisco Chronicle.* http://articles.sfgate.com/2007–10–08/business/17263912_1_virtual-worlds-conference-san-jose-s-gaia-san-francisco-s-second-life.

Levy, Ari. 2010. Zynga's value tops Electronic Arts as virtual-goods sales surge. *Bloomberg.* http://www.bloomberg.com/news/2010–10–26/zynga-s-value-at-5–5-billion-tops-electronic-arts-on-virtual-goods-surge.html.

Linden Lab. 2011. *Q1 2011 Linden Dollar economy metrics up, users and usage unchanged.* http://community.secondlife.com/t5/Featured-News/Q1–2011-Linden-Dollar-Economy-Metrics-Up-Users-and-Usage/ba-p/856693.

Ludlow, Peter, and Mark Wallace. 2007. *The Second Life Herald: The virtual tabloid that witnessed the dawn of the metaverse.* Cambridge, MA: MIT Press.

Magrino, Tom. 2010. Blizzard confirms next-gen MMOG called Titan. *GameSpot.* http://www.gamespot.com/pc/rpg/titan/news/6285568/blizzard-confirms-next-gen-mmog-called-titan.

Magrino, Tom. 2011. Blizzard's new MMOG to be "casual"—analyst. *GameSpot.* http://www.gamespot.com/pc/rpg/titan/news/6321832/blizzards-new-mmog-to-be-casual-analyst.

Malaby, Thomas. 2006. Parlaying value: Capital in and beyond virtual worlds. *Games and Culture* 1: 141–162.

Malaby, Thomas. 2009. *Making virtual worlds: Linden Lab and Second Life.* Ithaca, NY: Cornell University Press.

Mastrapa, Gus. 2009. *The Matrix Online* going offline. *Wired.* http://www.wired.com/gamelife/2009/07/matrix-online-closes/.

McCarthy, Caroline. 2007. Zwinky's virtual cash gets a real-world spin. *CNET News.* http://news.cnet.com/8301–17939_109–9779439–2.html.

McKenna, Katelyn Y. A., and John A. Bargh. 2000. Plan 9 from cyberspace: The implications of the Internet for personality and social psychology. *Personality and Social Psychology Review* 4: 57–75.

McNamara, Tom. 2004. World of Warcraft review: Blizzard does it again. *IGN.* http://pc.ign.com/articles/572/572070p1.html.

McNamara, Tom. 2006. Dungeons and Dragons Online: Stormreach: Is this the D&D MMO we've been looking for? *IGN.* http://pc.ign.com/articles/697/697669p1.html.

Michaels, Philip. 2010. Social entertainment network IMVU launches Mac client. *PCWorld.* http://www.pcworld.com/businesscenter/article/206524/social_entertainment_network_imvu_launches_mac_client.html.

Miller, Claire Cain, and Brad Stone. 2009. Virtual goods start bringing real paydays. *New York Times.* http://www.nytimes.com/2009/11/07/technology/internet/07virtual.html.

Miller, Greg. 2007. The promise of parallel universes. *Science* 317: 1341–1343.

Morales, Tatiana. 2002. EverQuest or Evercrack? *CBS News.* http://www.cbsnews.com/stories/2002/05/28/earlyshow/living/caught/main510302.shtml.

Morningstar, Chip, and F. Randall Farmer. 1991. The lessons of Lucasfilm's Habitat. In *Cyberspace: First steps,* ed. Michael L. Benedikt, 273–302. Cambridge, MA: MIT Press.

Mortensen, Torill Elvira. 2006. WoW is the new MUD: Social gaming from text to video. *Games and Culture* 1: 397–413.

Murdoch, Julian. 2010. Money for nothing, and your kicks for free. *GamePro*. http://www.gamepro.com/article/features/216227/money-for-nothing-and-your-kicks-for-free/.

Nardi, Bonnie. 2010. *My life as a night elf priest: An anthropological account of World of Warcraft*. Ann Arbor, MI: University of Michigan Press.

Ng, Brian D., and Peter Wiemer-Hastings. 2005. Addiction to the Internet and online gaming. *CyberPsychology and Behavior* 8: 110–113.

Onyett, Charles. 2007. The Lord of the Rings Online: Shadows of Angmar review: Turbine's latest MMORPG delivers. *IGN*. http://pc.ign.com/articles/787/787942p1.html.

Orland, Kyle. 2011. Turbine: Lord of the Rings Online revenues tripled as free-to-play game. *Gamasutra*. http://www.gamasutra.com/view/news/32322/Turbine_Lord_of_the_Rings_Online_Revenues_Tripled_As_FreeToPlay_Game.php.

Park, Andrew. 2011. E3 2011: Star Wars: The Old Republic updated hands-on preview. *GameSpot*. http://www.gamespot.com/pc/rpg/star-wars-the-old-republic/news/6317852/e3-2011-star-wars-the-old-republic-updated-hands-on-preview-high-level-play-on-tatooine?mode=previews.

Peckham, Matt. 2010. What'll be free and what won't in Lord of the Rings Online. *PCWorld*. http://www.pcworld.com/article/203674/whatll_be_free_and_what_wont_in_lord_of_the_rings_online.html.

Peters, Matthew. 2009. Dungeons and Dragons Online going free-to-play. *GameSpot*. http://www.gamespot.com/pc/rpg/dndonlineforsakenlands/news.html?sid=6211743.

Rausch, Allen. 2004. Reviews: *World of Warcraft*. *GameSpy*. http://pc.gamespy.com/pc/world-of-warcraft/571585p1.html.

Rausch, Allen. 2007. Reviews: *The Lord of the Rings Online: Shadows of Angmar*. *GameSpy*. http://pc.gamespy.com/pc/lord-of-the-rings-online-shadows-of-angmar/785884p1.html.

Robinett, Warren. 1994. Interactivity and individual viewpoint in shared virtual worlds: The big screen vs. networked personal displays. *Computer Graphics* 28: 127–130.

Saltzman, Marc. 2008. Review: Despite glitches, "Age of Conan" excites. *CNN*. http://articles.cnn.com/2008–06–24/tech/conan_1_hyborian-adventures-guilds-multiplayer?_s.

Schiano, Diane J. 1999. Lessons from LambdaMOO: A social, text-based virtual environment. *Presence: Teleoperators and Virtual Environments* 8: 127–139.

Schiesel, Seth. 2005. Conqueror in a war of virtual worlds. *New York Times*. http://www.nytimes.com/2005/09/06/arts/design/06worl.html.

Schiesel, Seth. 2008a. At play in a world of savagery, but not this one. *New York Times*. http://www.nytimes.com/2008/06/04/arts/television/04conan.html.

Schiesel, Seth. 2008b. A fantasy universe raises its broadsword against World of Warcraft. *New York Times*. http://www.nytimes.com/2008/10/11/arts/television/11hamm.html.

Schroeder, Ralph, Noel Heather, and Rachel M. Lee. 1998. The sacred and the virtual: Religion in multi-user virtual reality. *Journal of Computer-Mediated Communication* 4(2). http://jcmc.indiana.edu/vol4/issue2/schroeder.html.

Senior, Tom. 2011. Guild Wars 2 beta coming "in the second half of this year," 2012 release likely. *PC Gamer*. http://www.pcgamer.com/2011/05/18/guild-wars-2-coming-in-the-second-half-of-this-year-2012-release-likely/.

Shapiro, Andrew. 1998. The disappearance of cyberspace and the rise of code. *Seton Hall Constitutional Law Journal* 8: 703–723.

Shepherd, Tyche. 2011. *Second Life grid survey—Economic metrics*. http://gridsurvey.com/economy.php.

Shields, Mike. 2010. Zynga's betting the farm. *Adweek*. http://www.adweek.com/aw/content_display/news/digital/e3i5b647315f27310efe6cd981a4fd0cd06.

Sjöberg, Lore. 2005. Matrix Online: Gaming repackaged. *Wired*. http://www.wired.com/gaming/gamingreviews/news/2005/04/67088.

Spence, Jeremiah. 2008. Demographics of virtual worlds. *Journal of Virtual Worlds Research* 1(2). http://journals.tdl.org/jvwr/article/view/360/272.

Steen, Francis F., Patricia M. Greenfield, Mari Siân Davies, and Brendesha Tynes. 2006. What went wrong with *The Sims Online*: Cultural learning and barriers to identification in a massively multiplayer online role-playing game. In *Playing video games: Motives, responses, and consequences*, ed. Peter Vorderer and Jennings Bryant, 307–323. Mahwah, NJ: Lawrence Erlbaum.

Steinkuehler, Constance. 2007. Massively multiplayer online gaming as a constellation of literacy practices. *E-learning* 4: 297–318.

Stephenson, Neal. 1992. *Snow crash*. New York: Bantam Books.

Svensson, P. 2008. "Dungeons and Dragons" fights for its future. *MSNBC*. http://www.msnbc.msn.com/id/23903817/.

Tanner, Nicole. 2011. E3 2011: The Old Republic is an MMO for MMO haters. *IGN*. http://pc.ign.com/articles/117/1173952p1.html.

Tolkien, J. R. R. 1937. *The hobbit: Or, there and back again*. London: George Allen and Unwin.

Tolkien, J. R. R. 1954a. *The fellowship of the ring: Being the first part of the Lord of the Rings*. London: George Allen and Unwin.

Tolkien, J. R. R. 1954b. *The two towers: Being the second part of the Lord of the Rings*. London: George Allen and Unwin.

Tolkien, J. R. R. 1955. *The return of the king: Being the third part of the Lord of the Rings*. London: George Allen and Unwin.

Turkle, Sherry. 1994. Constructions and reconstructions of self in virtual reality: Playing in the MUDs. *Mind, Culture, and Activity* 1: 158–167.

Turnau, Theodore A., III. 2004. Infecting the world: Popular culture and the perception of evil. *Journal of Popular Culture* 38: 384–396.

VanOrd, Kevin. 2010. Star Trek Online review. *GameSpot*. http://www.gamespot.com/pc/rpg/startrekonline/review.html.

VanOrd, Kevin. 2011a. DC Universe Online review. *GameSpot*. http://www.gamespot.com/pc/rpg/dcuniverseonline/review.html.

VanOrd, Kevin. 2011b. Rift Review. *GameSpot*. http://www.gamespot.com/pc/rpg/rift-planes-of-telara/review.html.

Vinge, Vernor. 1981. True names. In *Binary star #5*, ed. James R. Frenkel. New York: Dell. Reprinted in *True names and the opening of the cyberspace frontier* (New York: Tor Books, 2001), ed. Vernor Vinge and James Frenkel, 239–330.

Williams, Dmitri. 2006. Virtual cultivation: Online worlds, offline perceptions. *Journal of Communication* 56: 69–87.

Williams, Dmitri, Scott Caplan, and Li Xiong. 2007. Can you hear me now? The impact of voice in an online gaming community. *Human Communication Research* 33: 427–449.

Williams, Dmitri, Nicolas Ducheneaut, Li Xiong, Yuanyuan Zhang, Nick Yee, and Eric Nickell. 2006. From tree house to barracks: The social life of guilds in World of Warcraft. *Games and Culture* 1: 338–361.

Wolf, Mark J. P. (ed.). 2008. *The video game explosion: A history from PONG to PlayStation and beyond*. Westport, CT: Greenwood Press.

Yee, Nicholas. 2001. *The Norrathian Scrolls: A study of EverQuest (Version 2.5)*. http://www.nickyee.com/eqt/report.html.

Yee, Nick, Jeremy N. Bailenson, Mark Urbanek, Francis Chang, and Dan Merget. 2007. The unbearable likeness of being digital: The persistence of nonverbal social norms in online virtual environments. *CyberPsychology and Behavior* 10: 115–121.

Yolan, Nick. 2010. Star Trek Online review: The good, the bad and the Trekkie. *IGN*. http://pc.ign.com/articles/106/1069985p1.html.

2

The Audience and Function of Virtual Worlds

To understand the growing societal role of virtual worlds, it is important to understand who uses virtual worlds, why users of virtual worlds spend time in them, how virtual worlds work, and where they come from. Although the number of virtual world users is large and growing, the audience of virtual worlds is not representative of the global population. This is due in part to the simple fact that the majority of the earth's population doesn't yet have access to the Internet, and many of those who do have access to the Internet lack the convenient access necessary to use virtual worlds regularly. Also, the features of many virtual worlds are more attractive to some potential users than others, such as the medieval fantasy-themed massively multiplayer online role-playing games (MMORPGs) that draw a substantial portion of the population of virtual world users. That said, the population of virtual worlds is more diverse than one might expect, and the typical virtual world user defies the popular stereotypical portrayal of young male video gamers toiling online in solitude (Williams, Yee, and Caplan 2008). This chapter reviews information about global access to virtual worlds, shares research results about virtual worlds' users and their motivations for using virtual worlds, and describes the development, function, and features of typical virtual worlds.

Access to Virtual Worlds

Global Access to the Internet

Based on the attention that virtual worlds receive from popular media and research, it might be easy to assume that the entire world is beginning to venture into these online environments. This, however, is not the case by any means. Although access to the Internet can be taken for granted by some, the majority of the world's population consists of people who are not Internet users.

Of more than six billion people on Earth, only 30% of them, or about two billion, are categorized as Internet users (International Telecommunications Union 2010b, 2011). Between 2005 and 2010, the number of Internet users worldwide doubled, but there are still great discrepancies between nations where many have Internet access and those where few do. In developed countries, more than two-thirds of the population uses the Internet, but less than one-fourth of the population in developing countries consists of Internet users. ("Developed" country is a term typically applied to countries that have a high level of well-being based on criteria such as levels of incomes, economic indicators, life expectancy, and literacy rate, while countries with lower levels of well-being based on such indicators are referred to as "developing" countries.)

Internet access is especially scarce in Africa, where only 10.8% of the population used the Internet in 2010 (International Telecommunications Association 2010b), but nations with limited Internet access are spread across the globe. In the Democratic Republic of Congo, Ethiopia, Guinea, Liberia, Myanmar, Niger, and Timor-Leste, less than 1% of the population had access to the Internet in 2010 (International Telecommunications Association 2011). Only 1–2% of the population had Internet access in Burkina Faso, Cambodia, Chad, Madagascar, and Papua New Guinea during 2010. Rates of access are presumed to be similarly low in several nations where such Internet access data are not available, such as Myanmar, North Korea, Sierra Leone, and Sudan. Internet access also varies widely within some geographic regions. In North America, 79% of the U.S. population and 81.6% of the Canadian population used the Internet in 2010, while only 8.4% of the population of Haiti, 10.5% of the population of Guatemala, and 11.1% of the population of Honduras had Internet access during that year. Although many of the world's

Internet users are from the nations with the highest Internet access rates, there are substantial populations of Internet users in some large nations that have lower rates of Internet access. Although only 34.3% of China's population had Internet access in 2010 (International Telecommunications Association 2011), China has the largest population of Internet users in any one country on earth (International Telecommunications Association 2010c).

Everyone with Internet access, though, does not have access to the technology needed to use virtual worlds. The above figures are based on a very loose definition of Internet access, including anyone who used the Internet at all from any device (including a mobile phone) during a given year (International Telecommunications Union 2010a). The number of people on Earth with sufficient access to computers and high-speed Internet connections to use virtual worlds is lower. Fewer than 1.6 billion people had access to the Internet at home in 2010 (International Telecommunications Union 2010c). Of about 1.8 billion households in the world, only about a third, or .6 billion, had a personal computer in them in 2010. In developed countries, 71.0% of households had a computer in 2010, but only 22.5% of households in developing countries had a computer during that year. Only about 29.8%, or .5 billion households, worldwide had a computer with Internet access in 2010.

Access to wired broadband Internet, which is usually necessary to facilitate the amount of online data exchange involved in using a virtual world, is also limited. Only 555 million people, or 8% of the world's population, had wired broadband access in 2010 (International Telecommunications Union 2010c). In developed countries, 24.6% of the population had fixed broadband access in 2010, but the rate was only 4.4% in developing countries. Less than 1% of Africa's population had wired broadband access in 2010.

Global Access to Virtual Worlds

For those who have adequate Internet and computer access to use virtual worlds, their access to a virtual world will depend on whether the virtual world is available in their region. While many commercial virtual worlds serve users in multiple countries, many are not accessible from all over the world. The popular MMORPG *World of Warcraft*, for example, is available in North America, Europe, China, South Korea, Singapore, Thailand,

Malaysia, Indonesia, the Philippines, Australia, New Zealand, and Argentina, as well as in some parts of Taiwan, Hong Kong, and Macau (Blizzard Entertainment 2010). The game is also provided in eight languages. Other virtual worlds, such as the preeminent social virtual world *Second Life,* can be played by anyone in the world with adequate computing and Internet resources.

There is some variation in how commercial virtual worlds, particularly commercial MMORPGs, tend to be accessed in different parts of the world. While a personal computer at home is the default method that many use to access virtual worlds, in some places it is very popular to access virtual worlds and other online communities from public locations that provide computer access for a fee. In South Korea, for example, many users pay hourly fees to use high-quality personal computers at comfortable Internet cafés called "PC bangs" (Huhh 2008). Although South Korea enjoys one of the highest broadband Internet access rates in the world, the public PC bangs remain a popular social area for recreational online game-playing. As a consequence, PC bangs draw extensive revenue from South Koreans who visit them for long sessions in virtual worlds, including popular virtual worlds developed in South Korea such as *Lineage, Lineage II, Guild Wars,* and *Aion,* and other massively popular online games developed in South Korea, such as the online strategy game *Star-Craft* and the MMORPGs *Ragnarok Online* and *MapleStory.*

Online game use at PC Bangs is so popular in South Korea that the country's professional online game leagues host entry-level competitions at PC bangs to identify potential future stars who will gain wealth and moderate fame as competitive online game players (Huhh 2008). While the typical payment structure for commercial virtual worlds in the United States is a monthly payment rate, many commercial virtual worlds capitalize on PC bangs' popularity in South Korea by allowing PC bangs to pay a flat subscription rate for all users, allowing patrons to avoid the typical monthly subscription costs associated with virtual worlds by instead paying hourly rates at a PC bang. Other providers from virtual worlds have gone further with this spirit of cooperation and explored sharing revenues from virtual goods bought in PC bangs with the PC bangs' proprietors.

Internet cafés are also a popular method for accessing virtual worlds in China, where the majority of the population do not own their own computers with Internet access (International Telecommunication Association 2010b). Online games, however, remain very popular through the use of Internet cafés. For example, as many as 5 million of *World of Warcraft*'s subscribers access the game from China, making it the only one of China's top 10 most popular online games not developed in China or South Korea (Fletcher 2009; Wines 2009). Responding to *World of Warcraft*'s massive audience in China, its developer, Blizzard Entertainment, has accommodated a number of demands from the Chinese government in a Chinese version of the game, including replacing skeleton characters with characters that have flesh and replacing dead player avatars with small graves.

Users of Virtual Worlds

Who Uses Virtual Worlds?

A precise estimate of how many people use virtual worlds is elusive for a number of reasons. Those who estimate how many virtual worlds there are often use different criteria to define the term, resulting in different numbers of applications, games, and environments being included in their estimates. Also, many virtual worlds do not release subscriber statistics, and it is difficult to estimate how many accounts in some virtual worlds are active at any time and how many accounts belong to unique people.

A 2010 report from consulting firm Kzero claimed that the number of virtual world accounts had exceeded one billion (Mastrapa 2010), and an analysis published in 2008 placed the total population of existing virtual worlds at approximately 194 million (Spence 2008), though these numbers included a large number of online communities and games that many would not consider actual virtual worlds using the criteria described in chapter 1 (Castronova 2001) while also excluding MMORPGs from their lists of virtual worlds (Spence 2008). An estimate of the total population of MMORPGs that was based on more than 70 such games, many of which were virtual worlds including social virtual worlds such as *Second Life*, placed the number of active subscriptions at about 21 million (Van Geel 2011). An online poll by Harris Interactive (2010) found that 78% of 8- to 12-year-olds, 52% of 13- to 17-year-olds, and 46% of 18- to 24-year-olds had played online games (not limited to virtual worlds specifically) in the past week. Despite such wide variety in estimates, it can be agreed that the number of virtual world users is large and growing.

The demographic makeup of virtual worlds varies among different types of virtual worlds. In general, the audience of virtual world users includes more players of massively multiplayer role-playing games than users of other social virtual worlds that are not games. By 2007, 6.5 million people had already entered *Second Life*, while *World of Warcraft* boasted 8.5 million active subscribers by that time (Bainbridge 2007). Males make up a disproportionately large segment of the audience for virtual worlds that are MMORPGs, but research indicates that the games' audience is fairly diverse in terms of demographics such as age, income, and relationship status.

A survey of *EverQuest* users conducted during 2000 and 2001, which was perhaps the first survey to provide demographic information about virtual world users, found that about 84% of players responding to the survey were male and 16% were female (Yee 2001). The average age of the *EverQuest* players was 25.6. Female players tended to be older than male players, with an average age of 29.0 years for females in the survey and an average age of 25.2 years for males in the survey. Of the players in the survey, 30% were students. Jobs in technology and related areas were also common among players in the survey, with 25% reporting employment in technology and another 4% reporting employment in engineering. The income of players in the survey was distributed across a broad range, with 27.6% reporting an annual household income below $30,000, 24.1% reporting an annual household income between $30,000 and $49,999, 20.4% reporting an annual household income between $50,000 and $74,999, and 27.8% reporting an annual household income of more than $75,000. The relationship status of players in the survey also varied, with 32.3% single and not dating, 29% single but dating, and 36.7% of them either married, engaged, or separated. Female players in the survey were more likely to be engaged, married, or separated than male players, and among single players females were more likely than males to be dating. A significant minority of the players in the survey, 19.1%, reported having children. This survey did not collect participants' location, but it can be presumed that its participants were mostly players from the United States and other countries where English is widely spoken because participants were recruited on English-language websites related to gaming.

Another online survey of *EverQuest* users, conducted in 2001, found similar results (Castronova 2001). Female players made up only 7.8% of players responding to the survey. The average age of players in that survey was 24.3. Of players in that survey,

43.4% reported working full-time, while 19.4% were working students and 15.6% were students who were not working. Players' education levels varied in the survey, with 31% having a college degree or more, 35.6% having a high school degree only, and 12.4% not having a high school degree. The average monthly wage of players in the survey was $3,154.12. While 60% of the players in the survey were single, another 22.8% were married or cohabitating, and 15.8% of the players in the survey had children they cared for daily. This and other surveys, though, did not tend to include players representing all regions of the world where the game was played, in part because the survey recruited participants on English-language websites. As a result of this recruitment method, 81.3% of players in the survey were from the United States, 6.6% were from Canada, and 8.9% were from Southern Europe.

A third survey of *EverQuest* users found that 81% were male and 19% were female (Griffiths, Davies, and Chappell 2004a, 2004b). Adolescents in the survey were 93.2% male and 6.8% female, while adults in the survey were 79.6% male and 20.4% female. The players in that survey had an average age of 27.9 years. Players in the survey had a variety of educational backgrounds, with 29% studying for a college degree or already having one, 13% having more advanced degrees, 23.5% having been educated at least to age 19, 20% having been educated at least to age 16, 14% having no education past age 11, and .5% claiming no formal education at all. The most common livelihoods reported by participants in that study were work in information technology and computing, which 28.7% of players in the survey held, and enrollment as a student, which was claimed by 20% of the players in the survey. A slight majority of the players in the survey, 55%, were single, while 30% were married, 10% lived with a partner, 3% were divorced, and 1.5% were separated. Among adult players in the survey, though, only 46% were single. This survey also recruited participants from English-language websites, so nations with English as a primary language provided most of the players in the survey, with 69.6% from the United States, 12% from the United Kingdom, 7% from Canada, 2.2% from Australia, 6% from New Zealand, and .4% from Ireland. The only nations without English as a primary language to provide more than 1% of the survey's participants were Germany, where 1.7% of the players in the survey lived, and Sweden, where 1.3% of the players in the survey lived. Only .6% of the players in the survey were from any country in Asia.

In a series of surveys targeting users of MMORPGs between 2000 and 2003 via English-language websites, 85.4% of the game-playing respondents were male (Yee 2006b, 2006c). The average age of MMORPG players in the survey was 26.57 years old, though the average age of male players (25.71 years) was younger than the average age of female players (31.72 years). Half of the players in the survey worked full-time, while 22.2% were full-time students and 13% were homemakers. More than a third of the players in the survey (36.3%) were married, and 22.1% of them had children. Only 25% of the players in the survey were teenagers.

Another online survey targeting users of MMORPGs through recruitment on English-language websites found that 88% of responding players were male (Ng and Wiemer-Hastings 2005). In that survey, 37% of players were students and 53% worked full-time. Their educational status was varied, with 29% holding a bachelor's degree and 44% holding a high school degree.

An online survey of players who used either the online role-playing game *Asheron's Call* or its sequel, *Asheron's Call 2*, found that responding players were 85.7% male and 13.8% female (Charlton and Danforth 2007). Male players in the survey ranged in age from 18 years old to 67 years old and had an average age of 28.83 years. Female players in the survey ranged in age from 18 years old to 50 years old and had an average age of 32.87 years. The survey recruited participants from an English-language website, and 85.7% of the responding players were from the United States or Canada, with 9.5% hailing from Europe, 3.4% living in Australia or New Zealand, and only 1.4% being from other countries.

Another online survey, conducted in 2006 and 2007 and targeting players of MMORPGs in North America and Europe, found that only 15.4% of responding players were female (Smahel, Blinka, and Ledabyl 2008). Players in that survey had an average age of 25 years, and only 26.9% of the players were 19 years of age or younger. Even though the results of that survey were similar to the results of other online surveys targeting users of MMORPGs, the makeup of participants in that survey was markedly different in that 64.2% of the players in the survey were from Europe, 33% were from North America, and less than 3% were from other regions of the world.

One survey of MMORPG users that recruited participants via both online gaming sites and e-mail messages to students at a university in the United Kingdom received more responses from female players than most surveys (Cole and Griffiths 2007). Its participating players were 70% male and 29% female. Despite this slightly higher rate of female players, other aspects of the demographic makeup of players in that survey were similar to those found in other surveys. Players in the survey ranged in age from 11 to 63 years, with an average age of 23.6 years. The average age of female players was 25 years, and the average age of male players was 23 years. The survey's players hailed from 45 countries, with 46% from the United States, 26% from the United Kingdom, and 5% from Canada. Students comprised 46.7% of the players in the survey, while 10.3% worked in the information technology industry.

A survey conducted within the game environment of the online role-playing game *EverQuest II* that also collected game server data found that male players made up 80.8% of the survey's respondents, while female players made up 19.2% of the respondents (Williams et al. 2008). Female players in the survey, however, tended to spend more hours per week playing *EverQuest II* compared to males, with game server data showing that the female survey respondents played for an average of 29.32 hours per week compared to an average of 25.03 hours per week for male respondents (Williams et al. 2009). Female players in the survey also tended to underestimate the amount of time they played per week more than their male counterparts, with the females underestimating their weekly play by 3.29 hours per week and the males underestimating their weekly play by an average of .93 hours per week. The average age of players in the survey was 31.16, with players ranging in age from 16 years old to 65 years old. Only 6.58% of players in the survey were younger than 18 years of age. The average age for male players in the survey was 32.82 years and the average age for female players in the survey was 33.49 years. The average household income for players in the survey was $84,715 per year. Players in the survey tended to have at least some university education, with 32.63% attending some college but not obtaining a degree, 16.93% having an associate's degree, 14.43% having a bachelor's degree, and another 14.7% claiming some graduate education. Only 15.62% possessed no more education than a high school degree, and a mere 7.67% reported not having completed high school. A large majority of the players in the survey, 87.62%, were white, with

3.34% Hispanic/Latino, 2.68% Asian/Pacific Islander, 1.74% Native American, and 1.55% black/African American.

Although these studies indicate that the populations of massively multiplayer role-playing games are predominantly male, at least in North America and Europe, other types of virtual worlds may attract different populations. A survey of *Second Life* users conducted in 2009 within the virtual world environment found different demographic trends in the social virtual world than had been found in the surveys of users of MMORPGs (Bell, Castronova, and Wagner 2009). In the *Second Life* survey, 51.4% of the respondents were female, while 43% of them were male. (Other users did not report their gender or reported that they were transgendered.) The age of *Second Life* users in the survey varied widely, with 35% reporting an age of 18–25 years, 32% reporting an age of 26–35 years, 18% reporting an age of 36–45 years, 10% reporting an age of 46–55 years, and 5% reporting an age of more than 55 years. Many participants in the survey reported lower levels of income than those observed by the above surveys of online game players, with 36% of the participating *Second Life* users reporting less than $10,000 in income per year, 15% reporting an income between $10,001 and $20,000, 29% reporting an income between $20,001 and $50,000, 16% reporting an income between $50,001 and $75,000, and 17% reporting an income of more than $75,000. For 57% of the participants in the survey, formal education ended between the ages of 18 and 25, while 25% had their education end between the ages of 26 and 35, 10% had their education end between the ages of 36 and 45, and 8% ended their educations at an age older than 45. The survey object placed in the *Second Life* environment asked questions in English, resulting in a group of participants that were mostly from English-speaking countries, with 40% from the United States, 9% from the United Kingdom, and 6% from Canada. Some other nations were also somewhat well-represented among survey participants, however, with 7% from Germany, 5% from France, 3% from the Netherlands, 3% from Spain, 2% from Brazil, 2% from Italy, and 22% from other countries.

Why Do People Use Virtual Worlds?

One of the aforementioned surveys of *EverQuest* users asked players to name their favorite feature of the game (Griffiths, Davies, and Chappell 2004a). The most popular answer, given by

24.6% of the players in the survey, was that *EverQuest* was a social game. Another 10.2% of the players in the survey noted being able to group together with others in the game, while 10% mentioned being a member of a "Guild" game group and another 10% named the fact that the game did not end as their favorite feature. Generally, social features of the game tended to be most often listed as favorites by both adolescent players and adult players in the survey (Griffiths, Davies, and Chappell 2004b).

The reasons for which virtual world users log on also appear to differ depending on users' demographics. In the aforementioned series of surveys targeting users of MMORPGs between 2000 and 2003, male and female players in the survey placed similar importance on socializing as a reason for playing, but male players tended to emphasize achievement and manipulation of others more than female players while female players tended to place more importance on forming relationships, immersing themselves in the environment, and using the virtual world to temporarily escape from real-life troubles (Yee 2006a, 2006b, 2006c). Younger male players placed more emphasis on achieving and manipulating others than older male players, and younger female players placed more emphasis on manipulating others and immersing themselves in the game environment than older players. The survey mentioned above that recruited MMORPG users found that male players were more likely than female players to play because of their "curiosity, astonishment, and interest" in the game, while female players were more likely than male players to play for "therapeutic refreshment" (Cole and Griffiths 2007, p. 579). The aforementioned survey of *EverQuest II* users found similar results, with male players more motivated by achievement than female players and female players more socially motivated than male players (Williams et al. 2009).

An online survey of *Second Life* users revealed different motivations compared to these surveys of MMORPG users (Zhou et al. 2010). Among popular motivations for the surveyed *Second Life* users were socializing, exploring the environment, learning, being entertained, and shopping. Female *Second Life* users were more motivated to shop and do research in the virtual world compared to male *Second Life* users, while males were more motivated by using the game to make money compared to females. Older users in the survey were more motivated by creating material in the world and by education compared to younger users, while younger users were more motivated by being entertained than older users. In general, the various studies examining motivations for using virtual worlds find that people use these environments for a wide range of reasons, and that the motivations users have for using virtual worlds tends to differ depending on characteristics of both the virtual worlds and characteristics of the users themselves.

The Function of Virtual Worlds

How a User Creates an Avatar and Enters a Virtual World

Although not all virtual worlds function the same way, the basic features of most are very similar. Most virtual worlds require their users to install some software on their computer to access the virtual world environment. This software is provided via a disc obtained from a physical store or other location or via download from the Internet. The installed software allows the virtual world application to operate quickly and efficiently on a user's computer. For some commercial virtual worlds, the user must pay for this software, while other virtual worlds provide free trial access for a limited time or are free to access altogether.

Although the hallmark of virtual worlds is their online interaction, most of the information a user's computer needs to display the virtual world is actually downloaded to the user's computer in advance rather than shared on the Internet while the user is in the virtual world. It would be far too cumbersome for a virtual world to send all of its information to a user's computer on the Internet as the user traveled, so much of that information is shared in advance through a user's initial installation of the virtual world software and small updates that are occasionally provided when a user logs in to the virtual world. Using that information in tandem with smaller amounts of information sent back and forth between a user's computer and a virtual world server (such as the user's location and the actions of other users in the virtual environment), the user's computer is able to present a rich and constantly updated representation of a virtual world.

Once a user has installed the software for a virtual world on a computer, the user typically selects a user name and password that can be used to access the account. This account creation process, which functions much like the process involved with creating an account with other popular online applications such as social networking websites and Web-based e-mail services, allows the user to access his or her account in the virtual world from any computer on which the virtual world software is installed, while also protecting against unauthorized use of the account by others. Some virtual worlds charge a fee for an account. In these cases, a monthly rate is the most common payment structure, except in some regions of the world where the use of virtual worlds in Internet cafés is common and other payment methods are more appropriate.

When a user first enters a virtual world, the user must create a customized avatar. The user can assign the avatar a unique name and choose the gender of the avatar, and most virtual worlds also give the user a broad range of choices in determining the avatar's physical characteristics such as height, build, hair color, eye color, and facial appearance. The available options can be extensive, with virtual worlds allowing many users to manipulate details of the character avatar's facial structure, eye shape and color, apparent age, and other nuances. Some virtual worlds, particularly MMORPGs, also allow the user to choose their avatar's species from a number of fanciful options.

In MMORPGs, users also often choose an avatar's class to determine the avatar's set of skills in the game. For example, a character from the hunter class might be able to attack other characters from a distance, while a shaman character might be able to use magic to heal other characters who are injured. Different classes might also have different levels of ability with regard to game-related traits. For example, a hunter might cause more damage with attacks on enemies than a shaman, but the shaman might recover from injury more quickly than the hunter. In social virtual worlds, avatars do not need such game-based virtual skills, so the avatar creation process involves only the determination of a character's identity and appearance. Many virtual worlds allow users to have more than one avatar per account, though the avatars cannot usually be actively present in the virtual world at the same time and some commercial virtual worlds may charge a premium for multiple characters.

Once a user has created an avatar, many virtual worlds require the user to choose from one of several versions of the virtual world, referred to by a number of names such as "servers" or "shards." In most cases, the general content of these different versions of the virtual world is identical, but they are often necessary because the group of computer servers hosting the virtual world online can only host a limited number of simultaneous users (often numbering in the thousands). To allow the virtual world to host more players than a server can handle, and to ensure that a virtual world is not overcrowded with avatars, multiple servers provide multiple versions of the virtual world. (Although each version of the virtual world might be called a "server," in many cases the virtual world version provided by the "server" is actually provided by a group of computer servers that manage different regions of the virtual world version.)

Sometimes, the virtual world versions provided by different servers are identical except for the piece of computer hardware on which they are hosted and the avatars who traverse the virtual environment they provide. In other cases, there are differences in the function of some virtual worlds on different servers, such as when an MMORPG provides some servers that allow player-versus-player combat and some that do not. Sometimes, the game functions and logistics are identical across different game servers, but they are assigned different roles by virtual world administrators to target players with different backgrounds and interests. For example, an MMORPG may dedicate a server to players who enjoy engaging in extensive role-playing activity with their avatar characters by typing long descriptions of character activity and dialogue in a fashion similar to users of multi-user dungeons (MUDs) and other text-based role-playing environments.

In some cases, an avatar based on one server cannot access versions of the virtual world that exist on other servers or interact with the avatars of virtual world users on other servers, but some virtual worlds allow a user to change the virtual world server accessed by an avatar. Alternately, some virtual worlds, such as *Second Life*, provide access to the same virtual world environment for all users so that all of the users' avatars can interact with one another and the same environment when they are simultaneously connected. In these cases, multiple computer servers are typically assigned to different virtual regions of the virtual world to manage user traffic, but the same virtual world environment is shared by all users.

How a User Navigates a Virtual World

When a user has created an avatar and entered a virtual world server, the virtual world environment will be visible on the user's video monitor. The back of the user's avatar is usually also visible on the screen because the user's point of view is from slightly behind the avatar. This perspective provides the user with a general first-person point of view of the environment while allowing the user to see the avatar's appearance and position in the environment clearly. Many virtual worlds provide the user with the option of using a true first-person perspective, with the screen showing an approximation of what the avatar's eyes would see, but this perspective is often less helpful to the user because it may be difficult to ascertain the avatar's precise position in the environment and the avatar's immediate surroundings.

In addition to a view of the virtual environment, most virtual worlds also display a number of other features on the user's screen. Many virtual worlds provide a text chat window in a corner of the user's screen that shows typed messages from nearby users and private messages sent specifically to the user's avatar by other users. Some virtual worlds include a miniature map in another corner of the user's screen that shows which direction the avatar is facing, some basic details of the virtual terrain around the avatar, and the relative location of some other nearby avatars and virtual objects. A number of other buttons are usually present on the screen, which the user can click to receive more information or execute commands. Additionally, many virtual worlds provide text information that visually floats over some elements of the environment, such as the names of other avatars or objects that the user can obtain or examine more closely.

A virtual world user typically navigates a virtual world environment using a standard keyboard and mouse (or game controller in the case of virtual worlds that are accessed from video game consoles). For example, a user might use the computer's arrow keys to walk forward, walk backward, and turn to the left and right, while using the computer mouse to examine and interact with other avatars and virtual objects. By using the keyboard and clicking the mouse on icons on the screen, the user can execute other commands such as typing chat messages, examining virtual items in the avatar's inventory, viewing a full map of the virtual environment, and making the avatar execute gestures. Many virtual worlds also provide audio voice chat between users whose computers are equipped with microphones.

Although the primary mode of travel in most virtual worlds is walking, other means are possible. In *Second Life,* users' avatars can float into the air and fly in order to travel quickly or see virtual areas from an elevated point of view. Many virtual worlds include virtual mounts or vehicles that accelerate an avatar's travel across virtual space, and others allow avatars to "teleport" to some or all virtual locations instantly.

When a virtual world user ends a session in a virtual world, the user's avatar is no longer visible to other users in the virtual environment. Other users' avatars can no longer perceive or interact with the avatar until the user returns. When the user returns for another session in the virtual environment, though, the user's avatar returns to the same place in the virtual world that it had occupied when the user ended the previous session. Although the location of the user's avatar does not change between sessions, any changes that have taken place in the virtual environment between sessions will still be in effect when the user returns to the virtual world. For example, if a user logs off of a virtual world in a virtual space and another user builds a virtual home near the location the logged-off avatar's user had been occupying, that virtual home will be present when the user returns to the virtual world.

Activities, Tasks, and Goals in Massively Multiplayer Online Role-Playing Games

In the MMORPGs that represent most virtual worlds, avatars typically complete tasks to advance the game's plot and advance the avatar character's abilities and status. The user's first session in an MMORPG is usually in an introductory area where the user completes a relatively simple task while being introduced to the game's premise, plot, and features. After this introductory stage, the avatar character is introduced to a larger segment of the virtual world. Most of the user's activity in the virtual world usually consists of accepting and completing quests, or short tasks, in order to advance the game's plot and receive "experience points" for the avatar character. Quests might include gathering items in the game world or defeating one or more minor computer-controlled characters. Some quests are required for the game's plot to advance, while others are optional. Users also have substantial latitude in deciding when to pursue different quests. Although some quests are part of quest chains, where some quests in the chain cannot be pursued until a prerequisite quest has been completed, a player may often choose from scores of available quests in even a small region. Alternately, a player may choose not to pursue a quest at all during a session, instead spending the time roaming the virtual environment, socializing with friends, or helping others with their own tasks.

While quests provide experience points, experience points are also usually granted for defeating computer-controlled characters, whether or not defeating such characters is part of an assigned quest, and they are also sometimes granted for other achievements such as exploring new regions. As experience points accumulate, the character avatar will gain increasingly higher-level status and gain accompanying abilities and skills. For example, an avatar character in a typical MMORPG will begin the game at level one, complete several quests that involve gathering virtual items or defeating minor computer-controlled enemy characters, and gain levels. As the levels accumulate, the character avatar will gain in attributes such as ability to attack and defend other characters, and in health or "hit points," which determine how much virtual damage a character can absorb in a battle before being defeated. Increasing level status will typically enable the avatar to acquire new skills and traits and grant the avatar access to increasingly larger and more challenging regions of the virtual world as the game's plot continues. Massively multiplayer online role-playing games typically have a maximum "level cap" beyond which a character cannot advance, but such high levels may require hundreds or thousands of hours of play to attain, and level caps are often raised as new content is added to the game to keep experienced users active and interested.

As a character avatar's status progresses, that avatar will also accumulate virtual currency and virtual weapons, armor, and other useful items. These objects are attained either as loot from defeated characters or through transactions with virtual stores and shops operated by computer-controlled characters. A character avatar is typically able to carry dozens of virtual items at once in an inventory, but some games limit the number of items a character avatar can hold at once. If a character avatar has reached the maximum number of virtual items that can be carried and wants to pick up another item, the avatar must discard an item. Some virtual worlds also provide banks where character avatars can store and retrieve items that are temporarily unneeded.

Although a character in an MMORPG might advance rapidly through several levels and quickly gain new items and skills, higher levels tend to take increasingly more effort and time to achieve and advanced items can be very difficult to obtain. This means that the player's character avatar will sometimes be defeated. Most MMORPGs allow a character avatar to return to the game environment if defeated. Given that players are required to invest substantial amounts of time to achieve high-level status and obtain rare virtual items for their avatar characters, it would be very discouraging for a user to be forced to start the game anew after a defeat. Therefore, it is a common practice for characters to be returned to a "safe" area after a defeat, from which they can continue the game. However, there is a penalty for in-game defeat in order to discourage recklessness and reward skilled players. This penalty usually consists of one or more minor inconveniences and temporary obstacles to progress in the game, such as a cost to repair damaged weapons and armor or a temporary reduction in the avatar character's abilities.

In addition to advancing the game's story and gaining levels, avatars in most MMORPGs also develop "crafting" skills. Depending on what abilities a character avatar has developed, characters can collect materials in the game and use them to forge weapons and armor, cook food, concoct potions, and more. The items that a player's character avatar crafts might be used by that same avatar, or the player might barter or trade them with other players in the game.

Most of these aspects of MMORPGs, such as quests, leveling, and accumulation of virtual currency and items, are consistent with those of role-playing computer games that can be played without the Internet. The unique aspect of MMORPGs, then, is their ability to bring players together in the virtual environment. This interaction sometimes comes in the form of combat between players, and some entire massively multiplayer role-playing games are devoted primarily to player-versus-player combat. In many games, though, combat between players is even disallowed or relegated to specific game regions.

Instead, most popular MMORPGs encourage cooperation between players. While many achievements in virtual worlds can be accomplished individually, many more are difficult or impossible to accomplish without the assistance of other players. Most MMORPGs allow the creation of temporary groups of a handful of character avatars who cooperate as allies while completing one or more quest tasks. These groups are often most effective when they include character avatars from different class types, such as a mix of character avatars who are skilled at combat and those who are skilled at healing other characters. Extremely challenging tasks might call for the creation of larger "raid" groups several times the size of common player groups. Players can also affiliate in longer-term relationships with larger groups in the form of guilds, which allow players to develop an enduring network with other players. Some guilds are very casual and loosely structured, while others maintain detailed schedules and organizational hierarchies and use websites outside of the game environment to manage their members and activities.

Although guilds are useful for organizing players who are trying to accomplish tasks in MMORPGs, uniting players to accomplish game objectives is not their only purpose for existing. Guilds also offer a social network for players who can communicate with their fellow guild members, both in the game environment and in other forums such as guild websites and sometimes even in-person arranged social gatherings. Some MMORPGs allow guilds to purchase virtual homes where players' avatars can gather together and socialize in their shared virtual space. Guilds may also organize events in games that do not accomplish game objectives, such as a party in a common game area or a public musical performance using virtual instruments.

Activities in Social Virtual Worlds

On the other hand, social virtual worlds such as *Second Life* function very differently than those virtual worlds that are MMORPGs. Although the basic visual interface and controls for social virtual worlds are very similar to those of MMORPGs, the users have no structured game to play. Without the presence of game objectives, story lines, and competition, social virtual worlds provide even more freedom than MMORPGs in terms of how a user may choose to experience the virtual environment. As with MMORPGs, social virtual worlds often place a user's avatar in an introductory area during the user's first session so that the user can become acquainted with commands and features. After the user's avatar leaves the introductory area, though, the user of a social world typically has few limits on where in the virtual world the avatar can travel or what the avatar can choose to do.

For some users, socializing with friends and meeting new people may be a primary activity, while others may enjoy visiting the virtual attractions that have been built in the virtual environment by its designers or users. Shopping and playing various games that exist within the virtual world are also options. In fact, some social virtual worlds like *Second Life* actually have MMORPGs that are operated by users in limited regions within the virtual world. The virtual venues and experiences available within social virtual worlds are as diverse as the virtual worlds' populations because most social virtual worlds allow and encourage their users to create content within the virtual world. For some users, this content creation is designed to make money within the virtual world. For example, a user might create a shop where virtual clothing designed by the user is sold to other users for their avatars. For other users, though, content is created merely to provide interesting places and objects for themselves and other users.

Although users are welcome, but not required, to create new content in social virtual worlds, some skills are required to create most virtual objects. In *Second Life,* for example, players can build new objects by creating, modifying, and combining rudimentary shapes such as cubes and cones (called "prims," which is short for "primitive" in reference to the objects' basic shapes). Building virtual objects in this fashion usually takes some practice in the virtual world environment, but advanced objects require additional aptitude. Most interactive objects require inclusion of code developed with programming knowledge, and attractive visual objects might require creation of image files using a graphics editing program. The challenges involved in creating advanced objects ensure an active economy within social virtual worlds, as users with advanced design skills can profit from making objects for users who lack advanced skills but want to enhance their virtual world experience.

Users' active role in content creation is also beneficial to administrators of social virtual worlds, as the users essentially provide thousands of hours of free design labor to enrich the virtual world with new content. Unlike MMORPGs, social virtual worlds typically rely on their users to create much or all of the virtual world environment and experience for one another. The administrators of social virtual worlds also often benefit from the transactions players make in the virtual environment by charging virtual entrepreneurs for the virtual space they use and by charging virtual buyers and sellers small fees for the exchange of their virtual currency to and from real currency.

Developers of Virtual Worlds

Creating and Managing a Commercial Virtual World

The MUDs that preceded virtual worlds could be developed through the efforts of a gifted university student or two (e.g., Bartle 2003, 2010), but creation of a large-scale commercial virtual world today requires a substantial commitment of resources (Castronova 2006). Thousands of hours of work from many different types of experts are required to develop an MMORPG. Among the specialists required to develop such a game are game designers, computer programmers, graphic and animation artists, and experts in database, network, and server architecture. These combined efforts mean that millions of dollars will be spent over the course of years by the time an MMORPG is ready to launch.

A 2003 estimate put the cost of developing an MMORPG at more than $10 million (Carpenter 2003). In 2010, Activision chief executive officer Bobby Kotick claimed that it would cost $500 million to $1 billion to develop a massively multiplayer online role-playing game that could compete with *World of Warcraft*'s dominance of the market (Welsh 2010). Social virtual worlds can cost less to develop than MMORPGs because of the large amount of game content that is developed by users at no cost to the virtual world's developer, but there are still substantial costs involved in developing a social virtual world's infrastructure, interface, and features. In addition to the initial costs of developing a virtual world, there are substantial costs associated with maintaining a virtual world's servers, addressing technical problems, providing support for users, and developing new content to hold users' interest.

Smaller-Scale Virtual Worlds

Despite the prohibitive costs involved in the creation and development of a successful commercial virtual world, there are means that allow a developer with modest resources to develop smaller and simpler virtual worlds. In 2002, Bioware and Infrogames released a computer role-playing game called *Neverwinter Nights*, named in homage to the first graphical online computer game, which had the same name and was released in 1991. Included with copies of the 2002 iteration of *Neverwinter Nights* was a software application called the Aurora tool set, which allowed users to create and play their own modules of the *Neverwinter Nights* game by designing areas, adding characters, and editing events and character behaviors (Kasavin 2002). Although *Neverwinter Nights* was not itself an online virtual world (though the game did allow players to connect online to play together), players could use the Aurora tool set to create and host their own online games with up to 96 players. In effect, then, the Aurora tool set could be used by players to create and host their own small and rudimentary virtual worlds. For example, a team of researchers used the Aurora tool set to create a prototype of a virtual world called *Arden,* the content of which was based on the works of Shakespeare, in order to examine the economic behavior of the virtual world's users (Castronova 2008; Castronova et al. 2008).

While the Aurora tool kit is an interesting example of a software platform that can be used to create small game-based virtual worlds, other platforms are being developed that can allow developers much more latitude in defining the purpose, size, structure, and function of the virtual worlds they create. In 1999, Duke University released Open Cobalt, a free software platform that can be used by individuals and organizations to make public and private virtual worlds. Open Cobalt is free to use, and users can adapt and modify its code to improve it. Open Cobalt provides the tools to build large-scale commercial virtual worlds like the social virtual worlds and MMORPGs in existence today, but developers can also use the software to build private virtual world environments, such as for students of a university.

More Users in More Worlds

A lot of different people use virtual worlds for a lot of different purposes, and both the number of people using virtual worlds and the number of different reasons they have for using them are continuing to grow. Although the development and maintenance of virtual worlds is a challenging and costly venture, the potential audience of dedicated users can justify the difficulties and risks involved. As long as virtual worlds remain popular and profitable, the future will likely bring more users from all over the world to explore the growing number of virtual worlds available. It is important to remember, though, that as ubiquitous as virtual worlds may seem to be, most of the world's population still lacks the convenient access to computing technology and Internet connectivity that are prerequisites for entry to the universe of virtual worlds.

References

Bainbridge, William Sims. 2007. The scientific research potential of virtual worlds. *Science* 317: 472–476.

Bartle, Richard A. 2003. *Designing virtual worlds.* Indianapolis, IN: New Riders.

Bartle, Richard A. 2010. From MUDs to MMORPGs: The history of virtual worlds. In *International handbook of Internet research,* ed. Jeremy Hunsinger, Lisbeth Klastrup, and Matthew Allen, 23–39. Dordrecht: Springer.

Bell, Mark W., Edward Castronova, and Gert G. Wagner. 2009. Surveying the virtual world: A large scale survey in Second Life using the Virtual Data Collection Interface (VDCI). http://papers.ssrn.com/sol3/papers.cfm?abstract_id=1418562.

Blizzard Entertainment. World of Warcraft subscriber base reaches 12 million worldwide. http://us.blizzard.com/en-us/company/press/pressreleases.html?id=2847881.

Carpenter, Adam. 2003. Applying risk analysis to play-balance RPGs. *Gamasutra: The art and business of making games.* http://www.gamasutra.com/view/feature/2843/applying_risk_analysis_to_.php.

Castronova, Edward. 2001. *Virtual worlds: A first-hand account of market and society on the cyberian frontier.* CESifo Working Paper No. 618, December. http://ssrn.com/abstract=294828.

Castronova, Edward. 2006. On the research value of large games: Natural experiments in Norrath and Camelot. *Games and Culture* 1: 163–186.

Castronova, Edward. 2008. *A test of the law of demand in a virtual world: Exploring the petri dish approach to social science.* CESifo Working Paper No. 2355, July. http://papers.ssrn.com/sol3/papers.cfm?abstract_id=1173642.

Castronova, Edward, Travis Ross, Mark Bell, Matthew Falk, Robert Cornell, and Matt Haselton. 2008. Constructing Arden: Life inside the machine. *Multimedia IEEE* 15(1): 4–8.

Charlton, John P., and Ian D. W. Danforth. 2007. Distinguishing addiction and high engagement in the context of online game playing. *Computers in Human Behavior* 23: 1531–1548.

Cole, Helena, and Mark D. Griffiths. 2007. Social interactions in massively multiplayer online role-playing gamers. *CyberPsychology and Behavior* 10: 575–583.

Fletcher, Owen. 2009. World of Warcraft allowed partial relaunch in China. *PCWorld*. http://www.pcworld.com/article/168817/world_of_warcraft_allowed_partial_relaunch_in_china.html.

Griffiths, Mark D., Mark N. O. Davies, and Darren Chappell. 2004a. Demographic factors and playing variables in online computer gaming. *CyberPsychology and Behavior* 7: 479–487.

Griffiths, Mark D., Mark N. O. Davies, and Darren Chappell. 2004b. Online computer gaming: A comparison of adolescent and adult gamers. *Journal of Adolescence* 27: 87–96.

Harris Interactive. 2010. YouthPulse 2010. *Trends and tudes* 9(2). http://www.harrisinteractive.com/vault/HI_TrendsTudes_2010_v09_i02.pdf.

Huhh, Jun-Sok. 2008. Culture and business of PC bangs in Korea. *Games and Culture* 3: 26–37.

International Telecommunications Union. 2010a. Definitions of world telecommunication/ICT indicators. http://www.itu.int/ITU-D/ict/material/TelecomICT%20Indicators%20Definition_March2010_for%20web.pdf.

International Telecommunications Union. 2010b. Key global telecom indicators for the world telecommunication service sector. http://www.itu.int/ITU-D/ict/statistics/at_glance/KeyTelecom2010.html.

International Telecommunications Union. 2010c. The world in 2010: ICT facts and figures. http://www.itu.int/ITU-D/ict/material/FactsFigures2010.pdf.

International Telecommunications Union. 2011. ICT statistics database. http://www.itu.int/ITU-D/icteye/Indicators/Indicators.aspx#.

Kasavin, Greg. 2002. Neverwinter Nights review. *GameSpot*. http://www.gamespot.com/pc/rpg/neverwinternights/review.html.

Mastrapa, Gus. 2010. Study says virtual world accounts number 1 billion. *Wired*. http://www.wired.com/gamelife/2010/10/virtual-world-accounts/.

Ng, Brian D., and Peter Wiemer-Hastings. 2005. Addiction to the Internet and online gaming. *CyberPsychology and Behavior* 8: 110–113.

Smahel, David, Lukas Blinka, and Ondrej Ledabyl. 2008. Playing MMORPGS: Connections between addiction and identifying with a character. *CyberPsychology and Behavior* 11: 715–718.

Spence, Jeremiah. 2008. Demographics of virtual worlds. *Journal of Virtual Worlds Research* 1(2). http://journals.tdl.org/jvwr/article/view/360/272.

Van Geel, Ibe. 2011. MMOData.net: Keeping track of the MMOG scene. http://mmodata.net/.

Welsh, Oli. 2010. $1 billion investment needed to take on World of Warcraft—Kotick. *Gamesindustry.biz*. http://www.gamesindustry.biz/articles/1-billion-investment-needed-to-take-on-world-of-warcraft-kotick.

Williams, Dmitri, Mia Consalvo, Scott Caplan, and Nick Yee. 2009. Looking for gender: Gender roles and behaviors among online gamers. *Journal of Communication* 59: 700–725.

Williams, Dmitri, Nick Yee, and Scott Caplan. 2008. Who plays, how much, and why? Debunking the stereotypical gamer profile. *Journal of Computer-Mediated Communication* 13: 993–1018.

Wines, Michael. 2009. Chinese agencies struggle over video game. *The New York Times*. http://www.nytimes.com/2009/11/07/world/asia/07china.html.

Yee, Nicholas. 2001. The Norrathian Scrolls: A study of EverQuest (Version 2.5). http://www.nickyee.com/eqt/report.html.

Yee, Nick. 2006a. Motivations for play in online games. *CyberPsychology and Behavior* 9: 772–775.

Yee, Nick. 2006b. The demographics, motivations, and derived experiences of users of massively multi-user online graphical environments. *Presence: Teleoperators and Virtual Environments* 15: 309–329.

Yee, Nick. 2006c. The psychology of massively multi-user online roleplaying games: Motivations, emotional investment, relationships and problematic usage. In *Avatars at work and play: Collaboration and interaction in virtual shared environments,* ed. Ralph Schroeder and Ann-Sofie Axelsson, 187–208. London: Springer.

Zhou, Zhongyun, Xiao-Lin Jin, Douglas R. Vogel, Yulin Fang, and Xiaojian Chen. 2010. Individual motivations and demographic differences in social virtual world uses: An exploratory investigation in Second Life. *International Journal of Information Management* 31: 261–271.

3

Societal Concerns and Opportunities

As virtual worlds become an increasingly popular medium for social, entertainment, and business use, discussion about the societal promise and perils of virtual worlds is also increasing. Research and notable news about issues related to virtual worlds continues to draw attention to more and more opportunities and concerns related to the developing medium. While much research focuses on potential problems virtual world users might face, such as overuse, there has also been some attention given to the potential benefits these environments might present for their users.

This discussion about the societal role of virtual worlds is also grounded in the context of broader conversations about the societal role of the Internet and video games. Virtual worlds all make use of the Internet, and many popular virtual worlds are video game environments, so research and public opinion about all three media are related to one another. This chapter reviews research and news anecdotes related to both the troubling concerns and the exciting opportunities presented by virtual worlds.

Problems and Concerns

Addiction and Problematic Use

"Addiction" is a common term used to describe some overuse of virtual worlds, as well as overuse of the Internet and video games. Researchers have argued that addiction to the Internet and addiction to video games should both be recognized as clinical disorders (Beard and Wolf 2001; Charlton and Danforth 2007; Griffiths 1991, 2000; Ko et al. 2005; Young 1998). Many users of virtual worlds are quick to describe their use of the environments as an addiction as well. In a series of surveys that generated responses from 30,000 users of massively multiplayer online role-playing games (MMORPGs) between 2000 and 2003, about half of one survey's respondents described themselves as addicted to an MMORPG (Yee 2006b; 2006c). A survey of users of the MMORPG *EverQuest* conducted during 2000 and 2001 found that a majority of respondents considered themselves to be either definitely or probably addicted to *EverQuest* (Yee 2001). In a 2007 survey of more than 1,000 U.S. youth ages 8–18 conducted by research group Harris Interactive (2007), 23% of the youth in the survey reported feeling addicted to video games.

Despite the term's popular use, though, experts disagree as to whether "addiction" is an appropriate term to describe overuse of media such as virtual worlds, the Internet, and video games (Griffiths 2008; Griffiths and Meredith 2009; Seay and Kraut 2007; Wood 2008; Yellowlees and Marks 2007). There is not even a complete consensus in medicine, psychology, and related fields as to how the term "addiction" is defined. In clinical use, the term "addiction" had traditionally been used to describe cases of physical dependency on a chemical substance, but in recent years some have used the term to describe some harmful behavioral compulsions such as eating disorders because these compulsions can induce similar chemical patterns in the brain as substance addictions. There is disagreement, though, as to whether behavioral disorders should be described with the term "addiction," or even what symptoms of dependency to a substance are necessary for addiction to be diagnosed (Goodman 1990; Holden 2001; Koob and Le Moal 2008; Wise and Bozarth 1987). The fifth edition of the American Psychiatric Association's *Diagnostic and Statistical Manual of Mental Disorders* will not list Internet or video game addiction in its "Addictions and Related Disorders" section, though the manual will include Internet addiction in an appendix as a topic for further investigation (Black 2010; Seib 2010).

To further complicate matters, the term "addictive" is also often used with a positive connotation by marketers and reviewers of interactive media like video games and virtual worlds (Seay and Kraut 2007). For them, "addictive" may be used to refer to products that provide an enticing, engaging, and enjoyable experience rather than a harmful one. Some research assessing dependency to the Internet and other computer-related compulsions may have also overestimated rates of harmful use by using criteria that confuse these feelings of high engagement, which are not necessarily negative for their users, with actual problematic compulsions (Charlton 2002; Charlton and Danforth 2007). The possibility that some heavy Internet use might be classified as a "positive addiction" that is beneficial to individuals without causing harm or competing with other healthy activities (Glasser 1976; Griffiths 1996; Shapira et al. 2003) also introduces confusion in how the term "addiction" might be applied to the use of the Internet, video games, and virtual worlds.

Given the difficulties surrounding the use of the term "addiction," some prefer to use the term "problematic use" to describe harmful overuse of media such as virtual worlds, video games, and the Internet (Beard and Wolf 2001; Caplan 2002; Caplan, Williams, and Yee 2009; Seay and Kraut 2007; Shapira et al. 2000; Shapira et al. 2003). Whatever term is used, though, there is certainly plenty of evidence that some users of virtual worlds can take their involvement and commitment to harmful extremes. Studies of problematic use of virtual worlds have primarily focused on those virtual worlds that are online games, primarily MMPORGs. These games' combination of the social features of the Internet and the engaging features of video games appear to make them particularly prone to abuse.

Research has found that people drawn to the forms of social interaction available on the Internet are at risk for patterns of problematic use (Byun et al. 2009; Caplan 2002, 2003; Caplan et al. 2009; McKenna and Bargh 2000; Morahan-Martin and Schumacher 2000; Young 1998). In a national telephone survey of U.S. adults conducted in 2004, 3.7% to 13.7% reported at least one behavior potentially indicative of problematic Internet use, and .3% to .7% were categorized as potential cases of problematic Internet use (Aboujaoude et al. 2006). Studies have also found that video games can have a potential for abuse (Griffiths 1997; Griffiths and Hunt 1995, 1998; Griffiths and Meredith 2009; Grüsser, Thalemann, and Griffiths 2007; Lemmens, Valkenburg, and Peter 2009). For example, data from Harris Interactive's aforementioned survey of U.S. youth ages 8–18 indicated that 7.9% to 19.8% of those who played video games at least occasionally exhibited traits that might categorize them as "pathological" game players (Gentile 2009). A similar study in Singapore conducted over the course of two years found comparable results, leading its author to conclude that that about 9% of the participants in a study of students in primary and secondary schools were pathological game players (Gentile 2011). Interestingly, the study conducted in Singapore did not find that online game playing was a specifically unique contributor to rates of pathological game play among participants, though participants in the study did tend to spend more time playing online games over the two-year duration of the study.

Given the potential for abuse that both the Internet and video games have exhibited, there is concern than online games can be particularly conducive to problematic use (Caplan et al. 2009; Griffiths, Davies, and Chappell 2004a; Griffiths and Meredith 2009; Hussain and Griffiths 2009). In early studies arguing for the existence of Internet addiction, even the text-based online role-playing games known as MUDs (multi-user dungeons), which were an early precursor to today's virtual worlds, were implicated as a computer application particularly prone to abuse by users (Beard and Wolf 2001; Morahan-Martin 2008; Ng and Wiemer-Hastings 2005). The newer MMORPGs, which represent many of the most popular virtual worlds, have elicited even more concern about their potential for problematic use. For such games, the long-term nature of the games' story lines, the somewhat unpredictable nature of major game events, and the social interaction and social status that can be achieved in the games are all features that can encourage overuse among players (Charlton and Danforth 2007; Griffiths and Meredith 2009; Hussain and Griffiths 2009; Ng and Wiemer-Hastings 2005; Young and Rogers 2007). Indeed, research on the brain activity of males who overused the MMORPG *World of Warcraft* indicated that when viewing images from the game, activity in various regions of their brains associated with cravings mirrored neurobiological patterns that have been associated with substance dependency (Ko et al. 2009).

Prominent examples of deaths related to online game overuse have received attention from popular media. A 28-year-old South Korean man collapsed and died in 2005 after playing the online multiplayer game *Starcraft*, which is a computer game played online but is not actually a virtual world or role-playing game, for 50 hours while stopping only to use the restroom and sleep for short periods (Naughton 2005). A 26-year-old Chinese man died in 2007 after playing unnamed online games frequently over the course of several days during the New Year holiday

(Spencer 2007), and a 30-year-old Chinese man died the same year after playing an unnamed online game for three days (Caron 2007). Excessive online game play has also been mentioned as a factor in parental neglect or abuse that resulted in the deaths of children, such as a four-month-old South Korean infant who died of suffocation in 2005 while her parents played *World of Warcraft* at a nearby Internet café (Hitora 2005; Lee 2005), a three-month-old South Korean infant who died from malnutrition in 2009 while her parents spent long hours playing the online game *Prius Online* at Internet cafés (Tran 2010), and a three-month-old baby in Florida whose mother shook him to death in 2010 when his crying interrupted her use of the social network game *Farm-Ville* (Martinez 2010).

Finally, problematic online game play has been speculatively linked in the media with the suicide of a 13-year-old boy in China who jumped to his death in 2004 after playing *World of Warcraft* for 36 consecutive hours (McDonald 2006) and the suicide of a 21-year-old man in Wisconsin who shot himself dead in 2001 while playing *EverQuest* (Kohn 2002; Patrizio 2002). Other anecdotal accounts of *EverQuest* overuse describe players who lost their jobs, were left by spouses and children, neglected their personal hygiene and household chores, and considered suicide due to their overuse of the game (Chappell et al. 2006). Although many of these cases involved online games that were not virtual worlds, they serve as powerful, if rare, examples of the potential harms that can accompany excessive use of virtual worlds and related online applications.

Of course, such extreme cases are not typical of those who use virtual worlds and online games. For a minority of virtual world users, though, their enjoyment of virtual worlds is problematic enough to disrupt their lives in harmful ways. A survey of *EverQuest* users conducted in 2000 and 2001 found that respondents played an average of 22.4 hours per week (Yee 2001). This commitment led 68.1% of the players in the survey to report having had dreams about *EverQuest*. Such results provide justification for the popular nickname that many users and those associated with users gave *EverQuest* at the height of its popularity: EverCrack (Morales 2002; Patrizio 2002).

In another online survey of *EverQuest* users conducted in 2001, players who responded to the survey reported playing an average of 28.9 hours in a typical week (Castronova 2001). Of adults in the survey, 31.5% of them reported spending more time in the game's virtual world of Norrath than at their jobs. Additionally, 58% of the players in that survey wished they could spend more time in Norrath, 39% of them reported that they would quit their jobs or studies if they could make a living by selling items in Norrath, 22% of them reported that they would spend all of their time in Norrath if they could, and 20% of them considered themselves to be full-time "residents" of Norrath. The users who considered themselves to be residents reported spending 36.1 hours per week playing *EverQuest*, and 44.1% of these so-called residents spent more time in Norrath than at work.

In a third survey of *EverQuest* users, players reported spending an average of 25 hours per week playing the game (Griffiths et al. 2004a). A minority of players in the survey reported spending much more time logged in per week, with 5.4% reporting 40–50 hours of play per week and 4% reporting more than 50 hours of play per week. Some players in the survey reported playing *EverQuest* for more than 70 hours per week. Adolescent players in the survey reported playing the game for an average of 26.25 hours per week, slightly more than the 24.7 hours per week reported by adult players in the survey (Griffiths, Davies, and Chappell 2004b). Although 22.8% of players in the survey reported that they didn't sacrifice any other aspects of their lives to play *EverQuest*, another 25.6% reported sacrificing another hobby or pastime to play, while 18.1% reported sacrificing sleep, 10.4% reported sacrificing socializing with friends, 9.6% reported sacrificing in their work or education, 5.4% reported sacrificing socializing with a partner, and 4.6% reported sacrificing family time (Griffiths et al. 2004a). Adult players in the survey were more likely than adolescent players to report sacrificing socializing to play *EverQuest*, while adolescent players in the survey were more likely than adult players to report sacrificing in their work or education (Griffiths et al. 2004b).

A series of surveys administered to users of MMORPGs between 2000 and 2003 found that players in the survey spent an average of 22.7 hours per week in their game of choice, with about 8% of them spending more than 40 hours per week playing (Yee 2006b; 2006c). Also, 60.9% of the players in the survey reported that they had spent at least 10 hours continuously playing an MMORPG before. Many players in the survey indicated being very emotionally invested in the online games they played, with 27% reporting that their most positive experience in the past week had taken place in their game and 33% reporting that their most negative experience in the past week had taken place in their online game. A large minority of the users appeared to exhibit patterns of problematic use, with 15% of players in the survey acknowledging that they became angry or irritable when they were unable to play and 30% of the players in the survey indicating that they continue to play their online game even when they are frustrated with it or not enjoying the game. Also, 18% of the players in the survey believed that their use of MMORPGs had caused problems with their academic success, personal health, financial status, or personal relationships (Yee 2006c).

In another online survey aimed at users of MMORPGs, 11% of responding players reported spending more than 40 hours per week playing the games and 80% reported spending more than eight continuous hours playing in one game session (Ng and Wiemer-Hastings 2005). Another such survey found that players spent an average of 27 hours per week in MMORPGs (Smahel, Blinka, and Ledabyl 2008). In one more survey of players of MMORPGs, responding players spent an average of 22.85 hours playing per week (Cole and Griffiths 2007). Of the players in that survey, 20.3% felt that their use of MMORPGs negatively affected their relationships with people who did not play online with them, and players who spent more hours per week playing were more likely to report that their playing negatively affected these relationships. Yet another online survey targeting users of MMORPGs categorized 7% of players in the survey as dependent players who were at risk of problematic usage (Hussain and Griffiths 2009).

An online survey of players who used either the online role-playing game *Asheron's Call* or its sequel, *Asheron's Call 2*, found that after excluding one participant who claimed to play for 100 hours per week, members of the survey reported playing online for an average of 18.64 hours per week (Charlton and Danforth 2007). About half of the players in the survey acknowledged that their online game play had caused them to lose sleep, and a substantial minority of participants in that survey reported that their online game play had caused arguments at home and disruptions in their social lives, work, and meal schedules.

A survey of *EverQuest's* successor, *EverQuest II*, which was conducted online within the game setting and paired with data from game servers, found that players in the survey spent an average of 25.86 hours per week playing *EverQuest II* (Williams, Yee, and Caplan 2008). The survey also revealed that players tended to underestimate the amount of time they played the game per week, particularly those players who were female (Williams et al. 2009). Female players in the survey tended to underreport their weekly play by 3.29 hours per week, while males tended to underreport their weekly play by an average of .93 hours per week.

Less research has explored overuse of social virtual worlds, such as *Second Life*, that are not online games. Similar concerns exist, though, regarding whether such social virtual worlds might also be prone to dysfunctional and problematic use (Hendaoui, Limayem, and Thompson 2008). Data from 2004 indicate that 25% of *Second Life* users were in the virtual world for more than 30 hours per week (Ondrejka 2004a). During the first quarter of 2011, about 794,000 accounts were logged into more than once, and users spent 104 million hours in the virtual world (Linden Lab 2011). Ignoring the relatively small number of hours spent by those users who logged into the virtual environment only once, this means that the 794,000 accounts spent an average of almost 131 hours in the game during that quarter—more than 43 hours per month or 10 hours per week. Although this average time commitment is lower than the typical average time commitment seen with users of MMORPGs, it appears that some users of social virtual worlds like *Second Life* are committing substantial amounts of time to their virtual world activity.

To complement the many surveys indicating the potential for abuse presented by MMORPGs, one laboratory experiment also indicates that MMORPGs may be more likely to encourage problematic use than video games that are not played online (Smyth 2007). Instead of seeking people who already played the games as with the surveys, the researchers conducting the experiment randomly assigned research participants to play either arcade video games using free arcade tokens, a console game on a PlayStation 2 game console, a computer video game that was not played online, or the MMORPG *Dark Age of Camelot*. Participants were instructed to play the game to which they were assigned for at least one hour per week for a month, but were given no further instructions about how much to play. Although there was no significant difference in the amount of time per week participants played video games per week before the study, in the last week of the study participants assigned to pay *Dark Age of Camelot* reported spending more time playing video games than the other groups and also reported worse overall health, lower sleep quality, and more interference with real-life socializing and schoolwork compared to the other groups.

In addition to displacing time spent on other life activities, the large amounts of time that some users spend in MMORPGs and other virtual worlds can have negative implications for their quality of life and mental health. A survey of college students in Taiwan found that heavier use of online games was associated with a decrease in the quality of interpersonal relationships and an increase in social anxiety (Lo, Wang, and Fang 2005), and a survey of *EverQuest II* players found that players had higher rates of depression and substance abuse than the general population (Williams et al. 2009). Studies have also found that online game play is correlated with problematic Internet use in general, meaning that people who play online games more are more likely to exhibit symptoms of problematic Internet use (Caplan et al. 2009; Ko et al. 2005; Morahan-Martin and Schumacher 2000), which is in turn is linked to outcomes such as anxiety, depression, loneliness, problems with social skills, and general decreases in quality of psychosocial health (Caplan 2002, 2003; Caplan et al. 2009; Morahan-Martin and Schumacher 2000; Young and Rogers 1998).

While sheer amount of time spent in virtual worlds is linked to problematic use (Yee 2006c), there is also evidence that some types of players might be more prone to problematic use than others. Given that more males use online games, males are more likely to experience problematic use (Morahan-Martin and Schumacher 2000). However, females who do use virtual worlds appear to spend more time in them than their more counterparts and underestimate their use more, so it may be that those females who do use virtual worlds are more at risk than the many males who use them (Williams et al. 2009). Though users of all ages are susceptible to problematic use, younger users may be more at risk for problematic use patterns than older players (Griffiths et al. 2004b; Smahel et al. 2008). Additionally, users who suffer from mood disorders appear to be more likely to exhibit potentially harmful use patterns (Yee 2006a).

The way users of virtual worlds interact with and respond to the environments also influences their likelihood of having problematic use patterns. Individuals who experience greater feelings of immersion and involvement while using virtual worlds tend to be more likely to exhibit problematic use tendencies (Caplan et al. 2009; Chou and Ting 2003), as do those who identify closely with the character avatar they use in a virtual world (Smahel et al. 2008). There is evidence that people who use microphones to engage in voice chat in virtual worlds are also more likely to have problematic use, possibly because these users are more socially involved with virtual worlds than users who do not use voice technology in virtual worlds (Caplan et al. 2009).

As evidence accumulates indicating that some users have problems managing their use of virtual worlds and related applications, clinical treatments have also been proposed. Although the necessity and effectiveness of these treatments is difficult to assess considering that problematic use of virtual worlds, the Internet, and video games is not universally recognized as a classifiable disorder, they have produced some results suggesting that they may be an appropriate course of action for some problematic users. Although some exploratory treatments for problematic online game play have been pharmaceutical, such as the use of methylphenidate on South Korean children with attention-deficit/hyperactive disorder (Han et al. 2009) and the use of the antidepressant buproprion on South Korean males who overused the online computer game *StarCraft* (Han, Hwang, and Renshaw 2010), a more frequently recommended approach to problematic use of the Internet and games is cognitive behavior therapy that targets and corrects thoughts and feelings behind problematic use (Griffiths and Meredith 2009; Grüsser et al. 2007). Although research on the clinical treatment of problematic use of the Internet and virtual worlds is still in its early stages, there are also a number of nonprofessional organizations that address problematic online game play. Many of them exist as online services and communities on the Internet and base their recommendations on existing substance abuse programs (Griffiths and Meredith 2009).

Aggression and Violence

Given that many virtual worlds are online games that feature violent combat as a prominent element, concern is growing about how virtual worlds' users are affected by exposure to virtual violence in the online environments. So far, there are a limited number of studies dealing specifically with the effects of violence in virtual worlds on aggression and violence in users (e.g., Williams 2006; Williams and Skoric 2005), but some understanding of these potential effects is provided by previous research dealing more generally with the effects of violence in the media and in video games. Researchers have produced hundreds of studies investigating the effects of violent media on aggression and violence in users (Anderson et al. 2003; Anderson and Bushman 2002a, 2002b; Bandura 1978; Bushman 1998; Bushman and Anderson 2001; Cantor 2000; Geen and Thomas 1986; Heath, Bresolin, and Rinaldi 1989; Huesmann 1986; Paik and Comstock 1994; Wood, Wong, and Chachere 1991). A large and growing body of research has focused more specifically on the effects of violent video games as well (Anderson 2004; Anderson and Bushman 2001; Anderson et al. 2010; Bensley and Van Eenwyk 2001; Dill and Dill 1998; Ferguson 2007a, 2007b; Griffiths 1999; Sherry 2001). Both of these general areas of research are pertinent to an understanding of virtual worlds' effects, particularly until there are more studies examining the issue in virtual worlds specifically.

Aggression has been defined as "any behavior directed toward another individual that is carried out with the *proximate* (immediate) intent to cause harm" (Anderson and Bushman 2002a, p. 28). Aggression has also been categorized into three subtypes (Anderson et al. 2003; Anderson et al. 2007; Crick and Grotpeter 1995; Scheithauer et al. 2006). The first subtype is physical aggression, which includes intentionally harmful physical acts such as punching, kicking, tripping, stabbing, and shooting. Violence, a specific extreme form of physical aggression, has been defined as "aggression that has extreme harm as its goal (e.g., death)" (Anderson and Bushman 2002a, p. 29). Another subtype of aggression is verbal aggression, which describes intentional harm by spoken or written means such as name-calling, hurtful electronic messages, and intentionally harmful evaluations of others. The third subtype of aggression is relational aggression, which involves harming others through damage to interpersonal relationships by means such as spreading rumors and socially ostracizing peers. Research dealing with the effects of violent content in virtual worlds, video games, and other media on aggression in users is concerned with how users' exposure to violent content influences all of these various forms of aggressive responses.

The possible role of violent video games has been mentioned in connection to many high-profile violent crimes, particularly in cases where the crimes bore resemblance to events in video games the perpetrators had been known to play. In 1997, a student at Heath High School in West Paducah, Kentucky, killed three students and injured five more in a mass shooting (Glaberson

2000). The parents of three victims brought an unsuccessful liability suit against video game manufacturers and other media companies based on the perpetrator's media habits, the first of many such unsuccessful suits to be filed against video game manufacturers by the victims of high-profile crimes and their families. In 1999, two students at Columbine High School in Littleton, Colorado killed 12 of their fellow students and a teacher in a mass shooting before killing each other in a mutual suicide (Brown 1999). The pair's affinity for the video game *Doom* was often mentioned as a potential influence on their crime, particularly given that one of the perpetrators mentioned the game in a video missive recorded before the crime occurred (Kohler 2007).

In 2003, an 18-year-old with no criminal history killed two police officers and an emergency dispatcher at a Fayette, Alabama, police station after stealing one of the officers' guns while at the station under suspicion of stealing a car (Smith 2005). The killer, who had been an avid player of the violent video game *Grand Theft Auto: Vice City,* then escaped in a police car before being apprehended. Also in 2003, two teenage boys from Newport, Tennessee, killed one motorist and wounded another when they used a rifle to shoot at vehicles on an interstate highway in apparent imitation of the video game *Grand Theft Auto III* (Kushner 2005). In 2004, a teenager who was reportedly fascinated with the violent video game *Manhunt* murdered another teenager in Leicester, England, with a hammer and knife (Millward 2004).

In 2007, an Ohio teenager shot his parents, killing his mother and seriously injuring his father, after they forbade him from playing the first-person shooter game *Halo 3* (Cavalli 2008a). In 2008, the violent video game *Grand Theft Auto IV* was mentioned in connection to a spree of armed robberies and attempted carjackings perpetrated by six teenagers in New York City (Cochran 2008), and also in connection to the stabbing murder of a taxi driver in Bangkok, Thailand (Buncombe 2008). A teenager who killed 15 students at a high school in Winnenden, Germany, in 2009 was described as a heavy video game player (Rayner and Bingham 2009).

Speculation about the role of violent video games after high-profile violent crimes has been so common that pundits have jumped to associate violent crimes to violent video game use even when there is no evidence that a perpetrator played violent video games. For example, when a Virginia Tech student murdered 32 students and faculty at the university in a mass shooting in 2007 before killing himself, activist attorney Jack Thompson repeatedly appeared in the popular media claiming that violent video games played a role in the crime despite limited evidence that the perpetrator owned or regularly played video games (Benedetti 2007). Thompson would be disbarred the following year for inappropriate conduct in unrelated cases (Cavalli 2008b).

Online games have also been mentioned in association with unusual instances of violent crime. In 2005, a man in Shanghai, China, murdered a friend who had been using a virtual weapon that the pair had jointly owned in the MMORPG *The Legend of Mir III* and who had sold it online without permission (Li 2005; Nolan 2010). The murderer had appealed to police before committing the murder, but had been told he had no legal recourse for the virtual item's theft. In 2007, a Russian who played the MMORPG *Lineage II* was killed by a man who was a member of a rival group in the game when members of two of the game's guild groups met to continue a dispute that originated in the virtual world (Haines 2008). In 2010, a French man plotted revenge for several months when his character in the online game *Counter-Strike* was killed by another player's character in a virtual knife battle, eventually arriving at the player's house and causing serious injury by stabbing him (Sheridan 2010).

Like the extreme examples of problematic overuse that received much media attention, the highly publicized examples of aggression and violence based on exposure to virtual worlds and video games are not typical. There is little evidence that violent content in media frequently causes violent crime, but that does not mean that violent content cannot lead to problematic outcomes in media users. Research investigating outcomes from exposure to violent media content, including violent video games and virtual worlds, suggests that there may be small but societally meaningful effects for many users.

The general conclusion of much research dealing with the effects of violence in television and film is that such violence can increase aggression in users, particularly younger users (Anderson et al. 2003; Anderson, Gentile, and Buckley 2007; Paik and Comstock 1994). This research is based primarily on findings from three types of studies. Cross-sectional surveys, which consist of a one-time survey questionnaire given to a large group of research participants, have tended to show a correlation between survey participants' reported exposure to violence media and their reported acts of violence and aggression. Laboratory experiments, which measure the responses of participants who are exposed to media violence to the responses of participants in a control group after randomly assigning participants to both groups in a controlled setting, have tended to show that exposure to violent media content can increase aggressive behavior in both children and adults. Laboratory experiments, however, typically focus on short-term responses because it is difficult to maintain a controlled setting over a long period of time. Longitudinal studies, which are rarer than cross-sectional studies and laboratory experiments because they consist of surveys repeated over a period of years and can present financial and logistical difficulties, have tended to show that violent media use during youth is associated with aggressive behavior as much as 10 to 15 years later.

As with research on violence in television and film, much research that is focused specifically on the effects of violent video games has found that violent video game content can increase aggressive responses in users (Anderson 2004; Anderson and Bushman 2001; Anderson et al. 2007; Anderson et al. 2010; Sherry 2001). Research on the effects of violent video games has relied primarily on cross-sectional surveys and laboratory experiments, and there is a lack of longitudinal studies specifically addressing violent video game content by collecting data on multiple occasions over a substantial period of time (i.e., several years) (Ferguson 2011). Cross-sectional surveys have tended to find that violent video game exposure is correlated with aggression and delinquency, including violence such as physical fights. Laboratory experiments have tended to find short-term effects of violent game content on aggression measures that can be measured in a laboratory setting, such as the length and intensity of a noise blast that a research participant is willing to give someone as punishment for losing in a competitive task. Most research on the effects of violent video game content on aggression has focused on three types of effects: effects on aggressive thoughts, effects on aggressive feelings, and effects on aggressive behavior (Anderson and Bushman 2001; Anderson et al. 2010). Generally, these studies have tended to find that exposure to violence in video games can influence all three of these types of aggressive responses.

Some researchers are concerned that violence in video games might have stronger effects on aggression than television and film because the violence in video games is more frequent, because the video game user is more attentive and involved when using games, and because video games encourage their users to identify more with the violent characters on the screen (Carnagey and Anderson 2004). However, research has not produced clear evidence that violence in video games has stronger effects on aggression than violence in television and film, and there is some evidence that the effects of violent games may even be weaker than the effects of violent television and film (Sherry 2001).

Although there is a body of research suggesting that violent video games and other violent media can increase aggression in users, it should be noted that some researchers have voiced disagreement with the conclusion that the existing research conclusively links violent video games, as well as other media, to aggressive responses (Ferguson 2007a, 2007b, 2010; Ferguson and Kilburn 2009; Sherry 2007). Arguments from this perspective claim that the body of research observing links between video game violence and aggression include flaws such as insufficiently validated measures of aggression, a failure to account for other factors that might influence aggression, a failure to acknowledge some contradictory findings, a failure to account for studies that may not have been published because they did not find effects, and observed effect sizes that are too small to be substantial and not based on any clinical standard. The strengths and weaknesses of the research related to violent video games and aggression have been a topic of continuing debate (Bushman, Rothstein, and Anderson 2010; Ferguson and Kilburn 2010), and are likely to be discussed for some time.

While most of our understanding of the potential effects of violence in virtual worlds on aggression in users comes from the body of research dealing with video games more generally, there have been some suggestions that virtual world games might be less conducive to aggression in users than some other types of video games because they encourage cooperation and social interaction between players (Anderson et al. 2007). There has also been some research focusing specifically on the effects of violence in virtual worlds. One prominent study (Williams and Skoric 2005) assigned a group of participants assigned to play the MMORPG *Asheron's Call 2* for one month, and asked them whether they had been in an argument with a friend or romantic partner before and after the month of play. The participants who played the assigned virtual world game did not show a significant increase in the amount of arguments they had over the month compared to a second group of participants assigned to a control group.

Although these results suggest that violence in virtual worlds may not influence users' aggression, the study's interpretability has been questioned in light of its high drop-out rate, lack of control over exposure to the game, and imprecise measure of aggression (Anderson et al. 2007). Given the limited amount of research addressing the effects of violence in virtual worlds specifically, more investigation is needed to explore how the vast and growing population of virtual world users might be influenced by those virtual worlds that contain violent content.

Distorted Perceptions of Social Reality

The potential negative effects of media violence are not limited to imitation of aggression and violence. Another, though less prominent, concern associated with exposure to violence in media is that long-term exposure to violent media might distort users' perceptions of the real world. A number of studies have found that heavy use of media such as television can have a "cultivation effect," skewing media users' perceptions of the real world so that the users see the real world as more like the world portrayed in the media (Gerbner et al. 1979; Gerbner et al.1980). For example, heavy television viewers have been found to make unusually high estimates of the frequency of violent crime compared to those who use less television because their judgment is influenced by the high frequency of violent acts portrayed on television (Romer, Jamieson, and Aday 2003). Such cultivation effects have also been found when comparing heavy television users' perceptions of political issues, expectations about work and marriage, and sex with the perceptions of those who use less television (Morgan, Shanahan, and Signorielli 2009; Segrin and Nabi 2002).

Although this phenomenon has been researched less with virtual worlds and video games, there is some evidence that these media can also distort perceptions of social reality. One study investigated whether research participants' exposure to violent video games was correlated with their perceptions of the frequency of violent crime and their feelings of safety, but no relationship was observed between violent video game use and these perceptions after controlling for participants' gender (Anderson and Dill 2000). Another study found some evidence for a relationship between the amount of time that participants spent playing video games and their estimates of violence and crime, though it did not distinguish between types of video games used (Van Mierlo and Van den Bulck 2004). A third study examined cultivation effects in users of virtual worlds (Williams, 2006). In that study, research participants who were assigned to play the MMORPG *Asheron's Call 2* for one month estimated higher rates of assault with weapons, a behavior frequently portrayed in the game, compared to a control group. These results suggest that the violence in virtual worlds could distort participants' perceptions of real worlds, though further research in the area is needed, particularly regarding effects of other types of content than violence on virtual world users' perceptions.

Harassment and Griefing

Aside from the various potential effects on users described above, a more general concern about users in virtual worlds is that they might be exposed to objectionable, disturbing, or otherwise undesirable content by other users. This is not a new concern in online communities. One of the most well-known incidents ever to occur in a text-based MUD (multi-user dungeon) environment was the infamous "rape in cyberspace" incident in the *LambdaMOO* virtual community (Dibbell 1998; MacKinnon 1997). In 1993, a player using the name "Mr. Bungle" appeared in the game environment "wearing" an offensive text description and used a coded object to type descriptions of behaviors that were attributed to other characters in the online environment without actually being typed by the users controlling those characters.

Mr. Bungle used this voodoo-doll object to depict other characters as engaging in a number of unusual, degrading, and violent sexual acts with themselves and with each other. Although the various indignities visited on the characters and their users took place only in briefly typed form on their computer screens, those involved in the incident were deeply disturbed. After the incident, Mr. Bungle was banned from *LambdaMOO* and a new system was put in place allowing users to quickly evict anyone involved in similar behavior, but discussion of the incident's implications for online social dynamics and policy extended far beyond the *LambdaMOO* community.

Although many virtual worlds share some of the interactive characteristics and user freedoms that characterized their MUD ancestors, most of them limit users' ability to control and influence other users' interactions enough to thwart any would-be Mr. Bungles of the virtual world era. The interactivity that virtual worlds present, however, still presents many opportunities for users with malicious intent to antagonize one another. These "griefers" derive pleasure from acts that inhibit other users' enjoyment of virtual worlds, which may include cheating and other instrumental exploitation or simply consist of harassment (Foo and Kovisto 2004). While much griefing consists of minor and silly interruptions, others are more offensive, such as a virtual recreation of the World Trade Center's destruction in *Second Life* (Dibbell 2008) or the *Second Life* user whose avatar visited the online campus of Ohio University in May 2007 to stage a virtual mass shooting in what was apparently a tasteless homage to the mass shooting perpetrated at Virginia Tech during the previous month (Bugeja 2007). While virtual worlds can place limits on player activity and provide users with tools to prevent and report griefing (for example, by blocking communication from a griefer and submitting the griefer's name to the virtual world's administrator), the open and interactive atmospheres that virtual worlds strive to provide will probably always leave them open to this type of abuse.

Opportunities and Benefits

Social Opportunities

Although the social nature of virtual worlds presents potential for problematic use and opens virtual worlds up to griefers, the opportunities for rich social interaction that virtual worlds provide are also a benefit. Online communities have provided unique opportunities for healthy social interaction and development. One of the earliest studies on the social impact of the Internet (Kraut et al. 1998) found that increased time online was associated with increased loneliness and depression, as well as a reduced local social network in a sample of users who were given access to the Internet for two years as participation in the study. Despite such observed problems for heavy Internet users, though, very different trends were observed for the entire group of participants in general. Overall, the group of members of the study tended to report lower levels of loneliness and depression and larger distant social networks after two years of Internet access (McKenna and Bargh 2000). The relative anonymity of online communities can allow users to safely explore their self-concept and identity, discuss topics they might otherwise find risky, embarrassing, or shameful, and form meaningful relationships that are not based on superficial appearances or the limitations of geography (Bargh and KcKenna 2004; Bargh, McKenna, and Fitzsimons 2002; McKenna and Bargh 2000; Turkle 1994; Walther 1996).

There is evidence that virtual worlds provide similar opportunities for self-exploration, beneficial social interaction, and relationship formation. A small survey of users of *World of Warcraft* found that players' characters tended to think of their characters' traits as similar to their own, but rated their characters as more like their ideal selves. Further, players with depression and low self-esteem considered their characters to be more similar to their ideal selves (Bessière, Seay, and Kiesler 2007). In another survey of players of MMORPGs, 34.6% of them felt that they could be "more themselves" in the game than they could be in real life (Cole and Griffiths 2007). These findings suggest that virtual worlds offer players an opportunity to explore their ideal selves regardless of their actual situation, though problems can occur if users isolate attributes of their online selves from their actual selves instead of taking the therapeutic opportunity to harmonize positive aspects of the self that are discovered and explored online by integrating them with the actual self (Morahan-Martin 2008).

In another survey of *World of Warcraft* users focusing on the dynamics of guild groups, about 60% of the participants reported belonging to a guild that was primarily social in purpose (Williams et al. 2006). In a series of surveys given to users of MMORPGs between 2000 and 2003, 39.4% of male players in the survey and 53.3% of female players in the survey rated their in-game friends as comparable to or better than friends they know from outside of the game environment (Yee 2006b, 2006c). The meaningfulness of those online relationships was underscored by the finding that 32.0% of female players in the survey and 22.9% of male players in the survey reported that they had told a personal secret or issue to a friend in an MMORPG that they had never told a real-life friend.

Also, 15.7% of the male players in the survey and 5.1% of the female players in the survey had become involved in a physical dating relationship with someone whom they had met in an MMORPG. The survey indicated that the games also facilitated some players' interaction in existing real-life relationships, with 59.8% of the female players in the survey and 15.8% playing an MMORPG with a romantic partner, and 39.5% of female players and 25.5% of male players playing with a sibling, parent, or child (Yee 2006b, 2006c). Players in the survey also found that their use of MMORPGs facilitated development of useful interpersonal skills, 10.7% claiming to have learned a lot about mediating conflict, 9.6% claiming to have learned a lot about motivating others, 5.8% claiming to have learned a lot about persuading others, and 10.7% claiming to have learned a lot about becoming a better leader. Another 44.5% reported learning a little about mediating conflict, while 38.8% reported learning a little about motivating others, 38.0% reported learning a little about persuading others, and 39.6% reported learning a little about becoming a better leader. Some potential employers appear to agree that virtual worlds can provide useful real-world skills, as a study conducted by business leader IBM indicated virtual worlds could be conducive to the development of real-world leadership skills (Miller 2007).

A different online survey of MMORPG users found similar trends (Cole and Griffiths 2007). In that survey, 76.2% of males and 74.7% of females reported making good friends in the games. The average number of good friends made by players in the games was seven; male players had made an average of 7.7 good friends while female players had made an average of 3.1 good friends. For 45.6% of the players in the survey, their online friends were seen as comparable to their real-life friends, while 16.8% were not sure. However, only 4.8% of participants in the survey found their online friends to be more trustworthy than their real-life friends, while 53.3% found their real-life friends more trustworthy, 36.7% found both types of friends to be equally trustworthy, and 5.3% were unsure. Players in the survey were comfortable disclosing to their online friends, with 39.3% acknowledging that they had discussed sensitive issues with in-game friends, including 46.7% of females and 36.2% of males. Additionally, 31.3% of the players in the survey had been attracted to another player, including 43.2% of the females and 26.2% of the males. Of these, 49.8% reported that the feeling had been mutual, including 47.1% of the males and 53.5% of the females. Of the players in the survey, 15.3% of the females and 7.7% of the males had dated another player in a game. The survey's players also shared the game in existing real-life relationships, as 26.3% played with family and friends, including 33.2% of the female players and 23.6% of the male players.

These results indicate that virtual worlds can provide a space for positive and healthy social interaction. In fact, some researchers have concluded that rather than being addicted, heavy players of MMORPGs are simply people who choose to pursue socialization online rather than offline, either as an alternative to other social opportunities or because other social opportunities are not available (Ng and Wiemer-Hastings 2005). Further, there is evidence that enhancements in virtual world technology are continuing to increase the strength of these online relationships formed between players. In one study, a group of research participants using voice chat features in *World of Warcraft* developed stronger and more trusting relationships over time than a control group that did not use the voice application (Williams, Caplan, and Xiong 2007). Considering that voice technology was linked to problematic Internet use in another study (Caplan et al., 2009), it is apparent that some of the features that encourage strong social relationships can also elicit intense relationships that may lead to problematic patterns for some users.

Such apparent paradoxes exemplify the complicated relationship between helpful and harmful aspects of virtual worlds and online games; these environments provide helpful social interaction opportunities, but many of the same social features that can be beneficial also provide potential for dependency and overuse (Allison et al. 2006). The satisfying social interaction that many find in virtual worlds also carries with it the risk that relationships may be developed online that are damaging to existing real-life relationships.

Perhaps the most prominent example of virtual social relationships damaging offline relationships is instances of virtual affairs (Kalning 2007), where a partner in a romantic relationship engages in virtual infidelity via avatars in a virtual world. Although it is unclear whether engaging in flirting, romantic dates, and even virtual sex in a virtual world like *Second Life* might be treated like real infidelity (or, more generally, mistreatment of a spouse) in a legal sense (Lastowka 2010), there are plenty of anecdotes in news items suggesting that whatever "virtual cheating" is, it can damage existing romantic relationships. Examples include a husband who interrupted family vacations for clandestine visits with a virtual girlfriend in *Second Life* (Kalning 2007), a man whose daily marathon sessions in *Second Life* included hours of leisure time with a virtual wife while his frustrated real-life wife served food to him at his computer (Alter 2007), and more than one case of a woman divorcing a husband after catching him engaged in virtual sex in *Second Life* (Lastowka 2010). Even text-based MUD games, virtual worlds' early ancestors, raised issues about the deleterious effect that virtual affairs could have on actual marriages (Dibbell 1998).

Educational Opportunities

The rich social environment provided by virtual worlds also makes them promising as an educational tool. There is evidence that even though popular MMORPGs are not designed for educational purposes, they may encourage players to become involved with reading and writing in online discussion forums related to the games and in fan fiction stories (Steinkuhler 2007; Steinkuhler and Duncan 2008). Virtual worlds that are not game-oriented, though, offer much greater opportunities for more direct delivery of education and learning.

Drawn by the opportunity to pursue new directions in teaching and research, more than 150 postsecondary institutions in more than a dozen nations created a presence in *Second Life* by leasing virtual land or islands from Linden Lab and building virtual classrooms, research laboratories, and more (Foster 2007). It can be easy for educators to develop a learning environment in *Second Life*, as Linden Lab provides support and resources targeting educators and other organizations, offering virtual space for lease in the virtual world that has ready-made virtual educational facilities (Boulos, Hetherington, and Wheeler 2007). *Second Life* can be an effective tool for distance education when face-to-face educational environments are not available (Childress and Braswell 2006; Ritzema and Harris 2008). Educational institutions must be cautious, though, about being prepared to protect students from harassment and other events that could happen in the open space of the virtual world—events for which some believe that the institution could be considered liable if students were compelled to use the virtual world as a required course element (Bugeja 2007).

In addition to providing opportunities for educating formally enrolled students, *Second Life* has also proved a rich platform for projects that educate virtual world users from the general public who are not students. Educational resources developed and deployed in *Second Life* by professionals from universities and health care organizations include a virtual facility dedicated to breast cancer awareness, a virtual museum with a variety of materials about the topic of genetics, a game that teaches how fast food consumption affects health, and simulations designed to help people understand the experiences of persons with conditions such as schizophrenia and neurological disease (Boulos et al. 2007; Yellowlees and Cook 2006).

Behavioral Research Opportunities

While users of virtual worlds can learn a lot in them, researchers can also learn a lot about human behavior from these virtual users. Some studies have indicated that virtual worlds' users exhibit a lot of the same behavioral tendencies in virtual worlds that they do in real life (Miller 2007). For example, research has found that avatars in *Second Life* tend to maintain personal space between one another in similar patterns to those of people in real life, even though the technology of *Second Life* allows avatars to stand in the same place or even walk through one another without consequence (Miller 2007). Avatars' demographic traits can also influence the behavior that virtual world users exhibit through those avatars in patterns that are similar to patterns observed in research conducted with people in real life. One study found that when pairs of avatars were standing together in *Second Life,* pairs of female avatars tended to stand closer to one another and make more eye contact than pairs of male avatars did (Yee et al. 2007). In general, avatars also tended to maintain less eye contact when they were standing closer together. These patterns were consistent with previous research observing real-life behaviors of males and females.

Considering the evidence showing that virtual world users display some similar behavior patterns through their avatars in virtual worlds, some researchers argue that virtual worlds are an ideal environment for research that would be very expensive, difficult, or unethical to conduct in real life (Bainbridge 2007; Castronova 2006; Miller 2007). Research where participants are asked to harm another person or research examining people's responses to serious dangers is not usually possible in traditional research environments, but virtual worlds can provide a useful setting. Events that occur naturally in virtual worlds can also provide guidance to researchers of real-world phenomena. For example, *World of Warcraft* experienced a virtual disease epidemic in 2005 when a virtual affliction called "corrupted blood," which had been intended to affect only players battling a difficult foe in a particular game area, rapidly spread across the game's population in a manner that was so unexpected and devastating that the game's administrators were forced to intercede with measures such as virtual quarantines (Balicer 2007; Lofgren and Fefferman 2007). After the unexpected outbreak, researchers lauded the potential of virtual worlds as tools to help us understand better understand the function and prevention of real-life disease epidemics.

Commercial Opportunities

Although *MUD1*, the early text-based ancestor of today's virtual worlds, had no in-game currency for fear of in-game inflation, most virtual worlds now use a virtual economy with currency and items that have in-game value (Manninen and Kujanpää 2007). Given the amount of effort and achievement that goes into the attributes, features, and virtual abilities of game characters, they have indirect economic value in the games as well. Research on transactions in the virtual economy of the MMORPG *EverQuest II* has found that users' economic behavior in the game mirrored economic patterns observed in the real world, suggesting that economies in virtual worlds and their real-world counterparts function similarly (Castronova et al. 2009).

In some virtual worlds, such as Turbine's multiplayer online role-playing games *Dungeons and Dragons Online* and *Lord of the Rings Online,* this in-game value translates into real-world value in the form of the small "microtransaction" payments players can make to buy game items from Turbine using real-world currency (Murdoch 2010; Peckham 2010). In others, the in-game value of resources has real-world value when it is sold in transactions between players. An economist followed the value of virtual goods in the MMORPG *EverQuest* by tracking sales of in-game items on the online auction site eBay (Castronova 2001). The analysis concluded that a user's play in *EverQuest*'s virtual world of Norrath produced an average hourly "wage" of virtual items and attributes worth $3.42, and that Norrath had a gross national product per capita that ranked somewhere between that of Russia and Bulgaria. This virtual exchange economy was stifled when Sony forbade players from selling in-game items and noted that all property created by players in the game was the property of Sony in its user agreement (Castronova 2003; Grimes 2006). Even after eBay stopped featuring *EverQuest* items in accord with an agreement with Sony and some other virtual worlds that followed Sony's example, many millions of dollars in virtual goods from other virtual worlds were sold on eBay (Ondrejka 2004b). The value of items in virtual worlds also translates into real-world value for many black-market enterprises that obtain game items through game play, then sell them to players in violation of many games' terms of service. These "gold farmers" and "power leveling" services, which primarily operate in MMORPGs where players receive resources in return for completing in-game tasks, often employ workers from less prosperous regions of the world to play the games and accumulate resources, then sell these resources at a profit to players from wealthier circumstances (Dibbell 2007). For example, prominent "gold farmers" selling virtual world items have employed workers to play the games in China and Mexico (Balkin 2004; Dibbell 2007).

Even though many MMORPGs seek to limit real-world sales of in-game resources, many social virtual worlds have economies that are set up to interact freely with real-life economies. Social worlds such as *Second Life* and *Entropia Universe* establish exchange rates with U.S. currency to facilitate easy transfer of resources in and out of virtual worlds (Bray and Konsynski 2008). These virtual economies offer real-life economic opportunity for both users and providers of virtual worlds. By 2011, $1 million was exchanged between users within the *Second Life* virtual world every day (Shepherd 2011).

While many of the people conducting transactions in social virtual worlds are spending or making a relatively insignificant amount of money, others are running very profitable enterprises. In 2006, a Chinese-born *Second Life* user in Germany called Ailin Graef became the first person to earn a million dollars in a virtual world through a virtual real-estate business involved in buying, developing, and selling virtual property (Hof 2006a, 2006b). In 2004, Australian David Storey spent $26,500 for a virtual island in *Entropia Universe,* an investment that earned him more than $100,000 yearly when he began to charge virtual hunters to hunt rare virtual animals on the virtual property (Chiang 2010b; Knight 2004). In 2005, British *Entropia Universe* user Jon Jacobs, nicknamed "Neverdie" after the name of his avatar in the virtual world, mortgaged his real-life home to buy a virtual asteroid in *Entropia Universe* for $100,000 (Bates 2010). Jacobs then built virtual leisure spot "Club Neverdie" on the asteroid, which he claimed earned him $200,000 yearly as users bought goods and services at venues on the asteroid including a shopping center and a stadium. In 2010, Jacobs sold the asteroid in parcels for a total of $635,000, including one $335,000 sale (Chiang 2010a; Tassi 2010). The legitimacy of Jacobs' claims of having conducted his virtual business independently from the *Entropia Universe* management have been questioned, though, because Jacobs identified himself as a spokesperson for the virtual world as early as 2004 and claimed to be in negotiations to purchase a virtual nightclub there as early as 2005 (Murray-Watson 2005). During a four-year period between 2004 and 2008, home-schooled high-school student Mike Everest and his mother made $35,000 making and selling virtual weapons in *Entropia Universe* from their home in Durango, Colorado (Alter 2008; Tiwari 2006). Proceeds from the online enterprise, which was supported by an initial investment of $6,000 from Everest's mother, were used to support the college educations of Everest and his two siblings.

These booming virtual economies also elicit concerns regarding how virtual worlds can protect users from theft and fraud and whether real-world governments should be able to regulate virtual worlds and tax economic transactions in them—and if so, how (Balkin 2004; Bray and Konsynski 2008). Corporations are also eager to use virtual worlds as a marketing tool, both by establishing an advertising presence in existing virtual worlds like *Second Life* and by creating their own branded "adverworlds" for users to visit (Hemp 2006). As commercial uses of virtual worlds grow more extensive and diverse, complex legal questions are not far behind. Cases probing legal issues dealing with virtual worlds' commercial content have included a lawsuit filed by Marvel Comics against NCSoft for failing to prevent users of its *City of Heroes* game from dressing their avatar characters like Marvel Comics characters (Loftus 2005), not to mention a lawsuit filed by one *Second Life* against another user for selling unauthorized imitations of a virtual "SexGen" bed developed and sold in the virtual world (Kirby 2009). So long as virtual worlds continue to present commercial opportunities, novel legal issues are likely to continue to arise.

Managing Concerns and Opportunities

The immersive technology and social setting of virtual worlds make them both a cause for concern and a potentially powerful tool for social good. How these environments are used, managed, and regulated will determine the ultimate influence of virtual worlds on their users and the population in general. As new virtual environments continue to spring up, arguments persist regarding how law and policy should govern them (Lastowka 2009, 2010; Lastowka and Hunter 2004; Tennessen 2009). Time will tell whether we are successful in taking advantage of the promise of virtual worlds while managing their dangers.

References

Aboujaoude, Elias, Lorrin M. Koran, Nona Gamel, Michael D. Large, and Richard T. Serpe. 2006. Potential markers for problematic Internet use: A telephone survey of 2,513 adults. *CNS Spectrums* 11: 750–755.

Allison, Sara E., Lisa von Wahlde, Tamra Shockley, and Glen O. Gabbard. 2006. The development of the self in the era of the Internet and role-playing fantasy games. *American Journal of Psychiatry* 163: 381–385.

Alter, Alexandra. 2007. Is this man cheating on his virtual wife? *Wall Street Journal.* http://online.wsj.com/article/SB11867016459239 3622.html.

Alter, Alexandra. 2008. My virtual summer job. *Wall Street Journal.* http://online.wsj.com/article/SB121088619095596515.html.

Anderson, Craig A. 2004. An update on the effects of playing violent video games. *Journal of Adolescence* 27: 113–122.

Anderson, Craig A., Leonard Berkowiz, Edward Donnerstein, L. Rowell Huesmann, James D. Johnson, Daniel Linz, Neil M. Malamuth, and Ellen Wartella. 2003. The influence of media violence on youth. *Psychological Science in the Public Interest* 4: 81–110.

Anderson, Craig A., and Brad J. Bushman. 2001. Effects of violent video games on aggressive behavior, aggressive cognition, aggressive affect, physiological arousal, and prosocial behavior: A meta-analytic review of the scientific literature. *Psychological Science* 12:353–359.

Anderson, Craig A., and Brad J. Bushman. 2002a. Human aggression. *Annual Review of Psychology* 53: 27–51.

Anderson, Craig A., and Brad J. Bushman. 2002b. The effects of media violence on society. *Science* 295: 2377–2378.

Anderson, Craig A., and Karen E. Dill. 2000. Video games and aggressive thoughts, feelings, and behavior in the laboratory and in life. *Journal of Personality and Social Psychology* 78: 772–790.

Anderson, Craig A., Douglas A. Gentile, and Katherine E. Buckley. 2007. *Violent video game effects on children and adolescents.* New York: Oxford University Press.

Anderson, Craig. A., Akiko Shibuya, Nobuko Ihori, Edward L. Swing, Brad J. Bushman, Akira Sakamoto, Hannah R. Rothstein, and Muniba Saleem. 2010. Violent video game effects on aggression, empathy, and prosocial behavior in Eastern and Western countries. *Psychological Bulletin* 136: 151–173.

Bainbridge, William Sims. 2007. The scientific research potential of virtual worlds. *Science* 317: 472–476.

Balicer, Ran D. 2007. Modeling infectious diseases dissemination through online role-playing games. *Epidemiology* 18: 260–261.

Balkin, Jack M. 2004. Virtual liberty: Freedom to design and freedom to play in virtual worlds. *Virginia Law Review* 90: 2043–2098.

Bandura, Albert. 1978. Social learning theory of aggression. *Journal of Communication* 28(3): 12–29.

Bargh, John A., and Katelyn Y. A. McKenna. 2004. The Internet and social life. *Annual Review of Psychology* 55: 573–590.

Bargh, John A., Katelyn Y. A. McKenna, and Grainne M. Fitzsimons. 2002. Can you see the real me? Activation and expression of the "True Self" on the Internet. *Journal of Social Issues* 58: 33–48.

Bates, Daniel. 2010. Internet real estate agent sells virtual nightclub on an asteroid in online game for £400,000. *Daily Mail.* http://www.dailymail.co.uk/sciencetech/article-1330552/Jon-Jacobs-sells-virtual-nightclub-Club-Neverdie-online-Entropia-game-400k.html.

Beard, Keith W., and Wolf, Eve M. 2001. Modification in the proposed diagnostic criteria for Internet addiction. *CyberPsychology and Behavior* 4: 377–383.

Benedetti, Winda. 2007. Were video games to blame for massacre? *MSNBC.* http://www.msnbc.msn.com/id/18220228/,

Bensley, Lillian, and Juliet Van Eenwyk. 2001. Video games and real-life aggression: A review of the literature. *Journal of Adolescent Health* 29: 244–257.

Bessière, Katherine, A. Fleming Seay, and Sara Kiesler. 2007. The ideal elf: Identity exploration in World of Warcraft. *CyberPsychology and Behavior* 10: 530–535.

Black, Rosemary. 2010. Sex addiction, obesity, Internet addiction not included in proposed changes to APA diagnostic manual. *New York Daily News.* http://www.nydailynews.com/lifestyle/health/2010/02/10/2010–02–10_sex_addiction_obesity_internet_addiction_not_included_in_proposed_changes_to_apa.html.

Boulos, Maged N. Kamel, Lee Hetherington, and Steve Wheeler. 2007. Second Life: An overview of the potential of 3-D virtual worlds in medical and health education. *Health Information and Libraries Journal* 24: 233–245.

Bray, David A., and Been R. Konsynski. 2008. Virtual worlds, virtual economies, virtual institutions. In *Proceedings of virtual worlds and new realities conference.* http://ssrn.com/abstract=962501.

Brown, Janelle. 1999. Doom, Quake and mass murder. *Salon.* http://www.salon.com/technology/feature/1999/04/23/gamers.

Bugeja, Michael J. 2007. Second thoughts about Second Life. *The Chronicle of Higher Education.* http://chronicle.com/article/Second-Thoughts-About-Second/46636/.

Buncombe, Andrew. 2008. Grand Theft Auto IV is pulled from Thai shops after killing of taxi driver. *The Independent.* http://www.independent.co.uk/news/world/asia/grand-theft-auto-iv-is-pulled-from-thai-shops-after-killing-of-taxi-driver-885204.html.

Bushman, Brad J. 1998. Priming effects of media violence on the accessibility of aggressive concepts in memory. *Personality and Social Psychology Bulletin* 24: 537–545.

Bushman, Brad J., and Craig A. Anderson. 2001. Media violence and the American public: Scientific facts versus media misinformation. *American Psychologist* 56: 477–489.

Bushman, Brad J., Hannah R. Rothstein, and Craig A. Anderson. 2010. Much ado about something: Violent video games and a school of red herring: Reply to Ferguson and Kilburn. *Psychological Bulletin* 136: 182–187.

Byun, Sookeun, Celestino Ruffini, Juline E. Mills, Alecia C. Douglas, Mamadou Niang, Svetlana Stepchenkova, Seul Ki Lee, Jihad Loutfi, Jung-Kook Lee, Mikhail Atallah, and Marina Blanton. 2009. Internet addiction: Metasynthesis of 1996–2006 quantitative research. *CyberPsychology and Behavior* 12: 203–207.

Cantor, Joanne. 2000. Media violence. *Journal of Adolescent Health* 27(Supplement): 30–34.

Caplan, Scott. 2002. Problematic Internet use and psychosocial well-being: Development of a theory-based cognitive-behavioral measurement instrument. *Computers in Human Behavior* 18: 553–575.

Caplan, Scott. 2003. Preference for online social interaction: A theory of problematic Internet use and psychosocial well-being. *Communication Research* 30: 625–648.

Caplan, Scott, Dmitri Williams, and Nick Yee. 2009. Problematic Internet use and psychosocial well-being among MMO players. *Computers in Human Behavior* 25: 1312–1319.

Carnagey, Nicholas L., and Craig A. Anderson. 2004. Violent video game exposure and aggression: A literature review. *Minerva Psichiatrica* 45: 1–18.

Caron, Nathalie. 2007. Chinese gamer dies of exhaustion after three-day binge. *Digital Journal.* http://www.digitaljournal.com/article/229820?noredir=1.

Castronova, Edward. 2001. *Virtual worlds: A first-hand account of market and society on the cyberian frontier.* CESifo Working Paper No. 618, December. http://ssrn.com/abstract=294828.

Castronova, Edward. 2003. *Theory of the avatar.* CESifo Working Paper No. 863, February. http://ssrn.com/abstract=385103.

Castronova, Edward. 2006. On the research value of large games: Natural experiments in Norrath and Camelot. *Games and Culture* 1: 163–186.

Castronova, Edward, Dmitri Williams, Cuihua Shen, Rabindra Ratan, Li Xiong, Yun Huang, and Brian Keegan. 2009. As real as real? Macroeconomic behavior in a large-scale virtual world. *New Media and Society* 11: 685–707.

Cavalli, Earnest. 2008a. Father, mother shot after taking *Halo 3* from son. *Wired.* http://www.wired.com/gamelife/2008/12/father-mother-s/.

Cavalli, Earnest. 2008b. Jack Thompson disbarred. *Wired.* http://www.wired.com/gamelife/2008/09/jack-thompson-d/.

Chappell, Darren, Virginia Eatough, Mark N.O. Davies, and Mark Griffiths. 2006. EverQuest—It's just a computer game right? An interpretive phenomenological analysis of online gaming addiction. *International Journal of Mental Health and Addiction* 4: 205–216.

Charlton, John P. 2002. A factor-analytic investigation of computer "addiction" and engagement. *British Journal of Psychology* 93: 329–344.

Charlton, John P., and Ian D.W. Danforth. 2007. Distinguishing addiction and high engagement in the context of online game playing. *Computers in Human Behavior* 23: 1531–1548.

Chiang, Oliver J. 2010a. Meet the man who just made a half million from the sale of virtual property. *Forbes.* http://blogs.forbes.com/oliverchiang/2010/11/13/meet-the-man-who-just-made-a-cool-half-million-from-the-sale-of-virtual-property/.

Chiang, Oliver J. 2010b. The world's most expensive island—online. *Forbes.* http://www.forbes.com/2010/02/17/farmville-facebook-zynga-technology-business-intelligence-virtual-goods.html.

Childress, Marcus D., and Ray Braswell. 2006. Using massively multiplayer online role-playing games for online learning. *Distance Education* 27: 187–196.

Chou, Ting-Jui, and Ting, Chih-Chen. 2003. The role of flow experience in cyber-game addiction. *CyberPsychology and Behavior* 6: 663–675.

Cochran, Lee. 2008. Teens say: Video game made them do it. *ABC News.* http://abcnews.go.com/TheLaw/story?id=5262689&page=1.

Cole, Helena, and Mark D. Griffiths. 2007. Social interactions in massively multiplayer online role-playing gamers. *CyberPsychology and Behavior* 10: 575–583.

Crick, Nicki R., and Jennifer K. Grotpeter. 1995. Relational aggression, gender, and social-psychological adjustment. *Child Development* 66: 710–722.

Dibbell, Julian. 1998. *My tiny life: Crime and passion in a virtual world.* New York: Henry Holt.

Dibbell, Julian. 2007. The life of the Chinese gold farmer. *The New York Times.* http://www.nytimes.com/2007/06/17/magazine/17lootfarmers-t.html.

Dibbell, Julian, 2008. Mutilated furries, flying phalluses: Put the blame on the griefers, the sociopaths of the virtual world. *Wired.* http://www.wired.com/gaming/virtualworlds/magazine/16-02/mf_goons.

Dill, Karen E., and Jody C. Dill. 1998. Video game violence: A review of the empirical literature. *Aggression and Violent Behavior* 3: 407–428.

Ferguson, Christopher J. 2007a. Evidence for publication bias in video game violence effects literature: A meta-analytic review. *Aggression and Violent Behavior* 12: 470–482.

Ferguson, Christopher J. 2007b. The good, the bad, and the ugly: A meta-analytic review of positive and negative effects of violent video games. *Psychiatric Quarterly* 78: 309–316.

Ferguson, Christopher J. 2010. Blazing angels or resident evil? Can video games be a force for good? *Review of General Psychology* 14(2): 68–81.

Ferguson, Christopher J. 2011. Video games and youth violence: A prospective analysis in adolescents. *Journal of Youth and Adolescence* 40: 377–391.

Ferguson, Christopher J., and John Kilburn. 2009. The public health risks of media violence: A meta-analytic review. *Journal of Pediatrics* 154: 759–763.

Ferguson, Christopher J., and John Kilburn. 2010. Much ado about nothing: The misestimation and overinterpretation of violent video game effects in Eastern and Western nations: Comment on Anderson et al. *Psychological Bulletin* 136: 174–178.

Foo, Chek Yang, and Elina M. I. Kovisto. 2004. Defining grief play in MMORPGS: Player and developer perceptions. In *Proceedings of the 2004 ACM SIGCHI International Conference on Advances in Computer Entertainment Technology*, 245–250. New York: ACM.

Foster, Andrea L. 2007. Professor Avatar. *Chronicle of Higher Education*. http://chronicle.com/article/Professor-Avatar/30018/.

Geen, Russell G., and Susan L. Thomas. 1986. The immediate effects of media violence on behavior. *Journal of Social Issues* 42(3): 7–27.

Gentile, Douglas. 2009. Pathological video-game use among youth ages 8 to 18. *Psychological Science* 20: 594–602.

Gentile, Douglas A., Hyekyung Choo, Albert Liau, Timothy Sim, Dongdong Li, Daniel Fung, and Angeline Khoo. 2011. Pathological video game use among youths: A two-year longitudinal study. *Pediatrics* 127: e319–e329.

Gerbner, George, Larry Gross, Michael Morgan, and Nancy Signorielli. 1980. The "mainstreaming" of America: Violence profile no. 11. *Journal of Communication* 30: 10–29.

Gerbner, George, Larry Gross, Nancy Signorielli, Michael Morgan, and Marilyn Jackson-Beeck. 1979. *Journal of Communication* 29: 177–196.

Glaberson, William. 2000. Finding futility in trying to lay blame in killings. *New York Times*. http://www.nytimes.com/2000/08/04/us/finding-futility-in-trying-to-lay-blame-in-killings.html.

Glasser, William. 1976 *Positive addiction*. New York: Harper and Row.

Goodman, Aviel. 1990. Addiction: Definition and implications. *British Journal of Addiction* 85: 1403–1408.

Griffiths, Mark D. 1991. Amusement machine playing in childhood and adolescence: A comparative analysis of video games and fruit machines. *Journal of Adolescence* 14: 53–73.

Griffiths, Mark D. 1996. Internet addiction: An issue for clinical psychology? *Clinical Psychology Forum* 97: 32–36.

Griffiths, Mark D. 1997. Computer game playing in early adolescence. *Youth and Society* 29: 223–237.

Griffiths, Mark D. 1999. Violent video games and aggression: A review of the literature. *Aggression and Violent Behavior* 4: 203–212.

Griffiths, Mark D. 2000. Does Internet and computer "addiction" exist? Some case study evidence. *CyberPsychology and Behavior* 3: 211–218.

Griffiths, Mark D. 2008. Videogame addiction: Further thoughts and observations. *International Journal of Mental Health and Addiction* 6: 182–185.

Griffiths, Mark D., Mark N. O. Davies, and Darren Chappell. 2004a. Demographic factors and playing variables in online computer gaming. *CyberPsychology and Behavior* 7: 479–487.

Griffiths, Mark D., Mark N. O. Davies, and Darren Chappell. 2004b. Online computer gaming: A comparison of adolescent and adult gamers. *Journal of Adolescence* 27: 87–96.

Griffiths, Mark D., and Nigel Hunt. 1995. Computer game playing in adolescence: Prevalence and demographic indicators. *Journal of Community and Applied Social Psychology* 5: 189–193.

Griffiths, Mark D., and Nigel Hunt. 1998. Computer game "addiction" in adolescence? A brief report. *Psychological Reports* 82: 475–480.

Griffiths, Mark D., and Alex Meredith. 2009. Videogame addiction and its treatment. *Journal of Contemporary Psychotherapy* 39: 247–253.

Grüsser, S. M., R. Thaleman, and Mark D. Griffiths. 2007. Excessive computer game playing: Evidence for addiction and aggression? *CyberPsychology and Behavior* 10: 290–292.

Haines, Lester. 2008. Online gamer murders rival clan member. *The Register*. http://www.theregister.co.uk/2008/01/17/gaming_murder/.

Han, Doug Hyun, Jun Won Hwang, and Perry F. Renshaw. 2010. Buproprion sustained release treatment decreases craving for video games and cue-induced brain activity in patients with Internet video game addiction. *Experimental and Clinical Psychopharmacology* 18: 297–304.

Han, Doug Hyun, Young Sik Lee, Churl Na, Jee Young Ahn, Un Sun Chung, Melissa A. Daniels, Charlotte A. Haws, and Perry F. Renshaw. 2009. The effect of methylphenidate on Internet video game play in children with attention-deficit/hyperactivity disorder. *Comprehensive Psychiatry* 50: 251–256.

Harris Interactive. 2007. Video game addiction: Is it real? http://www.harrisinteractive.com/NEWS/allnewsbydate.asp?NewsID=1196.

Heath, Linda, Linda B. Bresolin, and Robert C. Rinaldi. 1989. Effects of media violence on children: A review of the literature. *Archives of General Psychiatry* 46: 376–379.

Hendaoui, Adel, Moez Limayem, and Craig W. Thompson. 2008. 3D social virtual worlds: Research issues and challenges. *IEEE Internet Computing* 12(1): 88–92.

Hemp, Paul. 2006. Avatar-based marketing. *Harvard Business Review.* http://hbr.org/2006/06/avatar-based-marketing/ar/1.

Hitora, Kojiro. 2005. Child dies while parents play World of Warcraft. *1up.com.* http://www.1up.com/do/blogEntry?bId=5114271.

Hof, Rob. 2006a. My virtual life. *Bloomberg BusinessWeek.* http://www.businessweek.com/magazine/content/06_18/b3982001.htm.

Hof, Rob. 2006b. Second Life's first millionaire. *Bloomberg BusinessWeek.* http://www.businessweek.com/the_thread/techbeat/archives/2006/11/second_lifes_first_millionaire.html.

Holden, Constance. 2001. "Behavioral" addictions: Do they exist? *Science* 294: 980–982.

Huesmann, L. Rowell. 1986. Psychological processes promoting the relation between exposure to media violence and aggressive behavior by the viewer. *Journal of Social Issues* 42(3): 125–139.

Hussain, Zaheer, and Mark D. Griffiths. 2009. Excessive use of massively multiplayer online role-playing games: A pilot study. *International Journal of Mental Health and Addiction* 7: 563–571.

Kalning, Kristin. 2007. Is a virtual affair real-world infidelity? *MSNBC.* http://www.msnbc.msn.com/id/18139090/ns/technology_and_science-games/t/virtual-affair-real-world-infidelity/.

Kirby, Carrie. 2009. Avatars, attorneys in new world of virtual law. *SFGate.com.* http://articles.sfgate.com/2009-04-27/business/17194388_1_second-life-virtual-worlds-san-francisco-s-linden-lab.

Knight, Will. 2004. Virtual island sells for $26,500 in cyber assets. *New Scientist.* http://www.newscientist.com/article/dn6807.

Ko, Chih-Hung, Gin-Chung Liu, Sigmund Hsiao, Ju-Yu Yen, Ming-Jen Yang, Wei-Chen Lin, Cheng-Fang Yen, and Cheng-Sheng Chen. 2009. Brain activities associated with gaming urge of online addiction. *Journal of Psychiatric Research* 43: 739–747.

Ko, Chih-Hung, Ju-Yu Yen, Cheng-Chung Chen, Sue-Huei Chen, and Cheng-Fang Yen. 2005. Proposed diagnostic criteria of Internet addiction for adolescents. *Journal of Nervous and Mental Disease* 193: 728–733.

Kohler, Chris. 2007. How protests against games cause them to sell more copies. *Wired.* http://www.wired.com/gamelife/2007/10/how-protests-ag/.

Kohn, David. 2002. Addicted: Suicide over EverQuest? *CBS News.* http://www.cbsnews.com/stories/2002/10/17/48hours/main525965.shtml.

Koob, George F., and Michel Le Moal. 2008. Addiction and the brain antireward system. *Annual Review of Psychology* 59: 29–53.

Kraut, Robert, Michael Patterson, Vicki Lundmark, Tridas Mukophadhyay, and William Scherlis. 1998. Internet paradox: A social technology that reduces social involvement and psychological well-being? *American Psychologist* 53: 1017–1031.

Kushner, David. 2005. Grand death auto. *Salon.* http://www.salon.com/technology/feature/2005/02/22/gta_killers.

Lastowka, F. Gregory. 2009. Rules of play. *Games and Culture* 4: 379–395.

Lastowka, F. Gregory, and Dan Hunter. 2004. The laws of virtual worlds. *California Law Review* 92: 1–73.

Lastowka, Greg. 2010. *Virtual justice: The new laws of online worlds.* New Haven, CT: Yale University Press.

Lee, Yong-su. 2005. Infant daughter dies as parents play online game. *The Chosun Ilbo* (English ed.). http://english.chosun.com/site/data/html_dir/2005/06/14/2005061461037.html.

Lemmens, Jeroen S., Patti M. Valkenburg, and Jochen Peter. 2009. Development and validation of a game addiction scale for adolescents. *Media Psychology* 12: 77–95.

Li, Cao. 2005. Death sentence for online gamer. *China Daily.* http://www.chinadaily.com.cn/english/doc/2005–06/08/content_449494.htm.

Linden Lab. 2011. Q1 2011 Linden Dollar economy metrics up, users and usage unchanged. http://community.secondlife.com/t5/Featured-News/Q1–2011-Linden-Dollar-Economy-Metrics-Up-Users-and-Usage/ba-p/856693.

Lo, Shao-Kang, Chih-Chien Wang, and Wenchang Fang. 2005. Physical interpersonal relationships and social anxiety among online game players. *CyberPsychology and Behavior* 8: 15–20.

Lofgren, Eric T., and Nina H. Fefferman. 2007. The untapped potential of virtual game worlds to shed light on real world epidemics. *Lancet Infectious Diseases* 7: 625–629.

Loftus, Tom. 2005. Virtual worlds wind up in real courts. *MSNBC.* http://www.msnbc.msn.com/id/6870901/ns/technology_and_science-games/.

MacKinnon, Richard. 1997. Virtual rape. *Journal of Computer-Mediated Communication* 2(4). http://jcmc.indiana.edu/vol2/issue4/mackinnon.html.

Manninen, Tony, and Tomi Kujanpää. 2007. The value of virtual assets—The role of game characters in MMOGs. *Journal of Business Science and Applied Management* 2(1): 21–33.

Martinez, Edecio. 2010. FarmVille playing mom admits she killed infant who interrupted Facebook game. *CBS News.* http://www.cbsnews.com/8301-504083_162-20021079-504083.html.

McDonald, Joe. 2006. Parents sue over game boy's death leap. *The Age.* http://www.theage.com.au/news/world/screen-tragedy/2006/05/12/1146940734731.html.

McKenna, Katelyn Y. A., and John A. Bargh. 2000. Plan 9 from cyberspace: The implications of the Internet for personality and social psychology. *Personality and Social Psychology Review* 4: 57–75.

Miller, Greg. The promise of parallel universes. 2007. *Science* 317: 1341–1343.

Millward, David. 2004. "Manhunt" computer game is blamed for brutal killing. *The Telegraph.* http://www.telegraph.co.uk/news/uknews/1468088/Manhunt-computer-game-is-blamed-for-brutal-killing.html.

Morahan-Martin, Janet. 2008. Internet abuse: Emerging trends and lingering questions. In *Psychological aspects of cyberspace: Theory, research, applications,* ed. Azy Barak, 32–69. Cambridge, United Kingdom: Cambridge University Press.

Morahan-Martin, Janet, and Phyllis Schumacher. 2000. Incidence and correlates of pathological Internet use among college students. *Computers in Human Behavior* 16: 13–29.

Morales, Tatiana. 2002. EverQuest or Evercrack? *CBS News.* http://www.cbsnews.com/stories/2002/05/28/earlyshow/living/caught/main510302.shtml.

Morgan, Michael, James Shanahan, and Nancy Signorielli. 2009. Growing up with television: Cultivation processes. In *Media effects: Advances in theory and research* (3rd ed.), ed. Jennings Bryant and Mary Beth Oliver, 34–49. New York: Routledge.

Murdoch, Julian. 2010. Money for nothing, and your kicks for free. *GamePro*. http://www.gamepro.com/article/features/216227/money-for-nothing-and-your-kicks-for-free/.

Murray-Watson, Andrew. 2005. Real profits from virtual worlds. *The Telegraph*. http://www.telegraph.co.uk/finance/2903089/Real-profits-from-virtual-worlds.html.

Naughton, Philippe. 2005. Korean drops dead after 50-hour gaming marathon. *Times Online*. http://www.timesonline.co.uk/tol/news/world/article553840.ece.

Ng, Brian D., and Peter Wiemer-Hastings. 2005. Addiction to the Internet and online gaming. *CyberPsychology and Behavior* 8: 110–113.

Nolan, Rachel. 2010. Virtual world order. *Boston Globe*. http://www.boston.com/bostonglobe/ideas/articles/2010/12/19/virtual_world_order/.

Ondrejka, Cory. 2004a. Escaping the gilded cage: User created content and building the metaverse. *New York Law School Law Review* 49: 81–101.

Ondrejka, Cory. 2004b. Living on the edge: Digital worlds which embrace the real world. http://ssrn.com/abstract=555661.

Paik, Haejung, and George Comstock. 1994. The effects of television violence on antisocial behavior: A meta-analysis. *Communication Research* 21: 516–546.

Patrizio, Andy. 2002. Did game play role in suicide? *Wired*. http://www.wired.com/gaming/gamingreviews/news/2002/04/51490.

Peckham, Matt. 2010. What'll be free and what won't in Lord of the Rings Online. *PCWorld*. http://www.pcworld.com/article/203674/whatll_be_free_and_what_wont_in_lord_of_the_rings_online.html.

Rayner, Gordon, and John Bingham. 2009. Germany school shootings: Killer Tim Kretschmer warned of massacre on the Internet. *The Telegraph*. http://www.telegraph.co.uk/news/worldnews/europe/germany/4978990/Germany-school-shootings-Killer-Tim-Kretschmer-warned-of-massacre-on-internet.html.

Ritzema, Tim, and Billy Harris. 2008. The use of Second Life for distance education. *Journal of Computing Sciences in Colleges* 23: 110–116.

Romer, Daniel, Kathleen Hall Jamieson, and Sean Aday. 2003. Television news and the cultivation of fear of crime. *Journal of Communication* 53: 88–104.

Scheithauer, Herbert, Tobias Hayer, Franz Petermann, and Gert Jugert. 2006. Physical, verbal, and relational forms of bullying among German students: Age trends, gender differences, and correlates. *Aggressive Behavior* 32: 261–275.

Seay, A. Fleming, and Robert E. Kraut. 2007. Project massive: Self-regulation and problematic use of online gaming. In *Proceedings of CHI 2007*, 829–838. New York: ACM Press.

Segrin, Chris, and Robin L. Nabi. 2002. Does television viewing cultivate unrealistic expectations about marriage? *Journal of Communication* 52: 247–263.

Seib, Christine. 2010. Is there such a thing as Internet addiction? *The Times*. http://www.thetimes.co.uk/tto/life/article2463230.ece.

Shapira, Nathan A., Toby D. Goldsmith, Paul E. Keck, Jr., Uday M. Khosla, and Susan L. McElroy. 2000. Psychiatric features of individuals with problematic Internet use. *Journal of Affective Disorders* 57: 267–272.

Shapira, Nathan A., Mary C. Lessig, Toby D. Goldsmith, Steven T. Szabo, Martin Lazoritz, Mark S. Gold, and Dan J. Stein. 2003. Problematic Internet use: Proposed classification and diagnostic criteria. *Depression and Anxiety* 17L: 207–216.

Shepherd, Tyche. 2011. Second Life grid survey—Economic metrics. http://gridsurvey.com/economy.php.

Sheridan, Michael. 2010. Video gamer hunts down, stabs man who killed his online "Counter Strike" character. *New York Daily News*. http://www.nydailynews.com/news/world/2010/05/27/2010–05–27_video_gamer_hunts_down_stabs_man_who_killed_his_online_counterstrike_character.html.

Sherry, John L. 2001. The effects of violent video games on aggression. *Human Communication Research* 27: 409–341.

Sherry, John L. 2007. Violent video games and aggression: Why can't we find links? In *Mass media effects research: Advances through meta-analysis*, ed. Raymond W. Preiss, Barbara Mae Gayle, Nancy Burrell, Mike Allen, and Jennings Bryant, 231–248. Mahwah, NJ: Erlbaum.

Smahel, David, Lukas Blinka, and Ondrej Ledabyl. 2008. Playing MMORPGS: Connections between addiction and identifying with a character. *CyberPsychology and Behavior* 11: 715–718.

Smith, Tony. 2005. "Grand Theft Auto" cop killer found guilty: Gameplaying did not affect outcome. *The Register*. http://www.theregister.co.uk/2005/08/11/gta_not_guilty/.

Smythe, Joshua M. 2007. Beyond self-selection in video game play: An experimental examination of the consequences of massively multiplayer online role-playing play. *CyberPsychology and Behavior* 10: 717–721.

Spencer, Richard. 2007. Man dies after 7-day computer session. *The Telegraph*. http://www.telegraph.co.uk/news/worldnews/1544131/Man-dies-after-7-day-computer-game-session.html.

Steinkuehler, Constance. 2007. Massively multiplayer online gaming as a constellation of literacy practices. *E-learning* 4: 297–318.

Steinkuhler, Constance, and Sean Duncan. 2008. Scientific habits of mind in virtual worlds. *Journal of Science Education and Technology* 17: 530–543.

Tassi, Paul. 2010. Virtual Entropia Universe property sells for $335K real dollars. *Forbes*. http://blogs.forbes.com/insertcoin/2010/11/10/virtual-entropia-universe-property-sells-for-335k-real-dollars/.

Tennessen, Michael. 2009. Avatar acts: Why online realities need regulation. *Scientific American*. http://www.scientificamerican.com/article.cfm?id=avatar-acts.

Tiwari, Neha. 2006. Teen pays siblings' college fees by selling virtual weapons. *CNET News*. http://news.cnet.com/8301–10784_3–6124572-7.html.

Tran, Mark. 2010. Girl starved to death while parents raised virtual child in online game. *The Guardian*. http://www.guardian.co.uk/world/2010/mar/05/korean-girl-starved-online-game.

Turkle, Sherry. 1994. Constructions and reconstructions of self in virtual reality: Playing in the MUDs. *Mind, Culture, and Activity* 1: 158–167.

Van Mierlo, Jan, and Jan Van den Bulck. 2004. Benchmarking the cultivation approach to video game effects: A comparison of the correlates of TV viewing and game play. *Journal of Adolescence* 27: 97–111.

Walther, Joseph B. 1996. Computer-mediated communication: Impersonal, interpersonal, and hyperpersonal interaction. *Communication Research* 23: 3–43.

Williams, Dmitri. 2006. Virtual cultivation: Online worlds, offline perceptions. *Journal of Communication* 56: 69–87.

Williams, Dmitri, Scott Caplan, and Li Xiong. 2007. Can you hear me now? The impact of voice in an online gaming community. *Human Communication Research* 33: 427–449.

Williams, Dmitri, Mia Consalvo, Scott Caplan, and Nick Yee. 2009. Looking for gender: Gender roles and behaviors among online gamers. *Journal of Communication* 59: 700–725.

Williams, Dmitri, Nicolas Ducheneaut, Li Xiong, Yuanyuan Zhang, Nick Yee, and Eric Nickell. 2006. From tree house to barracks: The social life of guilds in World of Warcraft. *Games and Culture* 1: 338–361.

Williams, Dmitri, and Marko Skoric. 2005. Internet fantasy violence: A test of aggression in an online game. *Communication Monographs* 72: 217–233.

Williams, Dmitri, Nick Yee, and Scott Caplan. 2008. Who plays, how much, and why? Debunking the stereotypical gamer profile. *Journal of Computer-Mediated Communication* 13: 993–1018.

Wise, Roy A., and Michael A. Bozarth. 1987. A psychomotor stimulant theory of addiction. *Psychological Review* 94: 469–492.

Wood, Richard T.A. 2008. Problems with the concept of video game "addiction": Some case study examples. *International Journal of Mental Health and Addiction* 6: 169–178.

Wood, Wendy, Frank Y. Wong, and J. Gregory Chachere. 1991. Effects of media violence on viewers' aggression in unconstrained social interaction. *Psychological Bulletin* 109: 371–383.

Yee, Nicholas. 2001. *The Norrathian Scrolls: A study of EverQuest* (Version 2.5). http://www.nickyee.com/eqt/report.html.

Yee, Nick. 2006a. Motivations for play in online games. *CyberPsychology and Behavior* 9: 772–775.

Yee, Nick. 2006b. The demographics, motivations, and derived experiences of users of massively multi-user online graphical environments. *Presence: Teleoperators and Virtual Environments* 15: 309–329.

Yee, Nick. 2006c. The psychology of massively multi-user online roleplaying games: Motivations, emotional investment, relationships and problematic usage. In *Avatars at work and play: Collaboration and interaction in virtual shared environments,* ed. Ralph Schroeder and Ann-Sofie Axelsson, 187–208. London: Springer.

Yee, Nick, Jeremy M. Bailenson, Mark Urbanek, Francis Chang, and Dan Merget. 2007. The unbearable likeness of being digital: The persistence of nonverbal social norms in online virtual environments. *CyberPsychology and Behavior* 10: 115–121.

Yellowlees, Peter M., and James N. Cook. 2006. Education about hallucinations using an Internet virtual reality system: A qualitative survey. *Academic Psychiatry* 30: 534–539.

Yellowlees, Peter M., and Shayna Marks. 2007. Problematic Internet use or Internet addiction? *Computers in Human Behavior* 23: 1447–1453.

Young, Kimberly S. 1998. Internet addiction: The emergence of a new clinical disorder. *CyberPsychology and Behavior* 1: 237–244.

Young, Kimberly S., and Robert C. Rogers. 1998. The relationship between depression and Internet addiction. *CyberPsychology and Behavior* 1: 25–28.

4

Chronology

This chronology was completed in July 2011, so some events listed for the year 2011 are based on anticipated timelines available when the book went to press. Changes in video game companies' production schedules may have since altered the events anticipated for 2011 in this timeline.

Although the technologies necessary for the existence of virtual worlds have only existed for a relatively short period of time, the history of events related to the inspiration, conceptualization, and development of virtual worlds goes back much further into history. This chapter provides a brief chronology of events related to the history of virtual worlds and related technologies, organized by year.

1892	John Ronald Reuel (J. R. R.) Tolkien is born to British parents in Bloemfontein in the Orange Free State, part of present-day South Africa. Tolkien's epic fantasy novels will later heavily influence popular role-playing games, video games, online communities, and virtual worlds.
1937	J. R. R. Tolkien, a professor at the University of Oxford's Pembroke College, first publishes his novel *The Hobbit, or There and Back Again*. This first edition is published by George Allen and Unwin, Ltd., in the United Kingdom. Several more editions will be published over the next several decades, and the book will eventually be translated into more than 40 languages.

1938	Ernest Gary Gygax is born in Chicago, Illinois. Gygax will later become a cocreator of the *Dungeons and Dragons* fantasy role-playing game and be recognized as a pioneer in the role-playing game genre.
1947	David Lance Arneson is born in Minnesota. Arneson will later become a cocreator of the *Dungeons and Dragons* fantasy role-playing game.
1954	The first two volumes of J. R. R. Tolkien's epic novel *The Lord of the Rings*, titled *The Fellowship of the Ring* and *The Two Towers*, are published by George Allen and Unwin, Ltd., in the United Kingdom.
1955	The third and final volume of J. R. R. Tolkien's epic novel *The Lord of the Rings*, titled *The Return of the King*, is published by George Allen and Unwin, Ltd., in the United Kingdom.
1963	Computer scientist J. C. R. Licklider of the Advanced Research Projects Agency (ARPA) writes a memorandum to colleagues proposing an "intergalactic computer network" and outlining many of the ideas that will eventually lead to the development of ARPANET and the Internet.
1969	The first message is sent on ARPANET, a computer network that served as an ancestor of the Internet.
1973	J. R. R. Tolkien dies at the age of 81 in Bournemouth, England. Gary Gygax and Donald R. Kaye, with financial partner Brian J. Blume, found the role-playing game publishing company Tactical Studies Rules (TSR), Inc.
1974	*Dungeons and Dragons*, a paper-and-pencil fantasy role-playing game designed by Gary Gygax and Dave Arneson and inspired in part by the work of J. R. R. Tolkien, is first published in the United States by Tactical Studies Rules (TSR),

Inc. The initial run consists of 1,000 copies and sells out. Millions will buy *Dungeons and Dragons* game publications in subsequent years, and the game will be credited for inspiring other role-playing game publications as well as online games and virtual worlds.

1975   The computer network ARPANET is declared a success and converted from experimental to operational status.

1977   *The Silmarillion,* a collection of fictional mythology by J. R. R. Tolkien related to his popular works *The Hobbit* and *The Lord of the Rings,* is published posthumously by George Allen and Unwin, Ltd., in the United Kingdom. The collection is edited by Tolkien's son, Christopher Reuel Tolkien, with the assistance of Guy Gavriel Kay, and is compiled from manuscripts and notes written by the elder Tolkien as early as 1914.

Tim Anderson, Marc Blank, Bruce Daniels, and Dave Lebling, researchers at the Massachusetts Institute of Technology, complete the first version of the text-based computer game *Zork.* Among the acknowledged inspirations for *Zork* are the role-playing game *Dungeons and Dragons* and the novels of J. R. R. Tolkien.

1978   The first version of *MUD (Multi-User Dungeon),* a text-based online role-playing game influenced by the computer game *Zork* and the role-playing game *Dungeons and Dragons,* is developed by undergraduate computer science student Roy Trubshaw at the University of Essex in England. Trubshaw and fellow University of Essex computer science student Richard Allan Bartle continue to modify and develop the game substantially through 1980. In time, *MUD* will come to be called *Essex MUD* and *MUD1* to distinguish it from later versions and from adaptations created by other developers.

1980   The first "external" players from outside of the University of Essex network use Internet

1980 (*cont.*) precursor ARPANET to log on to *MUD*, the text-based online role-playing game developed by University of Essex undergraduate students Roy Trubshaw and Richard Bartle beginning in 1978. Trubshaw hands development and management of *MUD* and its successors completely over to Bartle.

The National Science Foundation funds CSNET, a network connecting computers in computer science departments at institutions that are not connected to ARPANET.

1981 Vernor Steffen Vinge, a professor at San Diego State University, first publishes his novella *True Names* in the fifth volume of Dell Publishing's *Binary Star* paperback series. *True Names* includes an early description of an online virtual world Vinge calls the "Other Plane."

1982 Novelist William Ford Gibson's short story *Burning Chrome*, which contains the first use of the term "cyberspace," is published in *Omni* magazine.

1983 *Scepter of Goth* (a.k.a. *Sceptre of Goth*) an early commercial MUD developed by University of Minnesota student Alan E. Klietz beginning in 1978 when he was a secondary-school student, is released. Users pay hourly fees to access the game via telephone modems.

1984 William Gibson's first novel, *Neuromancer*, is published by Ace Books and popularizes the term "cyberspace."

1985 Richard Bartle, codeveloper of the original *MUD* text-based online role-playing game, develops *MUD2*, an updated version of *MUD* designed for commercial release.

LucasFilm employees Chip Morningstar and F. Randall Farmer lead the design of the online community environment *Habitat*, which features a persistent two-dimensional graphical environment in which users can interact online.

The online role-playing game *Islands of Kesmai*, which approximates graphics using text characters, is made available on the CompuServe Internet service.

The National Science Foundation forms NSFNET, a project that expands on the range and speed of the computer networks begun by ARPANET and the related CSNET to eventually form much of the backbone for the Internet.

1988   The LucasFilm online community environment *Habitat*, originally created in 1985, is re-released to a broader audience with improved graphics and other modifications as *Club Caribe*.

1991   *Neverwinter Nights*, an online role-playing game from Stormfront Studios and Strategic Simulations, Inc., is made available to America Online users and becomes the first online role-playing game to feature graphics.

The National Science Foundation first allows some commercial use of the NSFNET computer network.

Silicon & Synapse, the company that will later become Blizzard Entertainment and produce *World of Warcraft*, is founded.

The text-based online virtual environment *LambdaMOO* is announced to the public.

The works of J. R. R. Tolkien, which have already provided inspiration for a number of online role-playing games, receive direct tribute in the form of *Elendor MUSH* (multi-user shared hallucination, a MUD variation) a noncommercial text-based online role-playing game featuring settings and characters from Tolkien's books.

1992   Writer Neal Town Stephenson's novel *Snow Crash* is published by Bantam Books. *Snow Crash*

1992 (*cont.*)	adapts the Hindu term "avatar" to describe the online representations that users control to interact with the novel's virtual environment known as the "Metaverse."

1993   The infamous "rape in cyberspace" incident occurs in the text-based *LambdaMOO* virtual community when an offensively described player using the name "Mr. Bungle" uses a coded "voodoo doll" to depict other character avatars as engaging in a number of unusual, degrading, and violent sexual acts with themselves and with each other. The incident prompts widespread discussion of the incident's implications for online social dynamics and policy. Mr. Bungle's character is permanently destroyed based on the decision of one *LambdaMOO* administrator. In the aftermath, another administrator, Pavel Curtis, creates a petition and voting system that allows *LambdaMOO* users to vote and determine all of the community's policies and actions in the future.

Amy Bruckman officially opens *MediaMOO*, a text-based online community for media researchers.

1994   Blizzard Entertainment and Interplay Entertainment release *Warcraft: Orcs and Humans*, a strategy computer game that is the first entry in what will become the very successful *Warcraft* computer game series. *Warcraft: Orcs and Humans* is not played online, though it includes themes, locations, and characters that will appear in the popular online role-playing game *World of Warcraft* a decade later.

1995   The online role-playing game *Meridian 59*, credited by many as the first true virtual world because it allowed users to interact with each other in a persistent environment represented in the first-person perspective with three-dimensional graphics, is released in incomplete form by Archetype Interactive.

NSFNET decommissions its management of the computer network it has developed since 1985, privatizing the network and thereby allowing full commercial use of the Internet.

1996   The online role-playing game *Meridian 59* receives a full commercial launch by The 3DO Company after being released in incomplete form the previous year.

Sierra Online releases the online role-playing game *The Realm*, which represents its environment with two-dimensional graphics.

Nexon releases the online role-playing game *Nexus: The Kingdom of the Winds* in South Korea. The game, which uses two-dimensional graphics, will eventually amass more than one million players and will be released in North America two years later. It is designed by Jake Song, who will later be one of the creators of the popular *Lineage* online role-playing game series.

Sony Corporation's Sony Interactive Studios America (SISA) begins work on what will become the online role-playing game *EverQuest*.

1997   Origin Systems and Electronic Arts release the online role-playing game *Ultima Online*, credited as the first virtual world to be a large-scale commercial success. *Ultima Online*'s creators are also credited with popularizing the term "virtual world" to describe it and similar games.

CipSoft releases *Tibia*, an online role-playing game that uses two-dimensional graphics.

Active Worlds, a virtual world initially intended to serve as a three-dimensional alternative to Web browsers, is launched to the public.

Blaxxun Interactive releases its *ColonyCity* virtual world (later called *Cybertown*) to demonstrate its Virtual Reality Modeling Language (VRML).

1998	The online role-playing game *Lineage* is released by the South Korean company NCSoft. Millions will eventually play the game in subsequent years, particularly in South Korea, where it is most popular.
	Ultima Online becomes the first massively multiplayer online role-playing game to amass more than 100,000 subscribers worldwide.
1999	Verant Interactive, a Sony brand, releases the online role-playing game *EverQuest*.
	Turbine and Microsoft release the online role-playing game *Asheron's Call*.
	Entrepreneur Philip Rosedale founds Linden Lab, the company that will eventually produce the virtual world *Second Life* years later, in San Francisco, California.
2000	The online role-playing game *Meridian 59*, credited by many as the first true virtual world, is shut down by LucasFilm.
2001	Mythic Entertainment releases the online role playing game *Dark Age of Camelot*, which popularizes the realm-versus-realm format wherein players allied with one group engage in virtual combat with players from a rival group instead of fighting indiscriminately against individual users' characters or solely against computer-controlled characters.
	Funcom releases the online role-playing game *Anarchy Online*, which has a science-fiction theme instead of the medieval fantasy theme employed by most commercial virtual world games previously released.
	Jagex Game Studio releases the online role-playing game *RuneScape*, which is unique among its peers because it charges no subscription fee and is playable in a standard Web browser without any need for the user to install game software onto the user's computer from a disc or the In-

ternet. *RuneScape* generates income from advertisements displayed at the top of users' computer screens and through optional subscription fees paid by some users in return for additional game features.

Sega's Sonic Team releases the online role-playing game *Phantasy Star Online,* which is played on the Sega Dreamcast console rather than on a personal computer like previous virtual worlds.

Blizzard Entertainment announces that it has begun development of *World of Warcraft,* an online role-playing game in its popular *Warcraft* computer game series.

Linden Lab begins work on *LindenWorld,* a prototype virtual environment that will eventually become the *Second Life* virtual world.

A 21-year-old man in Wisconsin commits suicide by shooting himself while playing *EverQuest.*

2002   Previously defunct online role-playing game *Meridian 59,* credited by many as the first true virtual world, is reopened by Near Death Studios.

Westwood Studios and Electronic Arts launch the online role-playing game *Earth and Beyond.*

Maxis and Electronic Arts release *The Sims Online,* an online virtual world based on the popular *The Sims* computer game series.

Turbine releases the online role-playing game *Asheron's Call 2,* a sequel to the popular *Asheron's Call* game released in 1999. The original *Asheron's Call* game remains active.

Linden Lab's prototypical virtual world *LindenWorld* is renamed *Second Life* as testing of the environment continues prior to its full public release.

2003   Linden Lab launches the online virtual world *Second Life* with the application's full public release.

2003 (*cont.*)   Unlike most commercial virtual worlds, *Second Life* is released with very little content created by Linden Lab. Instead, users are expected to create their own content and communities in the virtual world's environment by buying virtual land and creating virtual goods and services to share and sell. In addition to charging a monthly subscription fee (later changed to a one-time fee and eventually removed entirely in 2005), Linden Lab generates revenue from the virtual world by charging fees to those users who want to purchase virtual land and other premium services and by charging a small transaction fee for currency exchanges between the virtual world's "Linden Dollars" and real-life currency.

Square Enix releases the online role-playing game *Final Fantasy XI*, the first online edition of the long-running and globally popular *Final Fantasy* video game franchise, in the United States after releasing the game in Japan the previous year.

Sony Online Entertainment releases the online role-playing game *EverQuest Online Adventures*, a spin-off of the popular *EverQuest* computer game, for the PlayStation 2 console.

Crowd Control Productions releases the online role-playing game *EVE Online*.

Sony Online Entertainment and LucasArts adapt the popular *Star Wars* movie franchise into a virtual world by releasing the online role-playing game *Star Wars Galaxies*.

Wolfpack Studios and Ubisoft release the online role-playing game *Shadowbane*.

Wizet and Nexon release the two-dimensional online role-playing game *Maple Story* in South Korea before releasing the game in the United States two years later.

MindArk releases the virtual world *Entropia Universe*.

Makena Technologies launches the social virtual world *There*.

2004   Blizzard Entertainment releases *World of Warcraft*, an online role-playing game that continues the popular *Warcraft* game series launched a decade earlier. *World of Warcraft* has 200,000 subscribers within 24 hours of its release, but that number is just a hint at the millions who will play the game in subsequent years.

Sony Online Entertainment releases the online role-playing game *EverQuest II*, a sequel to the popular *EverQuest* game. The original *EverQuest* game remains active.

NCSoft releases the online role-playing game *Lineage II*, a prequel to the original *Lineage* game in the United States one year after its South Korean release. The original *Lineage* game remains active. NCSoft also releases the online role-playing game *City of Heroes* in cooperation with Cryptic Studios.

Square Enix releases a version of the online role-playing game *Final Fantasy XI* for the PlayStation 2 video game console in the United States. The release comes one year after a version of the game for personal computers was released in the United States and two years after the game was released in both formats in Japan.

The online role-playing game *Earth and Beyond* is shut down two years after its release.

The avatar-based graphical chat application Instant Messaging Virtual Universe (IMVU), developed by IMVU, Inc., is first made available.

A 13-year-old boy in China jumps to his death after playing *World of Warcraft* for 36 consecutive hours.

Australian David Storey spends $26,500 for a virtual island in the virtual world *Entropia Universe*,

2004 (*cont.*)   which he uses to earn more than $100,000 annually by charging virtual hunters to hunt rare virtual animals on the virtual property.

2005   ArenaNet and NCSoft release the online role-playing game *Guild Wars*, which differs from many popular virtual worlds in that it charges no monthly subscription fee to users once they pay the initial price to buy the game's software.

The virtual world *Second Life* abandons subscription fees, allowing users to create and use an avatar in the virtual world for no charge. With no subscription fees, Linden Lab generates its income primarily from economic activity between users in the virtual world.

The online role-playing game *World of Warcraft*, released in 2004, attracts more than 1 million subscribers.

A glitch in the online role-playing game *World of Warcraft* leads to a virtual plague when the "corrupted blood" disease spreads uncontrolled through the game's population, requiring intervention from Blizzard Entertainment representatives to halt the pandemic.

Sega and Monolith Productions release *The Matrix Online*, an online role-playing game based on the popular film *The Matrix* and its sequels.

The online role-playing game *Asheron's Call 2*, which never achieved the popularity of the original *Asheron's Call* game, is shut down.

A 28-year-old South Korean man collapses and dies after playing the online multiplayer game *Starcraft* for 50 hours while stopping only to use the restroom and sleep for short periods.

A four-month-old South Korean infant dies of suffocation while her parents play *World of Warcraft* at a nearby Internet café.

A man in Shanghai, China, murders a friend who had been using a virtual weapon that the pair had jointly owned in the massively multiplayer online role-playing game *The Legend of Mir III* and who sold it online without permission. The murderer had appealed to police before committing the murder, but had been told he had no legal recourse for the virtual item's theft.

British *Entropia Universe* user Jon "Neverdie" Jacobs buys a virtual asteroid in *Entropia Universe* for $100,000 and builds virtual nightclub "Club Neverdie" on the property.

2006 The beloved role-playing franchise *Dungeons and Dragons* is adapted into a virtual world by Turbine and Atari as *Dungeons and Dragons Online: Stormreach.*

Two additional campaigns for the popular *Guild Wars* online role-playing game, titled *Factions* and *Nightfall,* are released to add new content and features for *Guild Wars* users. The games can be purchased and played online independently or in conjunction with each other and the original *Guild Wars* game.

The Virtual World of Kaneva is released by Kaneva, Inc.

IAC Search and Media launches the avatar-based graphical chat application Zwinky.

Ailin Graef, a Chinese-born *Second Life* user in Germany, becomes the first person to earn a million dollars in a virtual world through a virtual real-estate business in *Second Life.*

The virtual world *Second Life* welcomes its millionth user.

2007 Turbine and Midway Games adapt J. R. R. Tolkien's *The Lord of the Rings* and elements from his other works into the online role-playing game *The Lord of the Rings Online: Shadows of Angmar.*

The first expansion of the online role-playing game *World of Warcraft,* titled *The Burning Crusade,*

2007 (*cont.*)   is released to provide new content and features to *World of Warcraft* users. More than two million users purchase the expansion within 24 hours of its release.

An expansion of the popular *Guild Wars* online role-playing game, titled *Eye of the North,* is released to add new content and features for *Guild Wars* users who already own one of the previous *Guild Wars* game or either of its additional campaigns *Faction* and *Nightfall.*

Entrepreneur Mark Pincus founds social network games company Zynga with cofounders Scott Sale and Kyle Stewart.

A 26-year-old Chinese man dies after playing online games frequently over the course of several days during the New Year holiday.

A 30-year-old Chinese man dies after playing an online game for three days.

A Russian who played the online role-playing game *Lineage II* is killed by a man who was a member of a rival group in the game when members of two of the game's guild groups meet to continue a dispute that originated in the virtual world.

A user of the virtual world *Second Life* visits the online campus of Ohio University in May 2007 to stage a virtual mass shooting in apparent reference to the tragic mass shooting perpetrated at Virginia Tech during the previous month.

2008   *Dungeons and Dragons* cocreator and role-playing game pioneer Gary Gygax dies at the age of 69 in Lake Geneva, Wisconsin.

The second expansion of the online role-playing game *World of Warcraft,* titled *Wrath of the Lich King,* is released to provide new content and features to *World of Warcraft* users. As with the first expansion released in the previous year, more than two million users purchase the expansion within 24 hours of its release.

The first expansion of the online role-playing game *The Lord of the Rings Online*, titled *Mines of Moria*, is released to provide new content and features to *The Lord of the Rings Online* users.

Funcom and Eidos Interactive release the online role-playing game *Age of Conan: Hyborian Adventures*, which is based on Robert E. Howard's popular fantasy stories featuring the character Conan the Barbarian.

Mythic Entertainment and Electronic Arts release the online role-playing game *Warhammer Online: Age of Reckoning*, an adaptation of the *Warhammer Fantasy* role-playing game series.

Sony Online Entertainment and Flying Lab Software release the online role-playing game *Pirates of the Burning Sea*.

BioWare and LucasArts announce that they have begun development of the online role-playing computer game *Star Wars: The Old Republic*.

The online role-playing game *The Sims Online* is shut down.

The virtual world *SmallWorlds* is released by Outsmart.

2009   The online role-playing game *Dungeons and Dragons Online: Stormreach* abandons monthly subscription fees for its users and releases the game in free-to-play form as *Dungeons and Dragons Online: Eberron Unlimited*. The game generates income by charging players for optional paid V.I.P. subscriptions and charging small fees for virtual items from an optional in-game store. After the change in cost structure, the game garners more than 2 million new users in 2009 and doubles its market share during that year.

The second expansion of the online role-playing game *The Lord of the Rings Online*, titled *Siege of Mirkwood*, is released to provide new content and features to *The Lord of the Rings Online* users.

2009 (*cont.*)   NCSoft releases the online role-playing game *Aion* in the United States, Europe, and Australia after releasing the game as *Aion: The Tower of Eternity* in South Korea the previous year.

The online role-playing game *The Matrix Online* is shut down.

The online role-playing game *Shadowbane* is shut down.

Zynga releases the social network games *Mafia Wars* and *Farmville*.

A three-month-old South Korean infant dies from malnutrition while her parents play the online game *Prius Online* at Internet cafés.

David Lance Arneson, codeveloper of the popular *Dungeons and Dragons* role-playing game franchise, dies in Saint Paul, Minnesota.

2010   The online role-playing game *World of Warcraft* serves more than 12 million subscribers worldwide.

The third expansion of the online role-playing game *World of Warcraft*, titled *Cataclysm*, is released to provide new content and features to *World of Warcraft* users. More than three million users purchase the expansion within 24 hours of its release.

The online role-playing game *The Lord of the Rings Online* abandons monthly subscription fees for its users and releases the game in free-to-play form, emulating the change in price structure implemented by online role-playing game (and fellow Turbine product) *Dungeons and Dragons Online* the previous year. The game generates income by charging players for optional paid V.I.P. subscriptions and charging small fees for virtual items from an optional in-game store. Game revenues triple after the change to the free-to-play format.

Cryptic Studios adapts the popular *Star Trek* science-fiction franchise with the release of the online role-playing game *Star Trek Online*.

The online role-playing game *Meridian 59*, credited by many as the first true virtual world, is made available to the public for no fee by original developers Andrew Kirmse and Chris Kirmse after previous developer Near Death Studios ceases operations.

Blizzard Entertainment acknowledges that it is developing the online role-playing game *Titan*.

The virtual world *There* is closed down.

Zynga releases the social network games *CityVille* and *FrontierVille*.

A three-month-old baby in Florida is shaken to death by his mother when his crying interrupts her use of the social network game *FarmVille*.

After plotting for months, a French man who had played the online game *Counter-Strike* visits another player's home and inflicts serious injury by stabbing him as revenge for the perpetrator's game character having been killed by the victim's character in a virtual knife battle.

British *Entropia Universe* user Jon "Neverdie" Jacobs sells his virtual asteroid-based nightclub in parcels for $635,000, including one sale for $335,000.

2011   BioWare and LucasArts release the online role-playing game *Star Wars: The Old Republic*, the second commercial virtual world based on the popular *Star Wars* film series.

Jagex Game Studio releases the online role-playing game *Stellar Dawn*.

Trion Worlds, Inc., releases the online role-playing game *Rift*.

2011 (*cont.*)   The third expansion of the online role-playing game *The Lord of the Rings Online*, titled *Rise of Isengard*, is released to provide new content and features to *The Lord of the Rings Online* users.

Sony Online Entertainment releases the online role-playing game *DC Universe Online*, which places characters in a virtual world featuring locations and characters from the DC Comics comic book series.

The online role-playing game *Star Wars Galaxies* is shut down.

North American servers for the original *Lineage* online role-playing game are shut down, though the game remains available in Asia.

5

Biographical Sketches

M any people have served important roles in the development and study of virtual worlds, whether through direct involvement as developers or researchers of virtual worlds, indirectly through development of applications that preceded them, or even more indirectly by inspiring virtual worlds and related applications with their ideas, games, and stories. This chapter provides a series of brief biographical sketches, in alphabetical order by surname, for a few of the many people who have played key roles in the long and ongoing history of virtual worlds.

Craig A. Anderson

Craig A. Anderson is a social psychologist who has conducted extensive research into the effects of violence in video game content on aggression in users. Anderson earned a PhD in 1980 from Stanford University, as well as an MA in 1978 from Stanford University and a BA in 1976 from Butler University. He has worked as a faculty member at Rice University, Ohio State University, and the University of Missouri and has been a professor at Iowa State University since 1999.

Anderson has published dozens of widely cited articles examining the relationship between exposure to violent video game content and aggressive thoughts, feelings, and behavior, along with other related responses. From this research, Anderson concludes that there is conclusive evidence that violent video game content has a causal influence on serious aggression and violence in video game players. Anderson's research has been widely lauded, but

123

he has also been subject to criticisms regarding whether he overstates the implications of his findings regarding serious acts of aggression and violence. Anderson's research related to video games has not tended to involve virtual worlds and other online games specifically, but has not tended to suggest there would be any distinction between the effects of violent content in online games and the effects of violent content in games not played online.

Timothy Anderson

Tim Anderson is a computer programmer who cocreated the early text-based role-playing computer game *Zork* beginning in 1977 while at the Massachusetts Institute of Technology. Anderson founded the software company Infocom in 1979 with *Zork* cocreators Marc Blank and Dave Lebling and several other cofounders. Anderson designed several other video games for Infocom and has since created video games for several other companies. Anderson has also written several historical accounts of *Zork* and Infocom for print and online publications.

David Lance Arneson

Dave Arneson was a game designer who cocreated the famed paper-and-pencil role-playing game *Dungeons and Dragons,* which has been widely credited as an inspiration for virtual worlds, the text-based online MUDs (multi-user dungeons) that came before them, and other video games, with Gary Gygax. Arneson met Gygax in 1969 while Arneson was a student at the University of Minnesota, and the pair would publish the original edition of the *Dungeons and Dragons* game in 1974 as a boxed set of three books with accompanying materials.

Arneson provided some of the original illustrations in that first edition. Arneson joined Tactical Studies Rules, Inc., the company cofounded by Gygax that published *Dungeons and Dragons,* in 1976, but left the company later that year. Arneson would later be involved in legal disputes with Tactical Studies Rules, Inc., over royalties from products derived from *Dungeons and Dragons.* After his initial work with *Dungeons and Dragons* and Tactical Studies Rules, Inc., Arneson founded his own game company, Adventure

Games, before selling it. He would also work in computer programming and education. Arneson died in 2009 at the age of 61.

Jeremy N. Bailenson

Jeremy Bailenson is an associate professor in the Department of Communication at Stanford University whose research focuses on representation, behavior, and responses of humans in virtual reality and virtual environments. He earned a PhD in cognitive psychology from Northwestern University in 1999, an MS in cognitive psychology in 1996, and a BA in cognitive science from the University of Michigan in 1994. Before joining the faculty at Stanford in 2003, Bailenson served as a postdoctoral fellow and an assistant research professor at the University of California, Santa Barbara.

Bailenson is the founding director of the Virtual Human Interaction Lab at Stanford. His research on virtual reality and virtual environments has been published in scores of articles in several fields, and he is the coauthor of the 2011 book *Infinite Reality: Avatars, Eternal Life, New Words and the Dawn of the Virtual Revolution* with Jim Blascovich. Bailenson has assisted organizations such as the Department of Defense, the National Research Council, and the National Institutes of Health with issues related to virtual reality and virtual environments. He also served as advisor to virtual worlds researcher Nick Yee during Yee's doctoral research at Stanford.

Richard A. Bartle

Richard Bartle is a British computer programmer, game designer, author, and researcher. Bartle is acknowledged as one of the codevelopers of *MUD* (Multi-User Dungeon), the original text-based online role-playing game that spawned a genre of related games and online communities known as "MUDs" in tribute. When Bartle was an undergraduate student in computer science at the University of Essex in 1978, he met fellow University of Essex computer science undergraduate Roy Trubshaw, who developed the basic structure of the *MUD* game in 1978 and worked on it with Bartle before passing it to Bartle to complete. Bartle was able to develop a more complete version of the game by 1980, at which time players from beyond the university were able to access *MUD* online.

He earned a BSc degree in computer science and a PhD in artificial intelligence from the University of Essex and has served on the faculty there on multiple occasions. Bartle produced a revision of *MUD* in 1985 and cofounded a game company called Multi-User Entertainment, Ltd., during the same year. He has worked with a number of other computing and game-related organizations since then. Among his publications is the book *Designing Virtual Worlds,* which has been an influential work in the area of game design.

Marc Blank

Marc Blank is a software engineer and game designer who cocreated the early text-based role-playing computer game *Zork* beginning in 1977 while at the Massachusetts Institute of Technology. Blank founded the software company Infocom in 1979 with *Zork* cocreators Tim Anderson and Dave Lebling and several other cofounders. Blank also earned an undergraduate degree from the Massachusetts Institute of Technology and a medical degree from the Albert Einstein College of Medicine of Yeshiva University. Blank has since worked for several other software companies and designed multiple games, including Sony's *Syphon Filter* game for the PlayStation console.

James J. Blascovich

Jim Blascovich is a professor of psychology in the Department of Psychological and Brain Sciences at the University of California at Santa Barbara who studies social behavior in virtual environments. He codirects the University of California at Santa Barbara's Research Center of Virtual Environments and Behavior. Blascovich has written numerous academic publications and is the coauthor of the 2011 book *Infinite Reality: Avatars, Eternal Life, New Words and the Dawn of the Virtual Revolution* with Jeremy Bailenson. He holds a PhD in social psychology from the University of Nevada at Reno and a BS in psychology from Loyola University at Chicago. Before joining the faculty at the University of California, Santa Barbara, Blascovich held positions at the University of

Nevada at Reno, Marquette University, and the State University of New York at Buffalo. He has received extensive research support from organizations such as the National Science Foundation, the National Institutes of Health, and the Army Research Laboratory.

Amy Susan Bruckman

Amy Bruckman is an associate professor in the School of Interactive Computing at Georgia Tech who was a pioneer in research related to online communities. Before joining Georgia Tech in 1997, Bruckman earned a PhD in media arts and sciences from the Massachusetts Institute of Technology, an MSVS in media arts and sciences from the Massachusetts Institute of Technology, and a BA in physics from Harvard University. While a doctoral student at the Massachusetts Institute of Technology, Bruckman founded *MediaMOO*, a text-based online community for media scholars and educators. Bruckman was named one of the world's top 100 innovators younger than 35 years of age by the magazine *Technology Review* in 1999.

Brad J. Bushman

Brad Bushman is a social psychologist who has conducted a large body of research dealing with the effects of violent media content on aggression. He holds a PhD in social psychology from the University of Missouri, an MA in psychology from the University of Missouri, an MA in statistics from the University of Missouri, an MEd in secondary education from Utah State University, and a BS in psychology from Weber State University. Bushman has been a professor at Ohio State University since 2010 and has also served on the faculty at Iowa State University, the University of Michigan, the Warsaw School of Social Psychology in Poland, and VU University Amsterdam in the Netherlands.

Bushman's research on the effects of violent media, particularly his work with Craig Anderson dealing with the effects of violent video games on aggression, has been cited widely. Like Anderson, Bushman concludes from his research that violence in video games is a significant causal risk influence on serious aggression and violence. Bushman has also conducted research suggesting that violent media do not tend to reduce users' aggression through catharsis. Bushman's research has not tended to deal with online games specifically or make distinctions between the effects of games played online and games that are not played online.

Edward Castronova

Edward "Ted" Castronova is an associate professor in the Department of Telecommunications at Indiana University. He has conducted prominent research on social and economic issues in virtual worlds, including some of the first empirical research describing users of massively multiplayer online role-playing games. Castronova earned a PhD in economics from the University of Wisconsin at Madison and a BS in international affairs from Georgetown University in 1985. Before joining the faculty at Indiana University, he served on the faculty at California State University, Fullerton, and the University of Rochester. Castronova has also worked in Germany studying issues related to German reunification.

In 2001, Castronova posted a research paper called *Virtual Worlds: A First-Hand Account of Market and Society on the Cyberian Frontier,* to an online research paper database called the Social Science Research Network. The paper included data from a large survey of users of the online role-playing game *EverQuest,* as well as an analysis of the real-life economic value of virtual goods produced in the game that was conducted by examining both production and trade of trade goods within the game and sales of virtual goods from the game on the Internet auction site eBay. The paper described *EverQuest*'s virtual world of Norrath as a place whose users dedicated significant amounts of time and energy to the game and produced goods with meaningful economic value. For example, the paper estimated that an *EverQuest*'s user produced virtual items and attributes worth an average of $3.42 per hour, and that Norrath had a gross national product per capita ranking between that of Russia and Bulgaria. Castronova's paper received much attention from the academic community and news media almost immediately upon its release.

Since the release of his groundbreaking paper on *EverQuest* users, Castronova has conducted extensive research involving a number of other virtual worlds ranging from *EverQuest II* to *Second Life.* Castronova also received $250,000 in funding from the

MacArthur Foundation to create a dedicated new virtual world in which research could be conducted regarding the social and economic behavior of its users. This virtual world, called *Arden: The World of Shakespeare,* was eventually released in incomplete form as a modification that could be added to the commercial *Neverwinter Nights* video game due to problems with the *Arden* game's development and design.

Castronova has published several academic articles, books, and book chapters on virtual worlds, and has also continued to post papers to the Social Science Research Network online. He also cofounded the website *Terra Nova,* a site featuring contributions about virtual worlds from scholars and industry professionals that describes itself as "an interdisciplinary weblog about the intersection of society, simulation, and play," in 2003 with Julian Dibbell, Dan Hunter, and Greg Lastowka. Castronova was born Edward Bird but changed his name when he was married in 2000.

Pavel Curtis

Pavel Curtis is a computer programmer who founded the online text-based social environment *LambdaMOO* in 1990 while he was working as a research scientist at Xerox PARC (Palo Alto Research Center). The "MOO" in *LambdaMOO* stands for "MUD, Object Oriented," a term describing text-based online environments that are a variation of MUDs (Multi-User Dungeons). *LambdaMOO's* opening was announced to the public in 1991.

Curtis was on a business trip during the days surrounding the infamous "rape in cyberspace" incident wherein a *LambdaMOO* user employed a coded object to make it appear as if other users' characters in the environment were performing obscene and degrading acts on each other and themselves, so he was not active in *LambdaMOO* during the incident and the online discussions immediately following the event. Upon his return from the business trip, Curtis developed and implemented a voting system in *LambdaMOO* that allowed all users to create petitions and vote on proposed actions and policy for the community, with the results being binding for *LambdaMOO* administrators.

Curtis has a PhD and an MS in computer science from Cornell University and a BA in music from Antioch College. He left Xerox PARC in 1996 and currently works at Microsoft.

Bruce K. Daniels

Bruce Daniels is a computer programmer and hydroclimatologist who was one of the creators of the early text-based role-playing computer game *Zork* beginning in 1977 while he was at the Massachusetts Institute of technology. Daniels earned an MA and a BS in computer science from the Massachusetts Institute of Technology and is expected to complete a PhD in earth sciences at the University of California, Santa Cruz, in 2012. After helping create the *Zork* game, he worked at a number of high-profile computer companies such as Apple, Sun Microsystems, and Oracle before returning to academic work pertaining to the impact of climate change on water systems. Daniels has also served in appointed and elected positions with government agencies in California related to management of water resources.

Julian Dibbell

Julian Dibbell is a journalist and author who as written articles and books on virtual communities and other online environments. In 1993, Dibbell wrote an article in New York City newspaper *The Village Voice* titled "A Rape in Cyberspace, or How an Evil Clown, a Haitian Trickster Spirit, Two Wizards, and a Cast of Dozens Turned a Database into a Society." The article describes an event in the text-based online community *LambdaMOO* wherein a character named "Mr. Bungle" entered the environment and used a coded virtual object to make it appear as if other characters in the environment were performing obscene and degrading acts on themselves and one another. Dibbell was not logged in on the virtual environment during the incident, but he attended a virtual meeting held in *LambdaMOO* three days later to discuss the event and what consequences should be visited on the Mr. Bungle character. Dibbell's article recounts both the event and the meeting that followed, along with other information gleaned from *LambdaMOO* participants, and prompted widespread discussion about the social and legal implications of events in virtual environments upon its publication.

In addition to the *Village Voice* article, Dibbell has written a book about his experiences in *LambdaMOO* titled *My Tiny Life: Crime and Passion in a Virtual World*. A reprinted version of the "A Rape in Cyberspace" article appears in that book. Dibbell is also the author of a book about virtual worlds titled *Play Money: Or, How I Quit My Day Job and Made Millions Trading Virtual Loot* and a number of widely read articles about virtual worlds, such as "The Life of the Chinese Gold Farmer," which appeared in *The New York Times* in 2007. Along with Edward Castronova, Dan Hunter, and Greg Lastowka, Dibbell cofounded of the website *Terra Nova,* a site featuring contributions about virtual worlds from scholars and industry professionals which describes itself as "an interdisciplinary weblog about the intersection of society, simulation, and play," in 2003. Dibbell holds a BA in English from Yale University.

F. Randall Farmer

F. Randall "Randy" Farmer is a computer programmer known for codeveloping the early graphical online community *Habitat* for LucasFilm with Chip Morningstar beginning in 1985. Farmer has since been involved with the development of other online communities and virtual worlds such as *WorldsAway, The Sims Online* and *Second Life* and has worked for other prominent online services such as Yahoo! and Answers.com. Farmer coauthored a paper with Morningstar titled "The Lessons of LucasFilm's Habitat" that was published in the edited book *Cyberspace: First Steps* in 1991.

Christopher J. Ferguson

Christopher Ferguson is an associate professor of psychology in the department of behavioral sciences at Texas A & M International University who is known for his research examining the positive and negative effects of violent video games. Ferguson joined the faculty at Texas A & M International University after earning a PhD in clinical psychology from the University of Central Florida. Unlike many researchers in the field of psychology examining the effects of violent video games, Ferguson has tended to conclude from his research that the effects of violent content in video games and other media on serious aggression and violence are limited.

Ferguson argues that the negative effects of violent content and its implications for policy are overstated by many researchers based on the existing evidence. Ferguson's somewhat unique views among his peers has brought attention to his work, but has also generated criticism from other researchers who disagree with his conclusions about the risk that violence in video games and other media pose. Although much of Ferguson's research on violent video games has dealt with video games generally rather than online games specifically, he has noted that online games involve socialization between players that may be associated with positive social outcomes such as interest in civic engagement.

Richard Garriott

Richard Garriott is a video game developer who developed the online role-playing game *Ultima Online*, which was released in 1997 and is credited by some as the first massively multiplayer online role-playing game based on the number of players it accommodated. After publishing his first computer game, *Akalabeth: World of Doom*, in 1980, Garriott released the popular *Ultima* series of role-playing computer games beginning in the same year. The *Ultima* series included nine primary games numbered I through IX that were released between 1980 and 1999, as well as a number of spin-off titles. The *Ultima Online* game is one such sequel.

Garriott self-published the first *Ultima* game, and the second was published by game company Sierra Online. In 1983, Garriott founded Origin Systems, Inc., with family members and fellow programmer Chuck Bueche to distribute the *Ultima* games. Origin Systems was sold to Electronic Arts in 1992. Garriott left Origin Systems and Electronic Arts in 2000 and cofounded Destination Games, Inc., with one of his brothers and a former member of the *Ultima Online* staff. He partnered with NCSoft in 2001 to develop the online role-playing game *Tabula Rasa*, which was released in 2007 and closed in 2009. Garriott left NCSoft in 2008.

The British-born son of an American astronaut, Garriott paid space tourism company Space Adventures for the opportunity to travel to space in 2008. Garriott had previously arranged a flight to space in 2001 that would have made him the first space tourist, but financial difficulties at that time had forced him to sell his seat on that spacecraft. Garriott attended the University of Texas at Austin, but did not complete a degree there.

William Ford Gibson

William Gibson is a science-fiction author whose novels and short stories greatly influenced the "cyberpunk" literary genre.

He introduced the term "cyberspace" to describe virtual worlds in *Burning Chrome*, a short story published in *Omni* in 1982, and popularized the term further in 1984 with his award-winning novel *Neuromancer*. The concepts and themes in his work are acknowledged as having influenced conceptual thinking regarding the development of computer technologies and online networks. Gibson earned a bachelor's degree in English from the University of British Columbia and holds honorary doctorates from Simon Fraser University and Coastal Carolina University. He was inducted to the Science Fiction Hall of Fame in Seattle, Washington, in 2008.

Ailin Graef

Ailin Graef is a Chinese-born entrepreneur known for becoming the first virtual millionaire while living in Germany in 2006 by earning more than one million dollars in profits through her virtual real estate business in the virtual world *Second Life*. Graef is also popularly known by the name of her *Second Life* avatar "Anshe Chung," and she sometimes uses the name as a pseudonym in real-life settings.

Before launching her online business, Graef was an educator. Based on her previous experience generating virtual money without real-life value in online role-playing games such as *Asheron's Call* and *Shadowbane*, Graef was able to generate real income in *Second Life* because *Second Life*'s virtual Linden Dollars could be exchanged for real currency. Graef engaged in a number of for-profit activities, including service as a virtual escort, to generate income in *Second Life* before making most of her online fortune through buying and selling virtual land in the virtual world. During her early work making money in *Second Life*, Graef used proceeds from the virtual world to support a disadvantaged young boy in the Philippines through a charity organization. Since making her fortune in *Second Life*, Graef has invested in a number of companies involved with online communities, including IMVU, Inc.

Ernest Gary Gygax

Gary Gygax was a game designer who co-created the famed paper-and-pencil role-playing game *Dungeons and Dragons*, which has been widely credited as an inspiration for virtual worlds, the text-based online MUDs (Multi-User Dungeons) that came before them, and other video games, with Dave Arneson. Gygax is widely recognized as the father of role-playing games.

Before creating *Dungeons and Dragons,* Gygax founded the gaming convention Gen Con in 1968. Gen Con remains a popular annual gaming industry event. Gygax created the medieval-themed game *Chainmail,* which contained some game elements that would be emulated later in the development of *Dungeons and Dragons,* in 1971 with hobby store owner Jeff Perren. In 1973, Gygax cofounded Tactical Studies Rules, Inc., with friend and fellow game enthusiast Don Kaye.

In 1974, Gygax created *Dungeons and Dragons* with Dave Arneson, whom he had met in 1969. The original edition of the *Dungeons and Dragons* game was published in a run of 1,000 copies, which sold out, as a boxed set of three books with accompanying materials. In 1977, Gygax expanded the original *Dungeons and Dragons* game with the publication of *Advanced Dungeons and Dragons.* Gygax left Tactical Studies Rules, Inc., in 1985, but created several more role-playing games during his lifetime. He died in 2008 at the age of 69.

Rod Humble

Rod Humble is a software developer who is the current chief executive officer of Linden Lab, producers of the virtual world *Second Life.* Before joining Linden Lab in 2011, he worked at multiple game companies including Electronic Arts, where he contributed to several games including some titles in the popular *The Sims* series, and Sony Online Entertainment, where games he was involved with included the *EverQuest* online role-playing game series and the online role-playing game *Star Wars: Galaxies.* Humble has worked in the video game industry since 1990.

Dan Hunter

Dan Hunter is a professor at the New York Law School who studies application of law to the Internet, including virtual worlds. Hunter has also served on the faculty at the University of Melbourne Law School in Australia and the Wharton School at the

University of Pennsylvania. He holds a PhD in legal reasoning from Cambridge University in England, an LLM in law from the University of Melbourne in Australia, and an LLB in law and a BS in computer science from Monash University in Australia. Hunter has published articles in several law journals and coauthored the book *Building Legal Intelligence Systems* in 1994. In 2003, Hunter cofounded the website *Terra Nova*, a site featuring contributions about virtual worlds from scholars and industry professionals and which describes itself as "an interdisciplinary weblog about the intersection of society, simulation, and play," with Edward Castronova, Julian Dibbell, and Greg Lastowka.

Jon Jacobs

Jon Jacobs is an English virtual worlds entrepreneur, commonly known by his online avatar name "Neverdie," who is known for his prominent purchases and sales of virtual property in the virtual world *Entropia Universe*. Jacobs purchased a virtual asteroid in *Entropia Universe* in 2005 for $100,000 in what was then recognized as the most expensive virtual item purchase ever. Jacobs took out a mortgage on his real-life home to finance the virtual property purchase. He founded a virtual nightclub and resort on the property called "Club Neverdie," which generated $200,000 annually for Jacobs through sales of various goods and services to *Entropia Universe* users. Jacobs sold his virtual asteroid property in separate portions in 2010 for a total of $635,000, including one sale totaling $335,000. The legitimacy of Jacobs' claims of having conducted his virtual business independently from the *Entropia Universe* management have been questioned, though, because Jacobs identified himself as a spokesperson for the virtual world as early as 2004 and claimed to be in negotiations to purchase a virtual nightclub there as early as 2005. Jacobs is also a film actor and director. He had an uncredited role in the film *Return to Oz* and appeared in an episode of the television series *Fame*.

Donald R. Kaye

Don Kaye was a cofounder of Tactical Studies Rule, Inc., the company that published the influential paper-and-pencil role-playing game *Dungeons and Dragons*. Kaye cofounded the company in 1973 with Gary Gygax, who had been his friend since childhood. Kaye and Gygax each invested $1,000 to found the company, with Kaye borrowing against a life insurance policy for his portion of the founding capital. *Dungeons and Dragons,* authored by Gygax and Dave Arneson, was published by Tactical Studies Rules in 1974 and is credited for widely influencing other role-playing games, including text-based online role-playing MUDs, role-playing video games, and virtual worlds. Kaye died unexpectedly from a heart attack in 1975 at the age of 36.

Kim Tack Jin

T. J. Kim is a South Korean software developer who founded the South Korean software company NCSoft, producer of the online role-playing games *Lineage, Lineage II, Guild Wars, City of* Heroes, and *Aion*. He serves as NCSoft's chief executive officer. Kim founded the company in 1997, and its first product was a hypertext programming language (HTML) editor for Web programming before NCSoft broke into the online role-playing game market with the 1998 release of *Lineage*. The company now has thousands of employees and subsidiaries in Taiwan, China, Japan, Europe, and the United States.

Andrew Kirmse

Andrew Kirmse is a computer programmer who, with his brother Chris Kirmse, was a primary creator of *Meridian 59,* an online role-playing game first released in 1995 and credited by many as the first true virtual world because of its three-dimensional, first-person graphical representation. Andrew first began developing what would become *Meridian 59* while he was a junior at the Massachusetts Institute of Technology, where he earned bachelor's degrees in physics, theoretical mathematics, and computer science, and also a master's degree in computer science. After developing *Meridian 59* with Archetype Interactive and The 3DO Company, Kirmse worked as a game programmer at LucasArts and worked with Internet company Google on the Google Desktop, Google Maps, and Google Earth applications. He and his brother currently provide access to *Meridian 59* free online after the last of a series of game companies stopped hosting the game commercially in 2010.

Chris Kirmse

Chris Kirmse is a computer programmer who, with his brother Andrew Kirmse, was a primary creator of *Meridian 59,* an online role-playing game first released in 1995 and credited by many as the first true virtual world because of its three-dimensional, first-person graphical representation. Chris first began developing what would become *Meridian 59* while he was a sophomore at Virginia Tech, where he earned a bachelor's degree in computer science. He later earned an MBA from San Jose State University. After developing *Meridian 59* with Archetype Interactive and The 3DO Company, Kirmse developed games for Internet company Yahoo! and was one of the inventors of Xfire, a networking system for video game players that allows users to send instant messages, join games, and use voice chat with friends. In 2011, he joined social games company Wild Needle. Kirmse and his brother Chris currently provide access to *Meridian 59* free online after the last of a series of game companies stopped hosting the game commercially in 2010.

Alan E. Klietz

Alan Klietz is a computer programmer who developed *Scepter of Goth* (a.k.a. *Sceptre of Goth*), an early commercial MUD (Multi-User Dungeon, a text-based online role-playing game). Klietz finished an early version of *Scepter of Goth* in 1978 as a secondary-school student, and the game was commercially released in 1983 while Klietz was an undergraduate student at the University of Minnesota, where Klietz earned a bachelor's degree in computer science in 1988. *Scepter of Goth* initially charged users an hourly rate of $2.99 per hour to log in and play via telephone modem, and the game was later licensed to franchisees who typically charged users similar rates.

Klietz was employed at GamBit Multisystems, Inc., a dial-up computer services company that provided dial-up computer services that initially provided *Scepter of Goth* to customers, from 1983 to 1985. Since then, he has worked for the Minnesota Supercomputer Center at the University of Minnesota and has been involved with multiple software companies.

Raphael Koster

Raph Koster is a game designer who led development of the on-line role-playing game *Ultima Online* and directed creation of the online role-playing game *Star Wars Galaxies*. Koster worked at Origin Systems from 1995 to 2000 and for Sony Online Entertainment from 2000 to 2006. He has written several books and articles on game design. Koster has an MFA degree in creative writing from the University of Alabama and a BA in English and Spanish from Washington College in Chestertown, Maryland. While a student, he was a developer of the text-based MUD (Multi-User Dungeon) games *Worlds of Carnage* and *LegendMUD*.

Greg Lastowka

Greg Lastowka is a professor in the School of Law at Rutgers University who studies issues related to intellectual property in on-line communities and virtual environments. Lastowka holds a BA from Yale University and a JD from the University of Virginia. He practiced law related to intellectual property and technology at the international law firm Dechert LLP before joining the faculty at Rutgers in 2004. In addition to his employment at Rutgers University, Lastowka has held visiting appointments at Columbia University and the University of Graz in Austria. He also served with the Peace Corps in Turkmenistan.

Lastowka has published several articles in law journals, as well as the book *Virtual Justice: The New Laws of Online Worlds*, which was published in 2010. He was also a cofounder of the website *Terra Nova*, a site launched in 2003 about virtual worlds that features contributions from scholars and industry professionals and describes itself as "an interdisciplinary weblog about the intersection of society, simulation, and play," with Edward Castronova, Julian Dibbell, and Dan Hunter.

P. David Lebling

Dave Lebling is a software engineer who cocreated the early text-based role-playing computer game *Zork* beginning in 1977 while working as a researcher at the Massachusetts Institute of Technology. Lebling founded the software company Infocom in 1979 with *Zork* cocreators Tim Anderson, Marc Blank, and several other cofounders. Lebling also earned an undergraduate degree in political science from the Massachusetts Institute of Technology. Lebling designed several other games with Infocom and has also worked for video and audio production company Avid and defense contractor BAE systems.

Joseph Carl Robnett Licklider

J.C.R. Licklider was a computer scientist and Internet pioneer who was one of the first to envision the Internet. Licklider earned a PhD in psychoacoustics from the University of Rochester in 1942, as well as an MA in psychology in 1938 from Washington University in St. Louis, Missouri, and a BA in physics, mathematics, and psychology in 1937 from Washington University as well. He worked at Harvard University from 1943 to 1950, after which he became an associate professor at the Massachusetts Institute of Technology.

In 1962, Licklider joined the U.S. Government's Advanced Research Projects Agency (ARPA), and in 1963 he sent his colleagues a memorandum proposing an "intergalactic computer network" and outlining many of the ideas that would eventually lead to the development of ARPANET, an Internet precursor. Licklider returned to the Massachusetts Institute of Technology in 1968 as the director of the Project on Mathematics and Computation (Project MAC), and he remained at the Massachusetts Institute of Technology until his retirement in 1985. In 1979, he was one of the cofounders of the software company Infocom, among whose other cofounders were several students and staff at the Massachusetts Institute of Technology including the creators of the early text-based role-playing computer game *Zork*. Licklider died in 1990 at the age of 75.

Thomas M. Malaby

Thomas Malaby is an associate professor of anthropology at the University of Wisconsin at Milwaukee who has conducted ethnographic research in virtual worlds. Malaby holds a PhD in anthropology from Harvard University, as well as master's and bachelor's degrees in anthropology from the same institution. In 2009, Malaby published the book *Making Virtual Worlds: Linden Lab and Second Life,* which was based on observational research he conducted over the course of a year at *Second Life* producers Linden Lab. He has also authored a book about gambling on the island of Crete and several academic articles and book chapters.

Brad McQuaid

Brad McQuaid is a video game designer who led development of the online role-playing game *EverQuest.* McQuaid designed his first game, the computer role-playing game *WarWizard* in 1989 with friend Steve Clover. McQuaid and Clover were both hired by Sony in 1996 to work on the online role-playing game that would become *EverQuest.* McQuaid was initially the lead programmer in *EverQuest*'s development before becoming its producer and a lead designer. He later became Sony Online Entertainment's chief creative officer. In 2002, McQuaid left Sony to become a cofounder of Sigil Games Online, Inc., which produced the online role-playing game *Vanguard: Saga of Heroes* in cooperation with Sony Online Entertainment until the company was acquired by Sony Online Entertainment.

Chip Morningstar

Chip Morningstar is a software developer who codeveloped the early graphical online community *Habitat* for LucasFilm with Randy Farmer beginning in 1985. Before working at LucasFilm, he was involved with Project Xanadu, an early attempt to develop hypertext before it became a standard method to linking documents on the World Wide Web. After working on *Habitat,* Morningstar was involved in the development of other games for LucasFilm before working for a number of other companies involved with software development, computer networking, and the Internet. Morningstar coauthored a paper with Farmer titled "The Lessons of Lucas-Film's Habitat" that was published in the edited book *Cyberspace: First Steps* in 1991. He earned a BS in computer engineering from the University of Michigan.

Bonnie Nardi

Bonnie Nardi is an anthropologist who has conducted ethnographic work related to a number of technology-related topics, including virtual worlds. One of her recent research interests is the online role-playing game *World of Warcraft*, which is the focus of her 2010 book *My Life as a Night Elf Priest: An Anthropological Account of World of Warcraft*. She has authored numerous other academic books, book chapters, and journal articles, most of which deal with topics other than virtual worlds. Nardi is a professor in the Department of Informatics at the University of California, Irvine. Before joining the faculty at the University of California, Irvine, Nardi worked at AT&T, Agilent, and Apple. She holds a PhD from the University of California at Irvine and a bachelor's degree from the University of California at Berkeley.

Cory Ondrejka

Cory Ondrejka is a software developer who was a cofounder of the virtual world *Second Life* and who served as chief technology officer of Linden Lab. While at Linden Lab from 2000 to 2007, Ondrejka was involved in development of the simple programming language that allows *Second Life* users to create content in the virtual world. Ondrejka was also instrumental in establishing *Second Life*'s policies of maintaining users' intellectual property rights for content generated in the virtual world and maintaining open access to the virtual world's programming code. Cory's *Second Life* avatar's name was Cory Linden.

Ondrejka earned a joint bachelor's degree in computer science and weapons and systems engineering from the U.S. Naval Academy and served as an officer in the U.S. Navy. Before starting work at Linden Lab in 2000, he was a programmer at the game company Pacific Coast Power and Light, the U.S. Department of Defense, and the U.S. National Security Agency. After leaving Linden Lab, Ondrejka worked for music company EMI until 2009.

Robert Pardo

Rob Pardo is a game designer who supervises the development and operation of the popular online role-playing game *World of*

Warcraft as vice president of game design for Blizzard Entertainment. Pardo joined Blizzard Entertainment in 1997 to work on the online strategy game *StarCraft*. Pardo would work on several other games for Blizzard Entertainment, including *Warcraft III: The Frozen Throne*, before becoming the company's vice president for game design and leading the development of *World of Warcraft*. Pardo holds a bachelor's degree in criminology, law, and society from the University of California, Irvine.

Mark Pincus

Mark Pincus is an entrepreneur who cofounded the online social games company Zynga, where he currently serves as chief executive officer, in 2007. The company takes its name from a bulldog that Pincus used to own called Zinga. Zynga develops Web-based social network games that are played by hundreds of millions of users, such as *Mafia Wars*, *FarmVille*, *CityVille*, and *FrontierVille*. Pincus has also held several positions in business and finance, and he has founded other companies specializing in social networking and Internet services. He earned an MBA from the Harvard Business School and a BS from the Wharton School at the University of Pennsylvania.

Howard Rheingold

Howard Rheingold is an author and educator who has written extensively on the social dimensions of the Internet and other communication technology. His 1993 book *The Virtual Community: Homesteading on the Electronic Frontier* details his experiences as a member and founder of several early online communities beginning in the 1980s. Among the virtual communities examined by Rheingold in *The Virtual Community* are the text-based online environments known as MUDs (multi-user dungeons).

The many other books written by Rheingold include *Tools for Thought: The History and Future of Mind-Expanding Technology*, *Out of the Inner Circle: A Hacker's Guide to Computer Security*, *Virtual Reality: Exploring the Brave New Technologies of Artificial Experience and Interactive Worlds from Cyberspace to Teledildonics*, and *Smart Mobs: The Next Social Revolution*. Rheingold also served as the first executive editor of *HotWired*, a website published by *Wired* magazine. He has faculty appointments in the Department of Communication at Stanford University and the School of Information at the University of California, Berkeley. Rheingold earned a bachelor's degree from Reed College in Portland, Oregon. One unique hobby of Rheingold's is hand-painting art on his shoes.

Philip Rosedale

Philip Rosedale is a technology entrepreneur who founded the virtual world production company Linden Lab in 1999 and led the creation of the virtual world *Second Life*. After initially focusing on prototypes for hardware to be used for interacting with computers, Rosedale and Linden Lab began developing an online virtual world environment called *LindenWorld* in 2001. *LindenWorld* was renamed *Second Life* in 2002 and given a full public launch in 2003. Rosedale's avatar in *Second Life* is called Philip Linden. He served as chief executive officer of Linden Lab until 2008, when he left that role to become a member of the company's board of directors. He resumed the role of chief executive officer in 2010 in a temporary interim role until 2011.

Rosedale has a BS degree in physics from the University of California, San Diego. Before founding Linden Lab, he worked as vice president and chief technology officer at RealNetworks.

John L. Sherry

John Sherry is an associate professor in the Department of Communication at Michigan State University who researches the effects of video games, the experiences of video game users, and the use of video games for educational purposes. He has conducted some prominent research on the effects of violent video game content on aggression, concluding that there is evidence for a link between exposure to violent game content and some aggressive responses but that the observed strength of this relationship in empirical studies is not as strong as the relationship observed in similar studies dealing with the effects of television violence. Before joining the faculty at Michigan State University, Sherry was on the faculty at Purdue University and the University of Arizona. He has a PhD in from the Mass Media Program at Michigan State University, an MFA from the School of Film at Ohio University, an MA from the Department of Communication at Wayne State University, and a BA from the Department of English at Wayne State University.

John Smedley

John Smedley is a software developer and executive who is currently the president of Sony Online Entertainment. He cofounded Verant Interactive, Inc., which developed the online role-playing game *EverQuest*. Verant Interactive was fully absorbed by Sony in 2000 after being previously affiliated with the entertainment company. In addition to the *EverQuest* series, Smedley was involved with development of the online role-playing game *Star Wars: Galaxies*. Smedley was first involved in the video game industry in 1989 as a programmer for ATG. He also founded a game company called Knight Technologies that developed several popular video games in the 1990s.

Song Jae-Kyeong

Jake Song is a South Korean computer programmer who was the lead creator of the online role-playing game *Lineage*. Song is credited by some as having contributed substantially to the prominent status of South Korea's video game industry. Before joining NCSoft, Song worked at Nexon and was a creator of the online role-playing game *Nexus: The Kingdom of the Winds*. In 2003, Song left NCSoft and founded XLGames, a company that is due to release the online role-playing game *ArcheAge* in 2012 in South Korea and at a time to be announced in North America and Europe. Song has a master's degree in computer science from KAIST (Korea Advanced Institute of Science and Technology) and completed some doctoral study there as well.

Jeffrey Steefel

Jeffrey Steefel is a game developer who has served video game company Turbine, Inc., as executive producer for the online role-playing game *The Lord of the Rings Online* since 2004. Before joining Turbine, he worked as a vice president at the virtual world and video game production companies There, Inc., Sony Online Entertainment, and 7th Level. Steefel has identified himself as a fan of author J. R. R. Tolkien's work and stated that his interest in developing an online role-playing game based on Tolkien's novels was a factor in his decision to work at Turbine. Steefel has a bachelor's degree in dramatic arts and engineering from the University of California, Davis. He worked as an actor before entering the games industry.

Neal Town Stephenson

Neal Stephenson is a science-fiction author whose 1992 novel *Snow Crash* is credited for adapting the Hindu term "avatar" to describe the online visual character that represents a virtual world user. In addition to several science-fiction novels and pieces of short fiction, Stephenson has written nonfiction articles for publications such as the technology magazine *Wired*. Some of Stephenson's fiction work has been written in collaboration with an uncle using the pen name Stephen Bury to represent both authors. Stephenson worked part-time for Blue Origin, an aerospace company created by Amazon.com founder Jeff Bezos, from the company's founding in 2000 until 2006. Stephenson holds a BA in geography from Boston University with a minor in physics.

John Ronald Reuel Tolkien

J. R. R. Tolkien was a British professor at the University of Oxford's Pembroke College and Merton College who wrote the fantasy classics *The Hobbit: Or, There and Back Again* and *The Lord of the Rings*. These works and Tolkien's other fiction have been credited as providing inspiration for role-playing games like *Dungeons and Dragons*, the text based online virtual role-playing games known as MUDs (multi-user dungeons), and online role-playing video games and virtual worlds. Tolkien's novels have sold hundreds of millions of copies worldwide, and *The Lord of the Rings* is recognized as the secondmost best-selling novel ever written after Charles Dickens' *A Tale of Two* Cities. In addition to his fantasy fiction, Tolkien published poetry and an extensive body of academic work, including literary criticism of British works such as *Beowulf*.

Posthumous work has also been published from his unfinished manuscripts and notes, some of it edited by his son Christopher.

Tolkien was born in South Africa and lived in England for much of his life after moving there at the age of three years. He earned a first-class honors degree in English Language and Literature from Oxford's Exeter College. He served in combat as an officer in the British Army in World War I. After his military service, Tolkien worked on the *Oxford English Dictionary,* then as a faculty member at the University of Leeds before becoming a professor at Oxford's Pembroke College in 1925. He moved to Oxford's Merton College in 1945 and remained there until his retirement from academia in 1959. He also served as an examiner for Ireland's University College Dublin. Tolkien was knighted as a Commander of the Order of the British Empire in 1972. He died in 1973 at the age of 82 and was buried in the same grave as his wife Edith.

Roy Trubshaw

Roy Trubshaw is a computer programmer who created the first version of the text-based online role-playing game *MUD (Multi-User Dungeon)*, an influential game that inspired an entire genre of online environments that became known as "MUDs" after Trubshaw's work. Trubshaw developed the basic structure of the *MUD* game while he was an undergraduate studying computer science at the University of Essex in 1978, working on it with fellow University of Essex computer science undergraduate Richard Bartle and eventually handing it over for Bartle to complete in 1980. Trubshaw earned a BSc in computer science from the University of Essex and has since worked in the information technology industry.

Sherry Turkle

Sherry Turkle is a professor of the social studies of science and technology at the Massachusetts Institute of Technology who has conducted research on the psychological and social dynamics of technology. Among her academic work related to online communities and virtual environments are a number of publications dealing with identity and social interaction in the text-based online environments known as MUDs (multi-user dungeons). She has written several books and numerous book chapters and journal articles on people's use of technology.

Turkle is the director of the Massachusetts Institute of Technology Initiative on Technology and Self. She has a PhD in sociology and personality psychology and a BA in social studies from Harvard University. Turkle is also a licensed clinical psychologist. She has also been awarded a Mellon Fellowship, a Rockefeller Humanities Fellowship, and a Guggenheim Fellowship, among other prestigious appointments and awards. Turkle was named Woman of the Year in 1984 by *Ms. Magazine*.

Ibe Van Geel

Ibe Van Geel is a Belgian information technology professional and video game analyst. He is the managing editor of MMO-Data.net, a website that provides data from Van Geel's research on subscription activity in online role-playing games. Van Geel launched the site in 2009 to continue the work begun by video game analyst Bruce Woodcock, who stopped updating his similar MMOGCHART.COM site in 2008. In addition to managing the MMOData site, Van Geel is employed in an information technology position. He has worked in the information technology industry for more than a decade and has a postsecondary education related to information technology.

Vernor Steffen Vinge

Vernor Vinge is an award-winning science fiction author and a retired professor of computer science and mathematics at San Diego State University. His 1981 novella *True Names* is acknowledged as portraying one of the earliest literary descriptions of an online virtual world. The setting of *True Names* includes a fictional virtual world known as the "Other Plane," which the novella's characters navigate. Several other science fiction novels, novellas, and short stories have received acclaim and awards, and he has been prolifically publishing science fiction work since the 1960s. Vinge holds a PhD from the University of California at San Diego and worked at San Diego State University from 1972 to 2000 before retiring to focus on his fiction writing.

Ryan G. Van Cleave

Ryan Van Cleave is an author and educator whose 2010 book *Unplugged: My Journey into the Dark World of Game Addiction* describes his increasingly harmful overuse of video games, which he ended after experiencing serious consequences for his social life and career incurred by his excessive game use. Van Cleave has also authored prose and poetry in several books and literary journal publications, and he regularly speaks on video game abuse and related topics. Van Cleave holds a PhD and an MA in American literature from Florida State University, as well as a BA in English from Northern Illinois University. He has served on the faculty at Clemson University, George Washington University, Eckerd College, and the Ringling College of Art and Design. Van Cleave was born Ryan Anderson, but changed his name in 2006 in homage to a group he was involved with in *World of Warcraft*.

Dmitri Williams

Dmitri Williams is an associate professor in the Annenberg School for Communication and Journalism at the University of Southern California who has conducted research on the use and effects of online role-playing games. In 2005, Williams published a journal article based on a month-long study of the effects of violence in the online role-playing game *Asheron's Call*, concluding that users of the game did not engage in acts of aggression significantly more than a control group who did not play the game. Williams also published several articles based on a study of the online role-playing game *EverQuest II*, conducted in cooperation with Sony Online Entertainment. In this study he and fellow researchers analyzed users' online behavior through data collected directly from *EverQuest II*, along with a large-scale survey distributed to the game's users. Williams conducted the study with an interdisciplinary group of researchers from several universities who formed a research team called the Virtual Worlds Observatory.

Williams earned a PhD from the Department of Communication Studies at the University of Michigan in 2004, an MA from the Annenberg School for Communication and Journalism at the University of Southern California in 1996, and a BA in English with a minor in business administration from the University of Southern California in 1993. Before joining the faculty at the Annenberg School for Communication and Journalism in 2007, Williams was an assistant professor in the Department of Speech Communication at the University of Illinois.

Bruce Sterling Woodcock

Bruce Woodcock is a video game industry consultant and analyst who developed a prominent database tracking subscriber activity in massively multiplayer online role-playing games, which he reported on his website MMOGCHART.COM. Woodcock began his research on activity in online games in 2002 and launched the MMOGCHART.COM site in 2004. He stopped updating the site in 2008, but its existing reports remain available there. Before entering the games industry as an investor, analyst, and consultant, Woodcock worked in information technology and systems administration. Woodcock studied physics, philosophy, and computer science at Purdue University but did not complete a university degree. Sterling also created and administered two text-based online role-playing MUD (multi-user dungeon) games.

Nicholas Yee

Nick Yee is a research scientist at the Palo Alto Research Center (PARC; formerly Xerox PARC) who researches social interaction in virtual worlds and psychological responses to virtual reality technology. Born in Hong Kong, Yee conducted seminal research into the users and social dynamics of virtual worlds with a survey of users of the online role-playing game *EverQuest*. He conducted the survey in 2000 and 2001 while he was an undergraduate student at Haverford College in Haverford, Pennsylvania. The project, titled *The Norrathian Scrolls: A Study of EverQuest*, received widespread attention as one of the first large-scale surveys of a virtual world when Yee made its results available online.

After earning a BA in psychology from Haverford with a concentration in computer science, Yee began a new series of surveys related to virtual worlds called *The Daedalus Project* while working in technology consulting with Accenture Technology Labs. Yee continued conducting surveys and reporting on them for the *Daedalus Project* while earning a PhD in Communication from Stanford

University between 2003 and 2007. Yee also published several articles and book chapters based on these surveys and other research conducted in Stanford's Virtual Human Interaction Lab
and elsewhere. Yee placed *The Daedalus Project* in hibernation in
2009, but continues his research related to virtual worlds and virtual reality.

6

Tables, Charts, and Images

To supplement the narrative descriptions about the virtual worlds and related technologies provided so far in this book, this chapter provides a series of tables, charts, and figures. These materials are included to provide visual depictions of data related to virtual worlds and provide some examples of the visual appearance of virtual worlds and related applications. The materials in this chapter deal with four topics: The visual appearance of virtual worlds, the population size of virtual worlds, research on users of virtual worlds, and information about the text-based games that preceded virtual worlds.

The Appearance of Virtual Worlds

There is some variety in how virtual worlds look to their users, both in terms of the appearance of the virtual environments represented and in terms of the interface elements that provide the user with information about the virtual world and allow the user to interact with the virtual world. Figure 6.1 is a screen image from *Second Life* captured while a user avatar is standing on the shore of a large body of virtual water. Although this image from *Second Life* shares similarities with the general appearance of other virtual worlds, the specific appearance of virtual worlds will vary. Online role-playing games, for example, will feature different windows related to commands that are specific to role-playing games (e.g., attacking, casting magic spells). Such windows are not featured in this *Second Life* image because many of the interface elements present in a massively multiplayer online role-playing

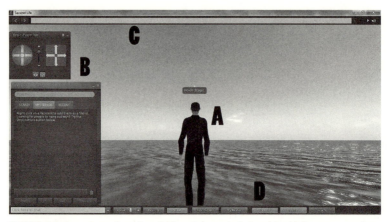

FIGURE 6.1 Screen image from *Second Life*, with letters A, B, C, and D added to image to indicate interface elements

game (MMORPG) are unnecessary in a social virtual world like *Second Life*.

Some features of the *Second Life* interface are indicated in the image with large capital letters (these letters were added to the screen image to indicate interface features and are not part of the actual *Second Life* interface). They are:

A. The user's avatar, with its name in *Second Life* listed above it. When a user creates a *Second Life* avatar, the user chooses a first name of the user's creation and selects a surname from a list of available surnames.

B. Menu windows. The top menu allows the user to control the avatar's movement and point of view. The bottom menu allows the user to see information about other users in the area, friends of the user, and people with whom the user has recently interacted. These and other menu windows can be opened and closed and moved to convenient locations on the screen.

C. Navigation bar. This tool works similarly to the navigation bar of a Web browser. Users can type a destination into the navigation bar or select it from a list of recently visited locations to virtually teleport there instantly.

D. Chat window, which allows user to use text chat and voice chat, perform gestures, and open other windows related to the user's avatar, its location, and the user's friends on the screen.

Populations of Virtual Worlds

It is difficult to determine the size of a commercial virtual world. Many virtual worlds do not release information about their number of subscribers very often, if at all. When virtual worlds do release such information, it is not easy to interpret because subscriber totals may be interpreted loosely by the virtual worlds' providers to inflate their size. For example, a virtual world may release a subscriber total that treats all accounts that have been created as active accounts even if the account holders have not accessed the virtual environment in months or only tried it once.

One well-known effort to track virtual world subscriber data was a website called *MMOG Chart* at http://mmogchart.com (Woodcock 2008), which was developed beginning in 2002 by video game industry analyst Bruce Woodcock to track activity in MMORPGs. Although Woodcock stopped updating *MMOG Chart* in 2008, a successor website called *MMO Data* at http://mmodata.net (Van Geel 2011) was created by information technology worker Ibe van Geel to carry on the analyses that had previously been conducted by Woodcock. Van Geel and a team of contributors collect official figures and estimates from a variety of sources to provide a regularly updated list of estimated populations of MMORPGs. Although the estimates cannot be validated with finality, they provide a useful picture of the populations of many popular virtual worlds, as well as the virtual world user population in general. Tables 6.1–6.3 are based on reports from Woodcock and Van Geel. Subscriber data reported here are rough estimates based on visual reports. Figures are estimates based on data available as of July 2011. Conflicting estimates may exist, and new data may change results.

Table 6.1 shows the variety in size of popular virtual worlds founded over the past several years, with the massively multiplayer online role-playing game (MMORPG) *World of Warcraft* dominating the market and only a few others garnering more than a million users. Also evident from the table is the tendency for most virtual worlds to peak in population within about a year of their release, though a few of the most successful virtual worlds have continued to grow in size for longer periods.

Most popular virtual worlds host their users on a number of different "shards" that provide identical versions of the virtual world on different grids of servers but do not allow users on different shards to interact. Some virtual worlds, however, are unique

TABLE 6.1

Partial List of Virtual Worlds and Estimated Peak Number of Active Subscribers

Virtual World	Developer/ Publisher	Year Released In U.S.	Estimated Peak Active Subscribers	Estimated Year of Peak Active Subscriptions
World of Warcraft	Blizzard Entertainment	2004	12,000,000	2010
Aion	NCSoft	2009	4,000,000	2009
Lineage	NCSoft	1998	3,250,000	2004
Lineage II	NCSoft	2004	2,100,000	2005
Runescape	Jagex	2001	1,250,000	2009
Second Life	Linden Lab	2003	805,000	2010
Warhammer Online	Mythic/ Electronic Arts	2008	800,000	2008
Age of Conan: Hyborian Adventures	Funcom/Eidos Interactive	2008	700,000	2008
Rift	Trion Worlds	2011	600,000	2011
Lord of the Rings	Turbine/Midway	2007	570,000	2010
EverQuest	Sony/Verant	1999	550,000	2004
EVE Online	Crowd Control Productions	2003	370,000	2011
EverQuest II	Sony	2004	325,000	2005
Star Wars Galaxies	Sony/LucasArts	2003	300,000	2004
Ultima Online	Origin Systems/ Electronic Arts	1997	250,000	2003
Dark Age of Camelot	Mythic	2001	250,000	2004
City of Heroes/ Villains	NCSoft	2004	190,000	2005
Asheron's Call	Turbine/Microsoft	1999	120,000	2001
Vanguard: Saga Of Heroes	Sony/Sigil Games	2007	120,000	2007
EverQuest Online Adventures	Sony	2003	114,000	2008
Dungeons and Dragons Online	Turbine/Atari	2006	109,000	2010

(*Continued*)

TABLE 6.1 (*Continued*)

Virtual World	Developer/ Publisher	Year Released In U.S.	Estimated Peak Active Subscribers	Estimated Year of Peak Active Subscriptions
Star Trek Online	Cryptic	2010	106,000	2010
The Sims Online	Maxis/Electronic Arts	2002	105,000	2003
Pirates of the Burning Sea	Flying Lab/Sony	2008	100,000	2008
Anarchy Online	Funcom	2001	60,000	2001
Asheron's Call 2	Turbine	2002	50,000	2003
Shadowbane	Wolfpack/Ubisoft	2003	50,000	2003
The Matrix Online	Sega/Monolith	2005	48,000	2005
Earth and Beyond	Westwood/ Electronic Arts	2002	38,000	2003
There	Makena	2003	17,000	2005

TABLE 6.2
Annual Peak Simultaneous User Trends in Virtual Worlds Hosted
on a Single Server/Shard (through 2010)

Virtual World	Approximate Peak Simultaneous Users for Year			
	2007	2008	2009	2010
Second Life	57,500	77,000	88,000	81,000
Eve Online	42,000	43,000	54,000	61,000

in that they place all of their users on the same shard, allowing every user who is online at the same time to potentially interact in the same virtual world.

Among virtual worlds that host all of their concurrent users on the same shard are the social virtual world *Second Life* and the science-fiction themed MMORPG *EVE Online*. Because most other large virtual worlds host their concurrent users on several different server shards, these virtual worlds provide the largest populations of virtual world users who are simultaneously present

TABLE 6.3
World of Warcraft Active Subscriber Trends by World Region, 2007–2010

Server Region	Approximate Peak Active Subscribers for Year			
	2007	2008	2009	2010
West	4.5 million	4.9 million	5.2 million	5.15 million
(Primarily North America, South America, and Europe)				
East	5.5 million	6.3 million	6.4 million	6.35 million
(Primarily Asia and Oceania)				
Global Totals	10 million	12 million	11.6 million	11.5 million

in the same virtual space. Table 6.2 shows estimates of the peak number of users each of these virtual worlds has had connected concurrently during the years 2007–2010.

As with all information about subscribers of virtual worlds, details about user populations from different world regions are elusive. Van Geel (2011), however, has been able to develop some information about the real-life locations of *World of Warcraft* users. Given that *World of Warcraft* is the most populous virtual world, information about the regions that provide its subscribers provides some indication of virtual worlds' popularity in general across the globe.

The region-based figures in Table 6.3 lack detail in terms of specific countries or even specific continents, but they still provide some insight about the significance of Asia among the population of virtual worlds. Even though *World of Warcraft* was developed in the United States and first released in North America, more *World of Warcraft* subscribers appear to hail from Asia and nearby regions than from the Americas and Europe.

Research on Users of Virtual Worlds

A number of surveys have explored the populations of virtual worlds. Although these surveys were conducted by highly trained social scientists from the academic community, most of these surveys did not use sampling methods that ensured a representative sample of the virtual world population. With exceptions, the users in most of the surveys chose to participate in the research after reading messages posted to English-language online websites related to virtual worlds. Given the recruitment methods of most of the surveys, their participants have in most cases been from the United States and, to a lesser extent, Europe. Very little data is available, on the other hand, describing the large audience of virtual worlds in Asia.

Despite these surveys' limitations in terms of how well they represent the true global audience of virtual worlds, they provide much of the most useful information we currently know about the users of virtual worlds. Tables 6.4–6.5 summarize the findings from several prominent surveys dealing with the users of virtual worlds.

TABLE 6.4

Gender and Age Reported by Virtual World Users in Survey Research

Survey Author(s)	Year(s) Conducted	Audience Recruited	%Male	%Female	Average Age
Yee (2001)	2000-2001	*EverQuest* users	84%	16%	25.6 years
Castronova (2001)	2001	*EverQuest* users	*	7.8%	24.3 years
Griffiths, Davies, and Chappell (2004a, 2004b)	Not Given (Published 2004)	*EverQuest* users	81%	19%	27.9 years
Yee (2006a, 2006b, 2006c)	2000-2003	MMORPG users	85.4%	*	26.57 years
Ng and Wiemer-Hastings (2005)	Not Given (Published 2005)	MMORPG users	88%	*	Not Given
Charlton and Danforth (2007)	Not Given (Published 2007)	*Asheron's Call* and *Asheron's Call II* users	85.7%	13.8%	28.83 years
Smahel, Blinka, and Ledabyl (2008)	2006-2007	MMORPG users	*	15.4%	25 years
Cole and Griffiths (2007)	Not Given (Published 2007)	MMORPG users	70%	30%	23.6 years
Williams, Caplan, and Lee (2008)	Not Given (Published 2008)	*EverQuest II* users	80.8%	19.2%	31.16 years
Bell, Castronova, and Wagner (2009)	2009	*Second Life* users	43%	51.4%	Not Given

* Some surveys only reported prevalence of one gender, though it can be inferred that all or nearly all of the remaining users in these surveys were of the other gender, excepting those reporting neither male or female gender and those who did not respond to questions about gender.

Although Table 6.4 indicates that there is some variety in the results of surveys assessing virtual world users' gender and age, the general trend is that users of MMORPGs are predominantly male, while there may be a greater proportion of female users in social virtual worlds. The average age of virtual world users tends to be in the 20s to early 30s, though this average is based on a broad range of ages among users in these surveys. More details about the demographics of virtual world users from these surveys can be found in chapter 2. More research is needed to determine whether these trends are similar in areas that have not been extensively researched, such as China.

Table 6.5 indicates that users of MMORPGs invest substantial time in their use of virtual worlds. Weekly averages, however, fail to capture the range of time commitments by these players, which include a significant minority whose time spent playing is enough to intrude substantially on other areas of life. More details about time spent by users in virtual worlds, all well as information about the prevalence of other indicators of problematic use and discussion of the consequences of overuse, can be found in

TABLE 6.5
Time Spent in Virtual Worlds Reported by Users in Survey Research

Survey Author(s)	Year(s) Conducted	Audience Recruited	Average Hours Per Week Using Virtual World
Yee (2001)	2000–2001	*EverQuest* users	22.4 hours per week
Castronova (2001)	2001	*EverQuest* users	28.9 hours per week
Griffiths, Davies, and Chappell (2004a)	Not Given (Published 2004)	*EverQuest* users	25 hours per week
Yee (2006a, 2006b, 2006c)	2000–2003	MMORPG users	22.7 hours per week
Charlton and Danforth (2007)	Not Given (Published 2007)	*Asheron's Call* and *Asheron's Call II* users	18.64 hours per week*
Smahel, Blinka, and Ledabyl (2008)	2006–2007	MMORPG users	27 hours per week
Cole and Griffiths (2007)	Not Given (Published 2007)	MMORPG users	22.85 hours per week
Williams, Caplan, and Lee (2008)	Not Given (Published 2008)	*EverQuest II* users	25.86 hours per week

*This survey excluded one case who reported using virtual worlds for 100 hours per week from its analysis.

chapter 3. Further research is needed to examine use trends in social virtual worlds to complement these surveys about MMOR-PGs, and studies of overuse in currently underresearched areas such as China are also needed.

MUDs and MUD-Type Text-Based Online Environments

Before the advent of graphical virtual worlds, text-based online environments required users to interact with the environment entirely through typed commands and text feedback displayed on the computer screen. In the decades since the first such environment, *Multi-User Dungeon (MUD,* later renamed *MUD1* to reduce confusion with the genre of many similar environments that would bear its name), was developed from 1978 to 1980, hundreds of these text-based online virtual environments have been created. Most of these virtual environments have used similar basic commands because most of them were developed using one of a few popular programming code infrastructures. These programming code infrastructures were in turn adapted from or inspired by the original *MUD* code.

To provide a better understanding of how users experienced the text-based online environments that preceded virtual worlds, Table 6.6 provides a list of common commands used in MUDs and related text-based virtual environments.

Although not every MUD and related text-based environment has used these precise commands, many have used these or something similar to facilitate users' navigation and interaction in the online environment.

Text-based MUDs lack rich graphics, so they use vivid descriptions to give their users a clear image of the online environment they represent. In some cases, the sense of environment provided by descriptions is further enhanced by extensive text descriptions of characters provided by role-playing MUD users. Tables 6.7–6.8 share examples of content that users would encounter in MUDs and MUD-type games, including typical descriptions of virtual rooms and their users. These examples are from *Elendor MUSH,* a nonprofit MUD-type game with a theme that honors the work of J. R. R. Tolkien. Elendor is a MUSH, or multi-user shared

TABLE 6.6

Common MUD Commands

Command (abbreviation)	Function
Help	Provides a list of frequently used commands and other information.
News	Provides a list of recently posted news and announcements from the MUD's administrators.
Who	Provides a list of connected users.
north/south/ east/ west/up/ down, etc. (n/s/e/w/ u/d)	Moves the user's character to another "room" in the environment, as long as there is an "exit" from the user's current location in the direction specified.
look/examine (l/ex)	When typed alone, will provide a description of the user's character's location. When followed with an object or direction (e.g., *look up, look table*) will provide a description of the location or object that is being looked at.
Description	When followed by a text description, changes the description that other users see when they look at the user's character.
Say (")	When followed by a string of text, user's character will say the text typed to other characters in the character's location (e.g., *Bill says, "Hello everyone."*).
emote (:)	When followed by a string of text, user's character will express the text as a state or behavior (e.g., *Bill sits down.*)
Shout	When followed by a string of text, user's character will say the text typed to all characters in nearby areas or, in some cases, the entire MUD.
Whisper	When followed by the name of another user's character and a string of text, user's character will say the text typed to only the specified character in the room. Other users will be aware that something was said between the characters, but will not be able to hear the message.
page/tell (p/t)	When followed by the name of another user's character and a string of text, user's character will send the text typed as a message to the specified character wherever that character is located.
Open	When followed by the name of an object that can be opened, will attempt to open the object to access its contents.
Close	When followed by the name of an object that can be closed, will attempt to close the object.
Unlock	When followed by the name of an object that can be unlocked, will attempt to unlock the object so that it can be opened.
Lock	When followed by the name of an object that can be locked, will attempt to lock the object so that it cannot be opened.
eat/drink	When followed by the name of an object that can be eaten or drunk, will use the item to heal injured character or for other purposes.
sleep/rest/sit	Causes character to recover from injury more quickly.

(*Continued*)

TABLE 6.6 (*Continued*)

Command (abbreviation)	Function
Inventory	Provides a list of items in the character's possession.
Take	When followed by the name of an object in the area, adds the object to the character's inventory.
Drop	When followed by the name of an object in the character's inventory, removes the object from the character's inventory and places it in the room.
Give	When followed by the name of an object in the character's inventory and the name of another character in the area, removes an object from the character's inventory and adds it to the other recipient character's inventory.
Wield	When followed by the name of a weapon in the character's inventory, places the weapon in the character's hand so that it can be used to attack.
Unwield	When followed by the name of a weapon in the character's inventory, removes the weapon from the character's hand so that it cannot be used to attack.
Wear	When followed by the name of a piece of clothing or armor in the character's inventory, places the armor on the character's body to increase the character's resistance to attack.
Remove	When followed by the name of a piece of clothing or armor in the character's inventory, removes the armor from the character's body so that it no longer protects the character.
Attack	When followed by the name of a character, will attempt an attack on the character with any weapon that is currently being wielded.
Stats	Provides the current status of the character
QUIT	Logs the user out of the virtual environment. When the next session begins, the user will typically be in the same place in the virtual environment.

hallucination, one type of MUD-type game with an emphasis on role-playing. A MUSH is one of many subcategories of MUD-type text-based online environments.

In MUD-type games, objects are created using typed programming code. In many cases, this code could only be programmed by users with special administrative privileges to prevent most users from causing problems with the games or programming objects that gave them an unfair advantage. For some objects and systems, the code can be very complicated, even for an experienced computer programmer. For other objects, the code can be relatively simple—at least for someone with relevant background and experience.

TABLE 6.7

MUD-Type Game Room Descriptions (from *Elendor MUSH*)

Sample Room Description 1 (seen when a user types "look" in the room):

Clearing

The dense forest opens into a large meadow, dominated by an enormous oak tree that seems to reach up to the clouds. The trunk of the oak tree is so immense that it would take a score of men, arm in arm, to encircle it. Its vast crown stretches out heavy branches to place most of the meadow in its shade. Nestled beneath the branches of the great oak near the trunk is a ramshackle cottage that had seen better years. To the side of the cottage is a large carefully maintained herb garden. To the west is a small structure. It appears to be a monument or shrine of some sort.

Obvious exits:
Path leads to Dark Wood.

Sample Room Description 2 (seen when a user types "look" in the room):

Common Room

A large room complete with two huge fireplaces that serve to keep the drafty room warm in the winter. A large table surrounded by chairs dominates the center of the room. The chair at the head of the table is exquisitely crafted and serves as the seat of the Chieftain. The walls are lined with banners depicting the crest of the Crow. Several doors lead out of the room, most of them leading to the sleeping quarters for the men and women of the clan.

Obvious exits:
Heavy Wooden Door leads to Courtyard

TABLE 6.8

MUD-Type Character Descriptions (from *Elendor MUSH*)

Character Description Example 1 (seen when a user types "look at [character name]"):
Before you is a muscular, hirsute man of moderate stature with an appearance somewhere between that of a warrior and a feral man. His garb is armor of thick iron rings over a simple tunic of roughly tanned hide, and his feet are clad in high leather boots. Green eyes, half-covered in dark clumps of matted hair, gaze angrily from beneath an iron helm that sprouts a pair of bullock's horns pointing to the fore. A nose broken many times lends testimony to his thirst for strife, as do battered lips, uneven teeth, and a beard interrupted by a long jaw-hugging scar. He wears a short sword at his side, and a round shield hangs from his back.

Character Description Example 2 (seen when a user types "look at [character name]):
Not as tall or slim as his brethren, the broad-shouldered elf before you has thick black hair that is tied behind his head in a knot. His eyes are a rich green, the color of summer leaves, and are deeply set. The elf's cheekbones are high, his cheeks full, and his mouth is wide.

Most often he wears a plain linen shirt, over which is draped a faded green tunic and a deerskin jerkin. His belt is black with a brushed silver clasp and his trousers are most often the same faded green as his tunic. The elf wears brown trail shoes that are tied with crossed laces winding from knee to the foot.

To provide something of an idea of the work behind the early MUD-type games, Table 6.10 shows most of the typical commands involved in creating a simple scimitar weapon, using the programming code system from the *Elendor MUSH* MUD-type game. The partial code is provided here not as an instructional programming guide, and the coded commands will not be explained here. The sample code is merely provided as an example of the programming code work involved in even a simple object in a MUD-type game. Certain elements of the code, though, such as the object's description and the messages sent to players who pick it up or drop it, are apparent even without the benefit of the relevant programming knowledge.

Although text-based MUDs were an ancestor of virtual worlds, there are still a large number of active MUDs in existence. The current audience of MUDs is dwarfed by the populations of popular virtual worlds, but some MUDs still accommodate scores, or even hundreds, of connected players at once. *MUDStats.com* is a site that posts activity data for several hundred MUDs based on frequent automatic updates conducted online. Table 6.10 features a list of the 30 most active MUDs according to *MUDStats.com*, ranked by the average number of users connected at any given time during a 30-day period from late June to last July 2011.

TABLE 6.9

Partial Sample Code to Create a Simple Weapon in a MUD-Type Text-Based Game (from *Elendor MUSH*).

```
@create Scimitar
@set Scimitar = NO_COMMAND
@set Scimitar = WEAPON
&CONDITION Scimitar=1000
&DAMAGE Scimitar=5 30
&EQ-DESCRIBE Scimitar= This is a fine weapon that was surely forged by a master craftsman. A blade of polished steel curves elegantly from the weapon's pommeled hilt, culminating in a gleaming point. The blade's handle is engraved with mysterious symbols of unknown meaning.
&EQ-DROP Scimitar=You let a scimitar slip from your grasp.
&EQ-ODROP Scimitar=lets a scimitar slip from his grasp.
&EQ-OSUCCESS Scimitar=picks up a scimitar.
&EQ-SUCCESS Scimitar=You pick up a scimitar.
&EQ-UNWIELD-MESSAGE Scimitar=sheaths a scimitar in a leather scabbard.
&EQ-WIELD-MESSAGE Scimitar=draws a scimitar from a leather scabbard.
&WEIGHT Scimitar=14
```

TABLE 6.10

The 30 Most Active Current MUDs (and MUD-Type Games) Based on Average Number of Connected Users (Excluding Adult-Themed MUDs)

#	Name	Genre	Average # of Users Connected
1	DragonRealms	Fantasy (Pay-To-Play)	418
2	AardwolfMUD	Fantasy	297
3	Gemstone IV	Fantasy (Pay-To-Play)	287
4	Achaea, Dreams of Divine Lands	Fantasy	271
5	Realms of Despair	Fantasy	177
6	BatMUD	Fantasy	150
7	Haunted Memories: Vienna by Night	Supernatural Horror	137
8	Medievia	Fantasy	128
9	Materia Magica	Fantasy	118
10	Discworld MUD	Fantasy	102
11	Multiverse Crisis MUSH	Multiple Themes	98
12	ZombieMUD	Fantasy	92
13	FiranMUX	Greco-Roman	82
14/15 (Tie)	Aetolia, the Midnight Age	Fantasy	78
14/15 (Tie)	New Worlds: Ateeran	Fantasy	78
16	Lusternia	Fantasy	77
17	3-Kingdoms	Sci-Fi/Fantasy	65
18	Threshold RPG	Fantasy	62
19	LambdaMOO	Social	58
20	AVATAR Mud	Fantasy	56
21/22 (Tie)	Dark and Shattered Lands	Fantasy	55
21/22 (Tie)	HellMOO	Cyberpunk	55
23	GreaterMUD	Fantasy	54
24	Final Fantasy MUSH	Fantasy	53
25/26 (Tie)	Serenity MUSH	Science Fiction	50
25/26 (Tie)	Alter Aeon	Fantasy	50
27	Imperian: The Sundered Heavens	Fantasy	48
28	M*U*S*H	Social	47
29/30 (Tie)	Legends of the Jedi	Science Fiction	44
29/30 (Tie)	Super Robot Taisen MUSH	Science Fiction	44

It should be noted that in the interest of providing a list that is useful to a broad audience, several adult-themed MUDs (including the MUD with the most traffic and the MUD with the second-most traffic when this analysis was performed) have been omitted from the listing.

Overall, *MUDStats.com* reported that all of the MUDs it tracks had a combined average of 8,000–10,000 or more users connected at any given time in late July 2011. Although that population doesn't rival the connection activity of virtual worlds, it suggests that MUDs do indeed still maintain a healthy audience.

References

Bartle, Richard A. 2010. From MUDs to MMORPGs: The history of virtual worlds. In *International handbook of Internet research*, ed. Jeremy Hunsinger, Lisbeth Klastrup, and Matthew Allen, 23–39. Dordrecht: Springer.

Bell, Mark W., Edward Castronova, and Gert G. Wagner. 2009. Surveying the virtual world: A large scale survey in Second Life using the Virtual Data Collection Interface (VDCI). http://papers.ssrn.com/sol3/papers.cfm?abstract_id=1418562.

Castronova, Edward. 2001. *Virtual worlds: A first-hand account of market and society on the cyberian frontier.* CESifo Working Paper No. 618, December. http://ssrn.com/abstract=294828.

Charlton, John P., and Ian D. W. Danforth. 2007. Distinguishing addiction and high engagement in the context of online game playing. *Computers in Human Behavior* 23: 1531–1548.

Cole, Helena, and Mark D. Griffiths. 2007. Social interactions in massively multiplayer online role-playing gamers. *CyberPsychology and Behavior* 10: 575–583.

Griffiths, Mark D., Mark N. O. Davies, and Darren Chappell. 2004a. Demographic factors and playing variables in online computer gaming. *CyberPsychology and Behavior* 7: 479–487.

Griffiths, Mark D., Mark N. O. Davies, and Darren Chappell. 2004b. Online computer gaming: A comparison of adolescent and adult gamers. *Journal of Adolescence* 27: 87–96.

Ng, Brian D., and Peter Wiemer-Hastings. 2005. Addiction to the Internet and online gaming. *CyberPsychology and Behavior* 8: 110–113.

Smahel, David, Lukas Blinka, and Ondrej Ledabyl. 2008. Playing MMORPGS: Connections between addiction and identifying with a character. *CyberPsychology and Behavior* 11: 715–718.

Van Geel, Ibe. 2011. MMOData.net: Keeping track of the MMOG scene. http://mmodata.net/.

Williams, Dmitri, Nick Yee, and Scott Caplan. 2008. Who plays, how much, and why? Debunking the stereotypical gamer profile. *Journal of Computer-Mediated Communication* 13: 993–1018.

Woodcock, Bruce Sterling. (2008). MMOGChart.com: Charting the future of the MMOG industry. http://www.mmogchart.com/.

Yee, Nicholas. 2001. The Norrathian Scrolls: A study of EverQuest (Version 2.5). http://www.nickyee.com/eqt/report.html.

Yee, Nick. 2006a. Motivations for play in online games. *CyberPsychology and Behavior* 9: 772–775.

Yee, Nick. 2006b. The demographics, motivations, and derived experiences of users of massively multi-user online graphical environments. *Presence: Teleoperators and Virtual Environments* 15: 309–329.

Yee, Nick. 2006c. The psychology of massively multi-user online roleplaying games: Motivations, emotional investment, relationships and problematic usage. In *Avatars at work and play: Collaboration and interaction in virtual shared environments,* ed. Ralph Schroeder and Ann-Sofie Axelsson, 187–208. London: Springer.

7

Organizations

There are a number of government agencies, nonprofit organizations, professional associations, and industry companies that conduct business, research, and other activity that is in some way relevant to virtual worlds and related technologies. This chapter lists some of these organizations and provides each organization's contact information along with a brief description of each organization and its activities related to virtual worlds and related technologies. Organizations' names, status, leadership, contact information, and activities may change over time, so be sure to seek updated information about each of these organizations if you wish to contact them or learn more about them. Also, be aware that some of the physical addresses listed for some organizations are not their primary mailing addresses.

Users of virtual worlds and related commercial software, such as online video games, should note that some contact information provided here for software companies is corporate information that should not be used for game customer support queries, product purchases, or other customer activities.

Government Organizations

Australian Classification Board
Donald McDonald, Director
Locked Bag 3 Haymarket
New South Wales
1240

Australia
(02) 9289 7100
http://www.classification.gov.au/

Founded in 1970, this is a body of the Australian government that classifies films, video games, and print publications with age ratings. The organization was part of Australia's Office of Film and Literature Classification until that office was discontinued in 2006. Ratings classifications assigned to video games by the board include G (General), PG (Parental Guidance recommended), M (Mature Audiences), and MA15 (Mature accompanied for those under 15). The Australian Classification Board can also refuse to classify a work, which amounts to an effective ban because an unclassified work cannot be sold in Australia or imported into the country.

Australian Classification Review Board
Victoria Rubensohn, Convenor
Locked Bag 3 Haymarket
New South Wales
1240
Australia
(02) 9289 7100
http://www.classification.gov.au/

This is an Australian government body that is entitled to review classifications that have been assigned to films, video games, and print publications by the Australian Classification Board. Like its sibling organization the Australian Classification Board, the Australian Classification Review Board was part of Australia's Office of Film and Literature Classification until that office was discontinued in 2006. Decisions to review classifications are made in response to appeals from organizations that have submitted materials for classification and would like the classification to be reconsidered, parties claiming to be aggrieved by ratings decisions, and by an attorney general of a state of the nation. Founded in 1970, the Australian Classification Review Board can change the rating of a film, video game, or printed work or effectively ban it by refusing classification because an unclassified work cannot be sold in Australia or imported into the country.

Federal Communications Commission (FCC)
Julius Genachowski, Chairman
445 12th Street SW
Washington, DC 20554
(888)225-5322
fccinfo@fcc.gov
http://www.fcc.gov

This is an independent United States government agency that regulates telecommunications. Goals of the agency include ensuring fair business practices, affordable access, and reliable function of telecommunication networks including radio, television, telephone, and Internet services. The Federal Communications Commission was created in 1934 by the Communications Act of 1934, at which time it replaced the Federal Radio Commission. The agency's role was updated by the Telecommunications Act of 1996. Activities conducted by the Federal Communications Commission that have been directly relevant to video games and virtual worlds have included an assessment of the video game industry's enforcement of its self-regulatory game ratings system, exploration of a possible universal ratings system to be used across media products, consideration of how central online video game use should be to the agency's definition of broadband services, and a statement from an agency commissioner about the possible influence of excessive online gaming on college dropout rates.

Federal Trade Commission (FTC)
John Leibowitz, Chairman
600 Pennsylvania Avenue, NW
Washington, DC 20580
(202)326-2222
http://www.ftc.gov

This is an independent United States government agency devoted to protecting consumers and regulating business practices. The Federal Trade Commission was founded in 1914 with the passage of the Federal Trade Commission Act. Issues investigated by the Federal Trade Commission include false and deceptive advertising, fraud, identity theft, behavioral targeting by online advertisers, and unfair competitive business practices. The Federal Trade

Commission has conducted studies examining some practices of the video game industry, including self-regulation of video games with age-restricted content to minors and the marketing of video games containing mature content to minors.
Game Rating Board (GRB)

Golden Bridge Bldg (120-708)
1F/2F/9F
31 Chungjeong-ro
Seodaemun-gu
Seoul
Korea
82-2-2012-7800
http://www.grb.or.kr

This is a South Korean government organization that assigns ratings to video games. The Game Rating Board was created in 2006, before which time the Korea Media Rating Board rated video games along with other media. Age ratings used by the Game Rating Board are ALL (suitable for all ages), 12 (not to be played by children under the age of 12 unless accompanied by an adult), 15 (not to be played by children under the age of 15 unless accompanied by an adult), and 18 (children under 18 cannot play).

Office of Film and Literature Classification (OLFC)
Andrew Jack, Chief Censor and Chief Executive Officer
4th Floor
BP House
20 Customhouse Quay
PO Box 1999
Wellington
New Zealand
+64 4 471 6770
information@censorship.govt.nz
http://www.censorship.govt.nz

This is a New Zealand government agency that assigns ratings classifications to films, print publications, and some video games. The Office of Film and Literature Classification was founded in 1993 and continues the work of various offices that have existed to serve similar roles since 1916. The organization assigns classification ratings to all films and print publications in New Zealand, but only assigns classification ratings to video games that contain restricted content. Classification ratings assigned to video games by the Office of Film and Literature Classification include R13 (restricted to persons 13 years of age and over), R15 (restricted to persons 15 years of age and over), R16 (restricted to persons 16 years of age and over), R18 (restricted to persons 18 years of age and over), and R (restricted to a particular group or for particular purposes).

Academic Associations and Other Nonindustry Organizations

American Academy of Child and Adolescent Psychiatry (AACAP)
Martin J. Drell, President
3615 Wisconsin Avenue, N.W.
Washington, DC 20016-3007
(202) 966-7300
http://www.aacap.org

This is a nonprofit professional organization founded in 1953 and dedicated to issues related to the psychiatric treatment of youth. The American Academy of Child and Adolescent Psychiatry publishes an academic journal, holds an annual professional meeting, and also publishes informational resources for families and medical professionals on its website. The association has produced several resources dealing with issues related to video games and virtual worlds, such as information about content and influence of video games.

American Academy of Pediatrics (AAP)
Errol R. Alden, Executive Director
141 Northwest Point Boulevard
Elk Grove Village, IL 60007-1098
(847) 434-4000
http://www.aap.org/

This is a professional organization focused on issues related to pediatric health care. Founded in 1930, the American Academy of Pediatrics publishes academic journals and a large number of other resources for medical professionals, patients, and parents. The organization has released both informational resources and position statements related to video games, the Internet, and other media.

American Psychiatric Association (APA)
Margaret Cawly Dewar, Association Governance Director
1000 Wilson Boulevard
Suite 1825
Arlington, VA 22209
(888) 357-7924
apa@psych.org
http://www.psych.org

This is a professional organization for psychiatrists founded in 1844. The American Psychiatric Association publishes several peer-reviewed academic journals devoted to research in the field of psychiatry, conducts research conferences, establishes guidelines for the profession, and publishes the *Diagnostic and Statistical Manual of Mental Disorders* (DSM) to aid psychiatrists and mental health professionals in diagnosis of psychiatric disorders. The association has considered including dependency on the Internet and video games as disorders in its *Diagnostic and Statistical Manual of Mental Disorders,* but has so far elected not to do so. An appendix in the upcoming fifth edition of the manual, however, will include Internet in an appendix as a topic meriting further investigation.

American Psychological Association (APA)
Suzanne Bennett Johnson, President
750 First Street, NE
Washington, DC 20002-4242
(800)374-2721
http://www.apa.org/

This is a scientific and professional organization for psychologists. The American Psychological Association was founded in 1892 and is made up of more than 50 divisions focusing on different topic areas related to the field. The association publishes scores of peer-reviewed academic journals and conducts a number of research conferences, many of which have featured research related to the content, use, and social and psychological dimensions of video games and virtual worlds. The American Psychological Association has also released formal statements about its positions regarding issues such as the possible effects of video game violence.

Annenberg Public Policy Center of the University of Pennsylvania (APPC)

Kathleen Hall Jamieson, Director
202 S. 36th St.
Philadelphia, PA 19104-3806
(215) 898-9400
info@annenbergpublicpolicycenter.org
http://www.annenbergpublicpolicycenter.org

This is a center dedicated to research on communication and media related to a range of issues including politics, youth development and behavior, health care, and civic engagement. The Annenberg Public Policy Center was founded in 1993. Researchers involved with the center have conducted research related to the content, use, and influence of video games and related media.

Association for Computing Machinery (ACM)

Alain Chesnais, President
2 Penn Plaza, Suite 701
New York, NY 10121-0701
(212) 869-7440
acmhelp@acm.org
http://www.acm.org

This is an academic organization related to computing. The Association for Computing Machinery was founded in 1947 and consists of hundreds of local university chapters and many area-specific special interest groups. The groups carry out most of the association's activity. The Association for Computing Machinery publishes a number of peer-reviewed academic journals and other publications, and several of the association's special interest groups conduct regular research conferences. Research related to virtual worlds and video games has been published in publications of the Association for Computing Machinery and presented at affiliated conferences, such as the Conference on Human Factors in Computing Systems (CHI) held by the association's Special Interest Group on Computer-Human Interaction (SIGCHI).

Association for Education in Journalism and Mass Communication (AEJMC)
Jennifer McGill, Executive Director
234 Outlet Pointe Blvd.
Columbia, SC 29210-5667
(803) 798-0271
aejmchq@aol.com
http://www.aejmc.org

This is an academic association for scholars dealing with issues related to news and other mass media. The Association for Education in Journalism and Mass Communication was founded in 1912 as the Association of Teachers of Journalism, renamed itself the Association for Education in Journalism in 1950, and took on its full current name in 1982. The association holds an annual conference and publishes three peer-reviewed academic journals. Several divisions of the association also publish peer-reviewed journals. Research appearing at the association's annual conference and in its publications has addressed video games and related technologies.

Association of Internet Researchers (AoIR)
910 W. Van Buren St., #142
Chicago, IL 60607
help@aoir.org
http://aoir.org

This is an academic organization for scholars interested in a broad range of social and cultural issues related to the Internet. The Association of Internet Researchers was founded in 1999. The organization holds an annual academic conference, proceedings of which are published each year, and promotes discussion via a popular electronic mailing list called AIR-L. The mailing list is open to anyone wishing to subscribe. Research presented at the association's annual conference has dealt with virtual worlds, video games, and related technologies.

Association for Psychological Science (APS)
Douglas L. Medin, President
1133 15th Street, NW

Suite 1000
Washington, DC 20005
(202) 293-9300
http://www.psychologicalscience.org

This is a scientific organization dedicated to research and scholarship in the field of psychology. The Association for Psychological Science was formed in 1988 as the American Psychological Society when it became independent from the American Psychological Association, then took on its current name in 2006. The Association for Psychological Science publishes several peer-reviewed academic journals and conducts an annual research conference, both of which have featured research related to video games and related online communities. The association has also released statements related to the psychological impact of video games.

Broadcast Education Association (BEA)
Heather Birks, Executive Director
1771 N Street NW
Washington, DC 20036-2891
(202) 429-5355
http://beaweb.org

This is an association for academics and professionals interested in research and scholarship dealing with electronic media. The Broadcast Education Association was founded in 1955 as the Association for Professional Broadcast Education, taking on its current name in 1973. The organization holds an annual convention and publishes two peer-reviewed academic journals. Research featured in the association's conferences and publications has dealt with online video games and related technologies.

Broadway Lodge
Brian Dudley, Chief Executive Officer
Totterdown Lane, Off Oldmixon Road
Weston-super-Mare
Somerset
BS24 9NN
United Kingdom
01934 812319
mailbox@broadwaylodge.org.uk
http://www.broadwaylodge.co.uk

This is a residential treatment center for addictions such as alcoholism, drug addiction, eating disorders, and gambling. In 2009, Broadway Lodge expanded its available services to include treatment for patients addicted to video games.

Cato Institute
Edward H. Crane, President and Chief Executive Officer
1000 Massachusetts Avenue, N.W.
Washington, D.C. 20001-5403
(202) 842-0200
http://www.cato.org

This is a libertarian nonprofit organization that conducts research and promotes policy encouraging limited government, individual rights and liberties, and free markets. The organization was founded in 1977. Consistent with its stance on other issues, the Cato Institute has released statements and policy positions against government regulation and censorship of video games, the Internet, and other media products and services.

**Center for Digital Ethics and Policy at Loyola
University Chicago**
Adrienne Massanari, Director
School of Communication
820 N. Michigan Ave
Water Tower Campus
Chicago, IL 60611
contact@digitalethics.org
http://digitalethics.org

This is an academic center promoting discussion, research, and policy recommendations related to ethical behavior in online communities and virtual environments. The Center for Digital Ethics and Policy publishes essays, book reviews, professional guidelines, and teaching resources on its website to serve scholars and professionals. Topics of published materials and interests of some affiliated research faculty include ethical issues related to video games and virtual worlds.

Children Now
Jane Gardner, Board Chair
1212 Broadway, 5th Floor

Oakland, CA 94612
(510) 763-1974
info@childrennow.org
http://www.childrennow.org

This is a nonprofit organization focused on research and advocacy to serve the interests of children. Children Now has produced a number of research reports related to media and children, including widely cited research on violence, gender, and race in the content of video games.

Coalition for Quality Children's Media
Ranny Levy, President
112 West San Francisco
Suite 350A
Santa Fe, NM 87501
kidsfirst@cqcm.org
http://www.kidsfirst.org

This is a nonprofit organization that works to ensure prominence and availability of quality children's media products and to provide children with the ability to apply critical skills when they use media. The organization administers a program called *KIDS FIRST!* whose volunteers review children's media products and endorse those products deemed to be high-quality for children. The organization also develops special programs targeting the needs of children with special circumstances such as low-income, hospitalized, and at-risk children. Many of the products reviewed by the organization are films and videos, and the organization holds an annual film festival, but the organization also reviews some video games and related software products.

Common Sense Media
James P. Steyer, Chief Executive Officer
650 Townsend, Suite 435
San Francisco, CA 94103
(415) 863-0600
http://www.commonsensemedia.org

This is a nonprofit organization that provides guidance to parents regarding media content by reviewing printed publications, films, music, websites, and video games. Common Sense Media's reviews of media products and programs report on violent content, sexual content, and profanity in them and provide ratings of what age groups may or may not be suited to use them. The organization has developed a rating system for movies and video games that uses different criteria and categories than systems used by the Motion Picture Association of America (MPAA) and the Entertainment Software Rating Board (ESRB). Common Sense Media's rating system is used by some online distributors of media products. The organization has also been active as an advocacy group regarding issues such as content of television advertising shown during family programs, children's privacy rights online, ratings assigned to some controversial video games by the Entertainment Software Rating Board, and proposed laws regulating sales of video games to minors.

Digital Games Research Association (DiGRA)
Helen Kennedy, President
http://www.digra.org

This is an international nonprofit organization for researchers from academia and industry who are interested in topics related to digital games. Digital Games Research Association was founded in 2003 and is registered in Finland. The organization holds a conference every other year.

Entertainment Consumers Association (ECA)
Hal Halpin, President
64 Danbury Road
Suite 700
Wilton, CT 06897-4406
(203) 761-6180
feedback@theeca.com
http://www.theeca.com

This is a nonprofit organization serving users of video games in the United States and Canada. The Entertainment Consumers Association was founded in 2006 as a consumer rights group focused on the interests of game players. The association claims that it is completely funded by member dues, that it does not give money to political candidates or parties, and that it is not funded by industry companies. The Entertainment Consumers Association's advocacy positions have sometimes been consistent with those of industry trade groups such as the Entertainment Software Association, but at other times the Entertainment Consumers Association has taken stances not mirrored by prominent industry groups or has confronted industry groups and game companies over issues related to game consumers' rights.

Henry J. Kaiser Family Foundation (KFF)
Drew E. Altman, President and Chief Executive Officer
2400 Sand Hill Road
Menlo Park, CA 94025
(650) 854-9400
http://kff.org

This is a nonprofit foundation that publishes research related to health and health care issues. Founded in 1948, the group commonly addresses topics such as health insurance policy and prominent diseases such as HIV/AIDS, but the group has also conducted research of significant relevance to video games and virtual worlds through its Program for the Study of Media and Mental Health. Research conducted by the foundation under this program has addressed the content of video games, children's use of video games and the Internet, and the effects of video games.

Institute of Electrical and Electronics Engineers (IEEE)
Gordon Day, President
445 Hoes Lane
Piscataway, NJ 08854-4141
(800) 678-4333
contactcenter@ieee.org
http://www.ieee.org

This is a nonprofit professional association involved with a broad range of fields related to electricity and electronics. The Institute for Electrical and Electronics Engineers was created in 1963 with the merger of the Institute of Radio Engineers (IRE), which had been founded in 1912, and the American Institute of Electrical Engineers (AIEE), which had been founded in 1884. The association publishes more than 100 peer-reviewed academic journals and also publishes several hundred conference proceedings each year. The association has hundreds of thousands of members, so its activities are divided among a few dozen groups known as societies and committees. Among societies of the Institute of Electrical and Electronics Engineers that are particularly relevant to virtual worlds and related technologies are its Computer Society, Computational Intelligence Society, and Consumer Electronics Society. The Institute of Electrical and Electronics Engineers conducts a large number of conferences and professional meetings each year, including some specifically focused on issues related to virtual worlds such as an international conference dealing with virtual reality and a symposium focused on virtual worlds.

International Communication Association (ICA)
Michael Haley, Executive Director
1500 21st Street NW
Washington, DC 20036
(202) 955-1444
icahdq@icahdq.org
http://www.icahdq.org

This is an international academic organization for academics involved with human communication. The association was founded in 1950 as the National Society for the Study of Communication (NSSC) and adopted its current name in 1969. The International Association is recognized by the United Nations as a nongovernmental organization. The association holds an annual research conference and publishes five peer-reviewed academic journals. Some research presented at conferences of the International Communication Association and published in the association's journals has dealt with online video games and virtual worlds. One of the organization's many divisions and interest groups is dedicated to the study of video games and related media.

International Telecommunications Union (ITU)
Hamadoun Touré, Secretary General
Place des Nations
1211 Geneva 20
Switzerland
+41 22 730 5111
itumail@itu.int
http://www.itu.int

This is an agency of the United Nations that coordinates and encourages international cooperation in development and use of communication technologies. The International Telecommunications Union was founded in 1865 as the International Telegraph

Union. Among the many telecommunication areas the agency is involved with that are relevant to virtual worlds and online communities is the development and growth of Internet infrastructures and access.

Iowa State University Center for the Study of Violence
Craig A. Anderson, Director
W112 Lagomarcino Hall
Department of Psychology
Iowa State University
Ames, IA 50011-3180
(515) 294-3118
csv@iastate.edu
http://www.psychology.iastate.edu/faculty/caa/csv/index.htm

This is a research facility dedicated to research dealing with causes and prevention of violence. The Center for the Study of Violence and its affiliated faculty have conducted extensive research on the effects of violent video games on aggression. The center has been supported by funding from the Centers for Disease Control and Prevention and the National Institutes of Health.

Kid Risk, Inc.
Kimberly Thompson, President
2 Seaport Lane, 11th Floor
Boston, MA 02210
(857) 383-4230
http://www.kidrisk.org/

This is a nonprofit organization dedicated to promoting research, public awareness, policy recommendation, and charitable activities related to management of risks faced by children. Kid Risk, Inc., has its roots in the Kids Risk Project, a related project conducted between 2000 and 2009. In 2009, Kid Risk, Inc. was created to continue to serve the mission of the earlier project. Among the research conducted by the Kid Risk Project and Kid Risk, Inc., was a series of studies investigating ratings and content of video games.

Massachusetts Institute of Technology Initiative on Technology and Self
Sherry Turkle, Director
77 Massachusetts Avenue
Building E51-296

Cambridge, MA 02139
sturkle@mit.edu
http://web.mit.edu/sturkle/techself/

This is a center devoted to research on social and psychological elements of technology. Its activities include a research program that has produced a series of edited books. The initiative has received support from the National Science Foundation and Intel Corporation.

Media Awareness Network
Jay Thomson, Executive Committee Chair
950 Gladstone Avenue
Suite 120
Ottawa, ON
K1Y 3E6
Canada
(613) 224-7721
info@media-awareness.ca
http://www.media-awareness.ca

This is a Canadian nonprofit organization dedicated to promoting education and awareness of issues related to media. Founded in 1996, the Media Awareness Network conducts and reports research related to young people's use of media and the content of media. The group has been funded by private sponsors, including partners Microsoft and Bell Canada, and the Canadian government. Among resources provided by the Media Awareness Network on its website are educational resources about violence in video games, guidelines for parents about supervision of children's video game use, information about positive effects of video games, discussion of issues related to gender and video games, information about issues related to online privacy, and reports about youths' use of video games.

Media Education Foundation (MEF)
Sut Jhally, Executive Director
60 Masonic St.
Northampton, MA 01060
(800) 897-0089
info@mediaed.org
http://www.mediaed.org

This is a nonprofit organization that creates and distributes documentaries and other materials pertaining to the societal impact of media. The Media Education Foundation was founded in 1992 and offers films related to such topics as commercialization in children's programming, media ownership, media and politics, media and gender norms and roles, sexual content in media, violence in media, and media and health. Documentaries from the Media Education Foundation that address topics related to video games and virtual worlds include *Beyond Good and Evil: Children, Media, and Violent Times; Consuming Kids: The Commercialization of Childhood; Game Over: Gender, Race, and Violence in Video Games; Generation M: Misogyny in Media and Culture; Remote Control: Children, Media Consumption & the Changing American Family;* and *Returning Fire: Interventions in Video Game Culture.* The Media Education Foundation offers discounted pricing of its products to high schools, community colleges, and nonprofit organizations, with a high rate charged to university-affiliated customers.

Media Watch
Ann Simonton, Director
P.O. Box 618
Santa Cruz, CA 95061
(831) 423-6355
info@mediawatch.com
http://www.mediawatch.com

This is a nonprofit organization that is dedicated to combating stereotyping and biased portrayals in the media related to racism, sexism, and violence. Media Watch produces print and video materials to inform media users about the content and influence of media. The organization has released statements related to the social responsibilities of video game publishers with regard to the content of games they produce.

National Communication Association (NCA)
Nancy Kidd, Executive Director
1765 N Street, NW
Washington, DC 20036
(202) 464-4622
inbox@natcom.org
http://www.natcom.org

This is an organization for scholars and professionals interested in the study of communication. The organization was initially concerned primarily with public speaking, but has since expanded its focus to include mediated communication. The National Communication Association was founded in 1914 as the National Association of Academic Teachers of Public Speaking and has changed its name several times before assuming its current title in 1997. The association holds an annual conference and publishes 10 academic journals. Research presented at National Communication Association conferences and published in the association's journals has addressed issues pertaining to virtual worlds, video games, and related media technologies.

On-Line Gamers Anonymous (OLGA)
Elizabeth Woolley, President
104 Miller Lane
Harrisburg, PA 17110
(612) 245-1115
olga@olganon.org
http://www.olganon.org

This is a nonprofit organization that aids people who have problems with online video game addiction. On-Line Gamers Anonymous was founded in 2002 by Elizabeth Woolley after her son Shawn Woolley committed suicide in 2001 while logged in on the online role-playing game *EverQuest*. The organization is operated by volunteers. The organization outlines a 12-step recovery program adapted from the Twelve Steps developed by Alcoholics Anonymous. On-Line Gamers Anonymous obtained permission to adapt the Alcoholics Anonymous program, but the two organizations are not affiliated. Support services provided by On-Line Gamers Anonymous include a telephone hotline, online message boards, online meetings, and other activities to support people who have problems with online games. A limited number of in-person meetings are also conducted by members of the organization.

Parents Television Council (PTC)
Tim Winter, President
707 Wilshire Boulevard #2075
Los Angeles, CA 90017

(213) 403-1300
editor@parentstv.org
http://www.parentstv.org

This is a nonprofit group that provides information and reports about the content of entertainment media programming and its potential influence on children. Founded in 1995, the group focuses primarily on issues related to television, but has also addressed video games and online media.

Pew Research Center
Donald Kimelman, Chairman
1615 L Street, NW Suite 700
Washington, DC 20036
(202) 419-4300
info@pewresearch.org
http://www.pewresearch.org

This is a nonprofit and nonpartisan organization that conducts polling, research, analysis of media content, and forums to examine issues and trends in a number of areas. It was established in 2004 as a subsidiary of the Pew Charitable trusts. The Pew Research Center is made up of seven projects. One of them, the Pew Internet and American Life Project, has released several reports focused on video games and online communities.

ReStart Internet Addiction Recovery Center
Hilarie Cash and Cosette Dawna Rae, Executive Directors
1001 290th Ave SE
Fall City, WA 98024-7403
(800) 682-6934
restart@netaddictionrecovery.com
http://www.netaddictionrecovery.com

This is a treatment center specializing in long-term (45 days or more) therapy for individuals suffering from addiction to the Internet and video games. Founded in 2009, the ReStart Internet Addiction Recovery Center claims to be the only treatment facility in North America dedicated specifically to treatment of this particular problem. In addition to treatment services, the center provides recommended reading, guidelines for recovering from addiction to the Internet and video games, and online recommendations for software and other tools that can be used to monitor and limit time spent using the Internet and video games.

Stanford University Virtual Human Interaction Lab (VHIL)
Jeremy Bailenson, Director
McClatchy Hall, Room 411
Department of Communication
Stanford University
Stanford, CA 94305-2050
(650) 736-8848
vhil-stanford@lists.stanford.edu
http://vhil.stanford.edu/

This is a research facility dedicated to empirical study of human behavior and interaction in virtual reality systems, virtual worlds, and other digital media settings. Research in the Virtual Human Interaction Lab has been supported by groups such as Cisco Systems and the National Science Foundation.

University of California, Santa Barbara Research Center for Virtual Environments and Behavior (ReCVEB)
Jim Blascovich, Director
Department of Psychology
University of California, Santa Barbara
Santa Barbara, CA 93106-9660
(805) 893-5798
blascovi@psych.ucsb.edu
http://www.recveb.ucsb.edu/

This center is devoted to researching human behavior in virtual environments. Research at the Center for Virtual Environments and Behavior has been funded by the U.S. Army, the National Science Foundation, and the Office of Naval Research.

University of Southern California Annenberg School for Communication and Journalism Center for the Digital Future
Jeffrey Cole, Director
11444 West Olympic Blvd., Suite 120
Los Angeles, CA 90064
(310) 235-4444
digitalcenter@digitalcenter.org
http://www.digitalcenter.org

This center conducts research related to the development and impact of media technology. One major activity of the Center for the Digital Future is a project titled *Surveying the Digital Future: A Longitudinal International Study of the Individual and Social Effects of PC/Internet Technology,* which is a long-term research project examining the societal impact of computers and the Internet.

Virtual Reality Medical Center
9565 Waples Street, Suite 200
San Diego, CA 92121
(866) 822-VRMC
frontoffice@vrphobia.com
http://www.vrphobia.com

This is a facility that uses virtual reality for therapeutic, educational, and training purposes. Specialties include treatment of posttraumatic stress disorder and medical training.

Virtual Worlds Institute
Jeremiah Spence, Director
4131 Spicewood Springs Road
Suite N-12
Austin, TX 78759
contact@vw-institute.org
http://www.vw-institute.org

This organization publishes the online publication *Journal of Virtual Worlds Research,* an open-access journal that publishes articles on a number of topics related to virtual worlds and related technologies.

Industry Organizations

Academy of Interactive Arts and Sciences (AIAS)
Jay Cohen, Chairman
23622 Calabasas Road, Suite 300
Calabasas, CA 91302
(818) 876-0850
http://www.interactive.org/

This is a nonprofit organization for video game industry professionals. Founded in 1996, the academy presents a series of Interactive Achievement Awards (IAAs) annually to recognize outstanding video games and industry members at its annual Design, Innovate, Communicate, Entertain (D.I.C.E.) Summit.

American Amusement Machine Organization (AAMA)
David Cohen, Chairman
450 E. Higgins Road, Suite 201
Elk Grove Village, IL 60007
(847) 290-9088
http://www.coin-op.org/

This is an international nonprofit trade organization that represents the coin-operated amusement machine industry in North America, including makers of arcade video games. It was founded in 1981. Although the American Amusement Machine Association is not involved with console and home computer games, the organization tends to serve as an advocate on issues pertaining to video games in general. The organization also applies a color-coded parental advisory rating system to coin-operated video game machines.

British Board of Film Classification (BBFC)
David Cooke, Director
3 Soho Square
London
W1D 3HD
United Kingdom
020 7440 1570
feedback@bbfc.co.uk
http://www.bbfc.co.uk

This is a British nongovernmental organization that assigns ratings to films and video games. Formed in 1912, the British Board of Film Classification is funded by the film industry. It assigned compulsory ratings to video games containing certain types of sensitive content until this responsibility was lifted from the organization by the Digital Economy Act in 2010. Currently, it dispenses advisory ratings for games about content of games that are voluntarily submitted by their publishers. Age ratings assigned to video games by the British Board of Film Classification include

U (Universal), PG (Parental Guidance), 12 (Age 12 and Over), 15 (Age 15 and Over), and 18 (Adults Only).

Consumer Electronics Association (CEA)
Kathy Gornik, Chair
1919 S. Eads Street
Arlington, VA 22202
(703) 907-7600
cea@ce.org
http://www.ce.org

This is an electronics industry organization that represents more than 2,000 member companies. The Consumer Electronics Association is an independent sector of the Electronic Industries Alliance (EIA), which was founded in 1924 as the Radio Manufacturers Association (RMA) and became the Radio-Television Manufacturers Association (RTMA) in 1950, the Radio-Electronics-Television Manufacturers Association (RETMA) in 1953, and the Electronic Industries Association (EIA) in 1957 before changing to its current name in 1998. The Consumer Electronics Association has been an independent sector of the Electronic Industries Alliance under its current name since 1999. The Consumer Electronics Association conducts market and consumer research, conducts the annual trade show called the International Consumer Electronics Show, and presents awards to industry people, organizations, and products.

Computer Entertainment Rating Organization (CERO)
http://www.cero.gr.jp/

This is a Japanese nonprofit organization that assigns age and content ratings to video games. The Computer Entertainment Rating Organization was founded by the Computer Entertainment Supplier's Association, its parent organization, in 2002. Age ratings assigned by the organization include A (All Ages), B (Ages 12 and Up), C (Ages 15 and Up), D (Ages 17 and Up), and Z (Ages 18 and Up). The Z rating is enforced by law. Some games with sexual content that are intended for adults only are not assigned ratings by the Computer Entertainment Rating Organization. These types of games are instead rated by two other Japanese organizations, the Contents Soft Association (CSA) and the Ethics Organization of Computer Software (EOCS).

Computer Entertainment Supplier's Association (CESA)
Yoichi Wada, Chair
http://www.cesa.or.jp/en/

This is a video game industry trade organization in Japan. Founded in 1996, the Computer Entertainment Supplier's Association organizes trade conventions such as the annual Tokyo Game Show. The Computer Entertainment Rating Organization (CERO) is a branch of the Computer Entertainment Suppliers' Association that was founded in 2002 and assigns age and content ratings to video games.

Entertainment Software Association (ESA)
Michael D. Gallagher, President and Chief Executive Officer
575 7th Street, NW
Suite 300
Washington, DC 20004
esa@theesa.com
http://www.theesa.com

This is the video game industry's primary trade association in the United States. The Entertainment Software Association was founded as the Interactive Digital Software Association (IDSA) in 1994 and took its present name in 2003. Members of the Entertainment Software Association include most notable publishers of video games distributed in the United States. The Entertainment Software Association supports the Entertainment Software Rating Board (ESRB), which assigns age and content ratings to video games and sets standards for video game industry practices related to advertising and online privacy. The Entertainment Software Association also actively works to combat software piracy and other intellectual property theft related to video games, as well as censorship and regulation of video games. Another prominent activity of the Entertainment Software Association is presenting the Electronic Entertainment Expo (a.k.a. E3), an annual video game industry trade show at which many video game companies exhibit new and upcoming software and hardware products.

Entertainment Merchants Association (EMA)
Bo Andersen, President and Chief Executive Officer
16530 Ventura Boulevard

Suite 400
Encino, CA 91436-4551
(818) 385-1500
http://www.entmerch.org/

This is a nonprofit trade association representing the interests of the international home entertainment industry involved with home distribution of products such as film, music, and video games. The Entertainment Merchants Association was founded in 2006 by merging two previous industry groups, the Interactive Entertainment Merchants Association (IEMA) and the Video Software Dealers Association (VSDA). The Entertainment Merchants Association successfully challenged a California law regulating sale of violent video games to minors in the United States Supreme Court case *Brown v. Entertainment Merchants Association*, which saw the Court strike down the law and on the grounds that video games were protected speech under the First Amendment.

Entertainment Software Association of Canada (ESAC)
Danielle LaBossiere Parr, Executive Director
130 Spadina Avenue, Suite 408
Toronto, ON M5V 2L4
(416) 620-7171
http://www.theesa.ca

This is a nonprofit trade association serving video game companies in Canada. The Entertainment Software Association of Canada conducts research related to the industry, works against piracy and intellectual property infringements related to video games, and acts as a liaison to the Canadian government for the industry. The organization was founded in 2004 to replace the Canadian Interactive Digital Software Association, which was founded in 1994.

Interactive Software Federation of Europe (ISFE)
Simon Little, Managing Director
15 Rue Guimard
B-1040 Brussels
Belgium
+32 2 612 17 72
info@isfe.edu
http://www.isfe-eu.org

This is a trade association serving interactive software companies in Europe. The International Software Federation of Europe was founded in 1998 by related national trade associations in the United Kingdom, France, Germany, and the Netherlands. In 2002, the organization expanded to represent the industry in all of the European Union and Iceland, Liechtenstein, Norway, and Switzerland. The Interactive Software Federation of Europe operates the Pan-European Game Information (PEGI) system, a self-regulatory rating system that assigns age and content ratings to video games. The Interactive Software Federation of Europe is also involved with providing reports from industry research, increasing awareness of the economic and cultural role of the interactive software industry in Europe, providing consumers with information about game content to protect children, working to establish industry representation at the national level in all member nations of the European Union, and working against software piracy.

Entertainment Software Rating Board (ESRB)
Patricia E. Vance, President
317 Madison Avenue, 22nd Floor
New York, NY 10017
http://www.esrb.org

This is a nonprofit video game industry organization that assigns age and content ratings to video games distributed in North America and enforces game industry standards for advertising and online privacy. The Entertainment Software Rating Board was formed in 1994 by the Interactive Digital Software Association (now the Entertainment Software Association). The organization's rating system is voluntary, but many game console makers and retail stores will not accept games that have not be submitted to the Entertainment Software Rating Board to receive ratings. Age ratings used by the organization currently include EC (Early Childhood), E (Everyone), E10+ (Everyone 10 Years of Age and Older), T (Teen), M (Mature), and AO (Adults Only).

International Games Developers Association (IGDA)
Gordon Bellamy, Executive Director
19 Mantua Road
Mt. Royal, NJ 08061
(856) 423-2990
http://www.igda.org

This is a nonprofit organization for video game creators. Founded in 1995 as the Computer Game Developers Association, the International Game Developers Association consists of a number of local chapters and special interest groups allowing members to form social and professional connections. The association function relies heavily on volunteer work from its large network of members.

Netherlands Institute for the Classification of Audiovisual Media (NICAM)
Hedwig d'Ancona, Governing Board President
Sumatralaan 45
1217 GP Hilversum
0900 1612600
The Netherlands
http://www.kijkwijzer.nl

This nonprofit group is one of two organizations that independently checks ratings assigned to video games by the Pan European Game Information (PEGI) rating system. The Netherlands Institute for the Classification of Audiovisual Media, founded in 1999, checks ratings for games assigned the age ratings 3 and 7, while the Video Standards Council in the United Kingdom checks ratings for games assigned the 12, 16, and 18 ratings.

Pan European Game Information (PEGI)
Antonio Xavier, PEGI Council Chairman
15 Rue Guimard
B-1040 Brussels
Belgium
+32 2 612 17 72
http://www.pegi.info

This is a European nonprofit video game industry association that assigns age and content ratings to video games sold in many European countries to provide consumers with information about game content. The Pan European Game Information system is run by the International Software Federation of Europe, which founded the system in 2003. The system is also recognized in some countries outside of Europe, such as Israel. The ratings system is independently checked for the organization by two independent groups: the Netherlands Institute for the Classification of Audiovisual Media (NICAM) from the Netherlands and the Video Standards Council (VSC) from the United Kingdom. Age ratings currently used by the system include 3, 7, 12, 16, and 18, with some variations used in certain countries.

Video Standards Council (VSC)
Gillian Shephard, President
Kinetic Business Centre
Theobald Street
Borehamwood
Herts WD6 4PJ
United Kingdom
0208 387 4020
vsc@videostandards.org.uk
http://www.videostandard.org.uk

Based in the United Kingdom, this nonprofit group is one of two organizations that independently checks ratings assigned to video games by the Pan European Game Information (PEGI) rating system. The Video Standards Council, founded in 1989, checks ratings for games assigned the age ratings 12, 16, and 18, while the Netherlands Institute for the Classification of Audiovisual Media in the United Kingdom checks ratings for games assigned the 3 and 7 ratings.

Industry Companies

Active Worlds, Inc.
Richard F. Noll, President and Chief Executive Officer
101 Convention Center Drive
Suite 700
Las Vegas, NV 89109
info@activeworlds.com
http://www.activeworlds.com/

This is a company that develops virtual worlds. Its virtual world platform called *Active Worlds* is used to operate virtual worlds owned by Active Worlds, Inc., such as its flagship virtual world *AlphaWorld*, as well as separate virtual worlds purchased by the company's customers.

ArenaNet
Mike O'Brien, President
3180 139th Ave SE
5th Floor
Bellevue, WA 98005
(425) 462-9444
press@arena.net
http://www.arena.net/

This is a video game developer owed by South Korean game company NCSoft. Founded in 2000 by former employees of Blizzard Entertainment, ArenaNet created the *Guild Wars* online role-playing game franchise.

BioWare
Ray Muzyka, Chief Executive Officer
BioWare Edmonton
200, 4445 Calgary Trail
Edmonton, Alberta
Canada T6H 5R7
(780) 430-0164
contact@bioware.com
http://www.bioware.com/

This is a Canadian video game developer that is owned by Electronic Arts. The company consists of four studios in Canada and the United States. Mythic Entertainment, creators of the online role-playing games *Dark Age of Camelot* and *Warhammer Online: Age of Reckoning* is now a BioWare studio called BioWare Mythic after Mythic's acquisition by Electronic Arts. Bioware released the online role-playing game *Star Wars: The Old Republic* with Electronic Arts and LucasArts.

Blizzard Entertainment
Michael Morhaime, President
Blizzard Entertainment
P.O. Box 18979
Irvine, CA 92623
(949) 955-1382
http://www.blizzard.com

This is an American video game company that developed the online role-playing game *World of Warcraft* as an online role-playing game adaptation of its *Warcraft* video game series. Founded in 1991 as Silicon & Synapse, the company became Blizzard Entertainment in 1994. Blizzard Entertainment also created the *Diablo* and *Starcraft* online game franchises.

CCP Games
Hilmar Veigar Pétursson, Chief Executive Officer
Grandagarður 8
101 Reykjavik
Iceland
+354 540 9100
http://ccpgames.com

This company (CCP stands for Crowd Control Productions) is an Icelandic video game developer founded in 1998. It developed the online role-playing game *EVE Online* and is currently developing the online game *Dust 514*.

Cryptic Studios
Jack Emmert, Chief Executive Officer
980 University Ave
Los Gatos, CA 95032-7620
(408) 399-1969
support@crypticstudios.com
http://www.crypticstudios.com/

This is a video game developer founded in 2000 and currently owned by the Chinese game company Perfect World. Among games Cryptic has developed are the online role-playing games *City of Heroes* (and its companion game *City of Villains*) and *Star Trek Online*.

Electronic Arts, Inc.
John Riccitiello, Chief Executive Officer
209 Redwood Shores Parkway
Redwood City, CA 94065
(650) 628-1500
http://www.ea.com/

This is a large video game publisher that was founded in 1982. Electronic Arts owns a number of prominent video game brands and studios, including online game developers BioWare and Maxis. The many online games Electronic Arts has been involved with include the online role-playing games *Ultima Online, Star Wars: The Old Republic, The Sims Online, Warhammer Online: Age of Reckoning,* and *Earth and Beyond.*

Flying Lab Software
Russell Williams, Chief Executive Officer
1905 Queen Anne Ave North, Suite 300
Seattle, Washington 98109-2549
(206) 272-9815
http://www.flyinglab.com

This is a video game developer that was founded in 1997. Flying Lab Software released the pirate-themed online role-playing game *Pirates of the Burning Sea* in 2008.

Funcom Productions A/S
Trond Arne Aas, Chief Executive Officer
Drammensveien 167
N-0277 Oslo
Norway
+47 22 92 59 00
pr@funcom.com
http://funcom.com

This is a Norwegian video game company that also has offices in the United States, Canada, Switzerland, and China. Funcom was founded in 1993. Games it has released include the online role-playing games *Anarchy Online* and *Age of Conan: Hyborian Adventures.*

IAC Search and Media, Inc
Barry Diller, Chief Executive Officer
555 12th Street
Suite 500
Oakland, CA 94607
(510) 985-7400
http://www.ask.com

IAC Search and Media is an Internet services company that is owned by InterActiveCorp. The company was founded in 1996.

IAC Search and Media provides the avatar-based graphical chat application *Zwinky*. When *Zwinky* users install the application on their computer, an advertising-supported IAC Search and Media search engine product is automatically installed as well. This practice has led to some criticism of IAC Search and Media and *Zwinky* among users and Internet security applications.

IMVU, Inc.
Cary Rosenzweig, Chief Executive Officer
PO Box 390012
Mountain View, CA
94039
(650) 646-3244
press@imvu.com
http://imvu.com

This company, founded in 2004, runs an avatar-based graphical instant messaging application. IMVU stands for Instant Messaging Virtual Universe.

Jagex, Ltd.
Mark Gerhard, Chief Executive Officer
St. John's Innovation Centre
Cowley Road
Cambridge
CB4 0WS
United Kingdom
press@jagex.com
http://www.jagex.com

This is a British game company specializing in free-to-play Web browser-based games. The company was founded in 2001, but the Jagex name has been in business use since 1999. Jagex developed the online role-playing games *RuneScape* and *Stellar Dawn*.

Linden Research, Inc.
Rod Humble, Chief Executive Officer
945 Battery Street
San Francisco, CA 94111
(415) 243-9000
presscontact@lindenlab.com
http://lindenlab.com

This is an Internet technology company that does business under the name Linden Lab. Linden Lab was founded in 1999 by Philip Rosedale. The company created the virtual world *Second Life*.

LucasArts Entertainment Company, LLC
Darrell Rodriguez, President
1110 Gorgas Avenue
San Francisco, CA 94129
(410) 568-3670
http://www.lucasarts.com

This is an entertainment software company that operates as a subsidiary of LucasFilm, Ltd. The company was originally founded in 1982 as LucasFilm games before changing to its current name in 1993. LucasArts was involved in the production of the online role-playing games *Star Wars Galaxies* and *Star Wars: The Old Republic*. As LucasFilm Games, the company also developed the early graphical online community *Habitat*.

Microsoft Corporation
Steve Ballmer, Chief Executive Officer
One Microsoft Way
Redmond, Washington
http://www.microsoft.com

This is a large company involved with a broad range of computer-related products and services. The company was founded in 1975 and is a dominant presence in the computer operating system market. Microsoft is also involved with video games and a number of other electronic industries. Microsoft was a publisher of the online role-playing game *Asheron's Call*.

MindArk PE AB
Jan Welter Timkrans, Chief Executive Officer
Jarntorget 8
SE 413 04 Gothenburg
Sweden
+46 (0)31 607 260
press@mindark.com
mindark.com

This company is a Swedish software company that created the virtual world *Entropia Universe*. MindArk was founded in 2003.

Monolith Productions
Samantha Ryan, Chief Executive Officer
10516 NE 37th Circle
Kirkland, WA 98033
(425) 739-1500
http://www.lith.com

Monolith Productions is a game developer founded in 1994 and currently owned by Warner Brothers. One of the games developed by the studio was the online role-playing game *The Matrix Online*.

Multi-User Entertainment Ltd. (MUSE)
Richard A. Bartle, Programming Director
Orchard House
Queens Road, West Bergholt
Essex
C06 3HE
United Kingdom
http://www.mud.co.uk/muse/

This is a dissolved company that was cofounded by the creators of the original *MUD* text-based online role-playing game to market their game-related products and services. Although the company was dissolved in 2007, its site remains a useful repository of information about the early online games the company's cofounders developed.

NCSoft
T. J. Kim, Chief Executive Officer
157-37 Samsung-dong
Kangnam-gu
Seoul 135-090
Korea
+82 2 2186 3300
webmaster@ncsoft.com
http://www.ncsoft.com

This is a South Korean video game company with subsidiaries in Taiwan, China, Japan, Europe, and the United States. NCSoft was founded in 1997 and has been involved with development of a number of games, including the *Lineage* online-role playing game franchise and the online role-playing games *Guild Wars*, *City of Heroes* (and the companion game *City of Villains*), and *Aion*.

Outsmart 2005, Ltd.
Unit 304
The Ironbank Building
150 Karangahape Road
Auckland, 1010
New Zealand
http://smallworlds.com

This is a New Zealand-based company that produces the graphical online social community *SmallWorlds*. The company was founded in 2008.

Palo Alto Research Center (PARC)
Stephen Hoover, Chief Executive Officer
3333 Coyote Hill Road
Palo Alto, CA 94304
(650) 812-4000
pr@parc.com
http://www.parc.com

This is a technology-related research company that has pioneered a number of developments related to computing and information technology. The organization was founded in 1970 as a division of Xerox, when it was called Xerox PARC, and became an independent subsidiary of Xerox in 2002. The company now works with a number of clients in addition to Xerox. Some of the organization's significant developments include the modern personal computer and the graphical computer interface. Notable figures in development and research related to virtual worlds and online communities, such as *LambdaMOO* founder Pavel Curtis and virtual worlds researcher Nick Yee, have worked for the Palo Alto Research Center. Since 2003, the Palo Alto Research Center has operated a large-scale project investigating social dimensions of online role-playing games titled *PlayOn*.

Sega Corporation
Hajime Sitomi, Chief Executive Officer
1-2-12 Haneda
Ohta-ku

Tokyo 144-8531
Japan
+81-3-5736-7111
http://sega.co.jp

This is a large Japanese video game software and hardware company that also has offices in the United States, the United Kingdom, Australia, and South Korea. Sega Corporation is a subsidiary of Sega Sammy Holdings, Inc. Sega Corporation was founded in Hawaii as Standard Games, a company that specialized in coin-operated amusement machines such as jukeboxes and slot machines. It was moved to Japan in 1951 and renamed Service Games, then reorganized as Sega Enterprises after a merger with another company. In 2000, the company took on its current name. The company has been involved with numerous video game hardware and software products, including the online role-playing game *Phantasy Star Online* for its Dreamcast console and the online role-playing game *The Matrix Online*.

Sony Online Entertainment (SOE)
John Smedley, Chief Executive Officer
8928 Terman Court
San Diego, CA 92121
(858) 577-3100
http://www.soe.com/

This is the online game development division of Japanese media company Sony Corporation. Sony Online Entertainment has roots in Sony Corporation's formation of Sony Interactive Studios America (SISA) in 1995. Sony Online Entertainment was created in 1998, while SISA became a division of Sony Corporation called 989 Studios that was focused on developing video games for Sony's PlayStation console. Development of online games was then assigned to Sony's Verant Interactive brand (briefly known as RedEye Interactive) until the Sony Online Entertainment division acquired Verant in 2000. Games from Sony Online Entertainment include the *EverQuest* online role-playing game franchise, including the original *EverQuest* game as initially released under the Verant brand, and the online role-playing games *Star Wars Galaxies, The Matrix Online, Vanguard: Saga of Heroes,* and *DC Universe Online*.

Square Enix Holdings Co., Ltd.
Yoichi Wada, Chief Executive Officer
Shinjuku Bunka Quint Bldg.
3-22-7 Yoyogi
Shibuya-ku
Tokyo 151-8544
Japan
http://square-enix.com
81-3-5333-1555

This is a Japanese video game producer and publishing company that also owns video game companies Taito Corporation and Eidos Interactive as subsidiaries. The company was originally founded as Enix in 1975 before becoming Square Enix after a merger with fellow video game company Square Co. in 1986. One of the many games the company has developed is the online role-playing game *Final Fantasy XI*, and its current subsidiary Eidos Interactive published the online role-playing game *Age of Conan: Hyborian Adventures* before being acquired by Square Enix.

Trion Worlds, Inc.
Lars Buttler, Chief Executive Officer
303 Twin Dolphin Dr. Ste. 500
Redwood City, CA 94065
communications@trionworlds.com

This is a video game publisher that was founded in 2006. Trion Worlds entered the online role-playing game market in 2011 with their release of *Rift*.

Turbine, Inc.
John Toomey, Software Development Manager
117 Kendrick Street Suite 300
Needham, MA 02494
(781) 407-4223
pr@turbine.com
http://www.turbine.com

This is a video game developer that is currently a subsidiary of Warner Brothers. The company was founded in 1994 as Cyber-Space, Inc., and was renamed Second Nature and Turbine Entertainment Software before changing its name to Turbine, Inc., in

2005. Turbine has developed the online role-playing games *Asheron's Call, Asheron's Call 2, Dungeons and Dragons Online,* and *The Lord of the Rings Online.*

Ubisoft Entertainment S.A.
Yves Guillemot, President and Chief Executive Officer
28 Rue Armand Carrel
93108 Montreuil Sous Bois Cedex
France
+33 (1) 48 18 50 00
http://www.ubi.com

This is a French video game company founded in 1986. Among the games published by Ubisoft was the online role-playing game *Shadowbane,* which was developed by Wolfpack Studios. Wolfpack Studios was also acquired by Ubisoft after the release of *Shadowbane.* In addition to its headquarters in France, Ubisoft also has several offices across Europe, Asia, North America, South America, Africa, and Australia.

Zynga
Mark Pincus, Chief Executive Officer
444 De Haro Street
Suite 125
San Francisco, CA 94107
(800) 762-2530
http://www.zynga.com/

This is a social network game company that was founded in 2007. The company is named after a dog that cofounder and chief executive officer Mark Pincus once owned. Some of the social network games Zynga has developed include *Mafia Wars, FarmVille, CityVille,* and *FrontierVille.*

8

Print and Online Resources

A number of books, book chapters, journal articles, and websites provide information about the history, function, users, and social role of virtual worlds or have served as inspiration for the creation and development of virtual worlds. Some of these resources are listed and briefly described in this chapter. Note that some of these works come from sources that are independent from the virtual worlds industry, such as academic scholars, while other resources are from persons and organizations with a vested commercial interest in one or more virtual worlds. When you consult and evaluate information from these resources, be sure to take the affiliations and interests of these sources into consideration.

Books

Anderson, Craig A., Douglas A. Gentile, and Katherine E. Buckley. 2007. *Violent video game effects on children and adolescents*. New York: Oxford University Press.

This book provides a history of violent video games, summarizes theoretical perspectives and research findings related to the effects of violence in video games on aggression, shares the results of three studies examining the effects of violent video games on users, and discusses implications of the research for public policy. Although the book mentions research dealing with the effects of online games, it does not otherwise include a focus on online games.

Bartle, Richard A. 2003. *Designing virtual worlds.* **Indianapolis, IN: New Riders.**

This book, authored by one of the creators of the original text-based online role-playing game called *MUD* (*Multi-User Dungeon*), describes the history and background of online games and virtual worlds, and provides a guide for developers of virtual worlds. The book provides guidelines regarding virtual worlds' technological structure, users, geography, physics, economics, social dynamics, and more.

Balkin, Jack M., and Beth Simone Noveck (eds.). 2006. *The state of play: Law, games, and virtual worlds.* **New York: NYU Press.**

This edited book includes chapters from scholars that explore a broad range of issues related to application of law to virtual worlds. Topics covered range from the rights of users in virtual worlds to punishment of virtual crime.

Blascovich, Jim, and Jeremy Bailenson. 2011. *Infinite reality: Avatars, eternal life, new worlds, and the dawn of the virtual revolution.* **New York: William Morrow.**

This book provides a thorough overview of research describing people's perceptions, psychological responses, and behavior in virtual reality simulations and online virtual environments. After discussing a history of visions and inventions related to virtual reality and describing the state of technology and research related to virtual reality, the authors speculate about future developments in the area and the technology's potentially dramatic effects on society.

Boellstorff, Tom. 2010. *Coming of age in Second Life: An anthropologist explores the virtually human.* **Princeton, NJ: Princeton University Press.**

In this book, the author applies his training as an anthropologist to the virtual world *Second Life,* describing findings from two years of personal observation conducted in the virtual world.

Castronova, Edward. 2005. *Synthetic worlds: The business and culture of online games.* **Chicago: University of Chicago Press.**

This book examines the function and social implications of virtual worlds, dealing with topics such as users of virtual worlds, rights and responsibilities in virtual worlds, the economics of virtual worlds, and the function of the virtual world game industry.

Dibbell, Julian. 1998. *My tiny life: Crime and passion in a virtual world.* **New York: Henry Holt and Company.**

This book recounts the author's personal experiences as a user of the text-based online community *LambdaMOO*. "MOO" stands for "MUD, Object Oriented," a term describing text-based online environments that are a variation of MUDs (multi-user dungeons). The book includes a description of the well-known "rape in cyberspace" incident in which a *LambdaMOO* member used coded commands to make it appear as if other users' characters were performing lewd and degrading acts on each other and themselves without the users' consent or control.

Gibson, William. 1984. *Neuromancer.* **New York: Ace Books.**

This science-fiction novel about computer hackers who ply their trade in a fictional virtual environment is credited with popularizing the term "cyberspace," which was the name given to the virtual environment in the novel. Gibson had used the term "cyberspace" in an earlier short story, but this award-winning novel introduced the term to a larger audience.

Heider, Don (ed.). 2009. *Living virtually: Researching new worlds.* **New York: Peter Lang.**

This book includes invited chapters from a number of scholars examining various social phenomena in virtual worlds such as *Second Life* and *World of Warcraft*. Chapters address topics including historical antecedents to virtual worlds, gender and identity in virtual worlds, business practices in virtual worlds, journalism in virtual worlds, and other related topics.

Ludlow, Peter, and Mark Wallace. 2007. *The Second Life Herald: The virtual tabloid that witnessed the dawn of the metaverse.* **Cambridge, MA: MIT Press.**

This book describes the development, operation, and impact of *The Second Life Herald*, an online newspaper covering events within the virtual world *Second Life*. The newspaper, created by one of the book's authors, elicited dramatic responses from the virtual world's community. Journalistic activity in other virtual worlds is also discussed.

Lastowka, Greg. 2010. *Virtual justice: The new laws of online worlds.* New Haven, CT: Yale University Press.

This book details the legal challenges introduced by the advent of virtual worlds by detailing recent cases, providing background on virtual worlds' development and operation, and discussing the present and future impact of virtual worlds on the laws that govern the real world.

Malaby, Thomas. 2009. *Making virtual worlds: Linden Lab and Second Life.* Ithaca, NY: Cornell University Press.

This book describes the decisions and difficulties involved in the development and management of the virtual world *Second Life* by Linden Lab, relating anecdotes from the author's experience during a year spent conducting observational research at Linden Lab.

Nardi, Bonnie. 2010. *My life as a night elf priest: An anthropological account of World of Warcraft.* Ann Arbor, MI: University of Michigan Press.

This book relates the author's experience during three years of research dealing with the online role-playing game *World of Warcraft* in both the United States and China. After describing her research method and providing background about *World of Warcraft*, the author discusses relevant concepts and theories and shares observations about social and cultural issues related to the game.

Rheingold, Howard. 1993. *The virtual community: Homesteading on the electronic frontier.* Reading, MA: Addison-Wesley.

This book, originally published in 1993 but since made available online by the author at http://www.rheingold.com/vc/book, recounts the author's personal experience and research related to a number of online virtual communities. One chapter focuses specifically on the text-based online environments called MUDs (multi-user dungeons), with some emphasis on their dynamics related to identity and social behavior. In addition to the original edition and the online version, a second edition of the book was published by MIT Press in 2000.

Stephenson, Neal. 1992. *Snow crash.* **New York: Bantam Books.**

This novel's story follows a group of computer hackers as they explore the mysterious and far-reaching effects of a fictional drug that has effects on its recipients in the real world as well as in a fictional virtual environment called the "Metaverse." The novel is credited with adapting the Hindu term "avatar" to describe the online character used by a virtual world user online.

Taylor, T. L. 2006. *Play between worlds: Exploring online game culture.* **Cambridge, MA: MIT Press.**

This book describes the author's experience during four years researching the online role-playing game *EverQuest.* The book details a number of social dynamics within and beyond the game environment and makes conclusions about strengths and weaknesses of the game's structure.

Tolkien, J. R. R. 1937. *The hobbit: Or, there and back again.* **London: George Allen and Unwin.**

This book is an acclaimed bestselling novel published by J. R. R. Tolkien, a professor at the University of Oxford's Pembroke College at the time of its writing. It has been translated into more than 40 languages, and millions of copies have been printed. It is the first novel to introduce many of the characters and settings in Tolkien's renowned body of work that would later be credited with influencing paper-and-pencil role-playing games such as *Dungeons and Dragons,* role-playing video games, and virtual worlds.

Tolkien, J. R. R. 1954. *The fellowship of the ring: Being the first part of the Lord of the Rings.* **London: George Allen and Unwin.**

Tolkien, J. R. R. 1954. *The two towers: Being the second part of the Lord of the Rings.* **London: George Allen and Unwin.**

Tolkien, J. R. R. 1955. *The return of the king: Being the third part of the Lord of the Rings.* **London: George Allen and Unwin.**

These books comprise the three volumes of J. R. R. Tolkien's beloved fantasy epic *The Lord of the Rings,* which was begun as a sequel to his novel *The Hobbit* but grew to become a three-volume novel written over the course of more than a decade. The series was written while Tolkien was a professor at the University of Oxford's Pembroke College and Merton College. The epic has sold more than 150 million copies worldwide and has been lauded as one of the most popular books of all time by several polls held in multiple countries. The theme, characters, and settings of Tolkien's work have been credited with influencing paper-and-pencil role-playing games such as *Dungeons and Dragons,* as well as role-playing video games and virtual worlds.

Van Cleave, Ryan G. 2010. *Unplugged: My journey into the dark world of video game addiction.* Deerfield Beach, FL: Health Communications.

The author details his own struggles with excessive use of video games, culminating with abuse of the online role-playing game *World of Warcraft,* which had crippling consequences for his health, and family, and career. The author also provides information about other traumatic events in his background and describes his recovery from excessive video game use.

Vorderer, Peter, and Jennings Bryant (eds.). 2006. *Playing video games: Motives, responses, and consequences.* Mahwah, NJ: Lawrence Erlbaum.

This edited volume includes chapters from scholars describing research in a number of areas related to the users, content, and effects of video games. Topics covered that are relevant to online games and virtual worlds include the history of video games, social interaction in online games, and the function of online role-playing games.

Young, Kimberly S., and Cristiano Nabuco de Abreu (eds.). 2010. *Internet Addiction: A handbook and guide to evaluation and treatment.* Hoboken, NJ: Wiley.

This edited book provides a thorough review of the state of research in the emerging and disputed area of Internet Addiction. The book includes contributions from the editors as well as invited authors from multiple fields. Chapters of the book outline theoretical mechanisms related to Internet addiction, methods used for diagnosis and treatment, and the case for formal recognition of Internet addiction as a clinical disorder. One chapter of the book is dedicated to online role-playing games specifically.

Book Chapters and Contributions to Edited Volumes

Bartle, Richard A. 2010. From MUDs to MMORPGs: The history of virtual worlds. In *International handbook of Internet research,* ed. Jeremy Hunsinger, Lisbeth Klastrup, and Matthew Allen, 23–39. Dordrecht: Springer.

This book chapter, authored by one of the creators of the original text-based online role-playing game called *MUD* (*Multi-User Dungeon*), outlines a history of virtual worlds from 1978 to the time of the chapter's publication. The chapter also serves as a useful example of the variety in definitions and criteria used to describe what is a virtual world and what is not, as the author's conceptualization of virtual worlds includes some applications that others do not consider virtual worlds, such as online games that do not include three-dimensional graphics or any graphics at all.

Morahan-Martin, Janet. 2008. Internet abuse: Emerging trends and lingering questions. In *Psychological aspects of cyberspace: Theory, research, applications,* ed. Azy Barak, 32–69. Cambridge, United Kingdom: Cambridge University Press.

This chapter reviews concepts and research related to Internet abuse, including abuse of specific Internet applications. The chapter provides a brief history of online games from the early text-based online game *MUD* (*Multi-User Dungeon*) to virtual worlds and describes elements that can make these games particularly conducive to abuse.

Morningstar, Chip, and F. Randall Farmer. 1991. The lessons of LucasFilm's Habitat. In *Cyberspace: First steps,* ed. Michael L. Benedikt, 273–302. Cambridge, MA: MIT Press.

This chapter describes the online community *Habitat,* which the authors developed for LucasFilm as one of the first attempts at a large-scale commercial virtual environment, and shares a number of recommendations about the development and function of online communities based on the authors' experiences with *Habitat.*

Yee, Nick. 2006. The psychology of massively multi-user online roleplaying games: Motivations, emotional investment, relationships and problematic usage. In *Avatars at work and play: Collaboration and interaction in virtual shared environments*, eds. Ralph Schroeder and Ann-Sofie Axelsson, 187–208. London: Springer.

This chapter describes results from a series of surveys of more than 30,000 users of online role-playing games that investigated a number of social issues related to the games' users and their activities within the game. Findings from the surveys indicated that users spanned a broad range of ages and backgrounds, played the games for many different reasons, spent an average of more than 20 hours per week playing the games, and experienced meaningful experiences and social relationships when using the games.

Vinge, Vernor. 1981. True names. In *Binary Star #5*, ed. James R. Frenkel. New York: Dell. Reprinted in *True names and the opening of the cyberspace frontier*, ed. Vernor Vinge and James Frenkel, 239–330. New York: Tor Books, 2001.

This science-fiction novella describes users of a fictional virtual reality technology known as the "Other Plane" which is recognized as one of the earliest visions of an online virtual world recorded in literature.

Articles

Allison, Sara E., Lisa von Wahlde, Tamra Shockey, and Glen O. Gabbard. 2006. The development of the self in the era of the Internet and role-playing fantasy games. *American Journal of Psychiatry* 163: 381–385.

This article provides a case study of an 18-year old male, "Mr. A," with a prior history of psychiatric treatment who received a psychiatric evaluation after his parents expressed concern about his obsessive use of online computer games. "Mr. A" reported playing the games for 12 to 16 hours each day.

Anderson, Craig A. 2004. An update on the effects of playing violent video games. *Journal of Adolescence* 27: 113–122.

This article summarizes existing research related to the effects of violent video games, concluding that violent video games can in-

crease aggressive thoughts, feelings, and behavior, increase car-
diovascular arousal, and decrease helping behavior. The article
does not address online games specifically.

**Anderson, Craig A., Leonard Berkowitz, Edward Donnerstein,
L. Rowell Huesmann, James D. Johnson, Daniel Linz, Neil M.
Malamuth, and Ellen Wartella. 2003. The influence of media
violence on youth. *Psychological Science in the Public Interest*
4: 81–110.**

This article reviews research on the effects of violence in television,
films, video games, and music and concludes that media violence
has a substantial influence on aggression and violence in media
users. The article does not address online video games specifically.

**Anderson, Craig A., and Brad J. Bushman. 2001. Effects of vio-
lent video games on aggressive behavior, aggressive cognition,
aggressive affect, physiological arousal, and prosocial behavior:
A meta-analytic review of the scientific literature. *Psychological
Science* 12:353–359.**

This article describes a meta-analysis (a study that statistically
combines and summarizes the findings from a large group of studies examining the same variables) assessing the effects of violent
video games and aggressive thoughts, feelings, and behaviors,
physiological arousal, and helping behavior. Based on an analysis
including 54 studies from 35 reports, the authors conclude that
violent video games increase aggressive thoughts, feelings, and
behavior, increase physiological arousal, and decrease helping
behavior. The article does not mention online video games specifically.

**Anderson, Craig A., and Brad J. Bushman. 2002. The effects of
media violence on society. *Science* 295: 2377–2378.**

This article briefly summarizes research dealing with the effects
of media violence on aggression in media users, arguing that the
effects of media violence on users' aggression are stronger than
the observed effects of calcium intake on bone mass and of lead
exposure on children's IQ scores. The article briefly mentions
research on the effects of video games, though not online video
games.

Anderson, Craig A., and Karen E. Dill. 2000. Video games and aggressive thoughts, feelings, and behavior in the laboratory and in life. *Journal of Personality and Social Psychology* 78: 772–790.

This article describes two studies investigating the effects of violence in video games on aggression in games' users. The first study was a survey that found violent video use to be related to aggression and delinquency and that academic achievement was negatively related to overall video game use, while the second study was an experimental finding that exposure to a violent video game in a laboratory increased aggressive thoughts and behavior in users. The studies did not examine online video games specifically.

Anderson, Craig. A., Akiko Shibuya, Nobuko Ihori, Edward L. Swing, Brad J. Bushman, Akira Sakamoto, Hannah R. Rothstein, and Muniba Saleem. 2010. Violent video game effects on aggression, empathy, and prosocial behavior in Eastern and Western countries. *Psychological Bulletin* 136: 151–173.

This article describes a meta-analysis (a study that statistically combines and summarizes the findings from a large group of studies examining the same variables) exploring the effects of violent video games on aggressive thoughts, feelings, and behaviors, physiological arousal, desensitization, and helping behavior. This study examined 130 research reports and included research from both Japan and Western countries to examine cultural differences in the effects of violence in video games. The study found that violent video games increase aggressive thoughts, feelings, and behavior, as well as arousal and desensitization, while reducing helping behavior, and that these effects were similar across cultures. Online video games are not mentioned specifically in the article.

Andreatos, Antonios. 2007. Virtual communities and their importance for informal learning. *International Journal of Computers, Communications and Control* 2(1): 39–47.

This article provides a definition and categorization of virtual communities and discusses their educational potential as a tool for continuing education. Gaming communities such as MUDs (multi-user dungeons) and related applications are mentioned as examples of virtual communities that promote interaction, discussion, and relationships between users.

Bainbridge, William Sims. 2007. The scientific research potential of virtual worlds. *Science* **317: 472–476.**

This article briefly summarizes research being conducted using virtual worlds such as *Second Life* and *World of Warcraft* and describes the unique opportunities these online environments can provide for exploration of a number of social phenomena.

Balicer, Ran D. 2007. Modeling infectious diseases dissemination through online role-playing games. *Epidemiology* **18: 260–261.**

This article discusses the potential of online role-playing games as a resource for research on how infectious diseases spread through communities and how they can be prevented, citing the "corrupted blood" epidemic in the online role-playing game *World of Warcraft* as an example of an online phenomenon that could inform research on disease outbreaks in the real world.

Balkin, Jack M. 2004. Virtual liberty: Freedom to design and freedom to play in virtual worlds. *Virginia Law Review* **90: 2043–2098.**

This article provides recommendations regarding how law and policy should be applied to virtual worlds regarding issues such as players' free speech rights, intellectual property rights, and rights to privacy.

Bargh, John A., Katelyn Y. A. McKenna, and Grainne M. Fitzsimons. 2002. Can you see the real me? Activation and expression of the "True Self" on the Internet. *Journal of Social Issues* **58: 33–48.**

This article describes three studies that examine how people perceive and express their concept of self in online interaction. The study does not examine or discuss online interaction in virtual worlds specifically.

Bargh, John A., and Katelyn Y. A. McKenna. 2004. The Internet and social life. *Annual Review of Psychology* **55: 573–590.**

This article describes the history of the Internet in the context of other technologies and reviews research on the effects of Internet use on social interaction and behavior. The article does not address social interaction in virtual worlds specifically.

Beard, Keith W., and Eve M. Wolf. 2001. Modification of the proposed diagnostic criteria for Internet addiction. *CyberPsychology and Behavior* 4: 377–383.

This article proposes changes to the criteria previously used by some researchers in diagnosing and exploring the concept of Internet addiction. Findings from some researchers that online games can be particularly conducive to overuse are mentioned.

Bensley, Lillian, and Juliet Van Eenwyk. 2001. Video games and real-life aggression: A review of the literature. *Journal of Adolescent Health* 29: 244–257.

This article reviews existing research on a possible relationship between violence in video games and real-life violence, concluding that there is not adequate evidence to justify concern that video game violence is a substantial cause of real-life violence but that further research might provide more support for such concern. The article does not address effects of online games specifically.

Bessière, Katherine, A. Fleming Seay, and Sara Kiesler. 2007. The ideal elf: Identity exploration in World of Warcraft. *CyberPsychology and Behavior* 10: 530–535.

This article describes a study investigating how users of the online role-playing game *World of Warcraft* practice identity exploration online, finding that users described their game as more similar to their ideal self than they described themselves—particularly users with poor psychological well-being.

Biocca, Frank. 1992. Communication within virtual reality: Creating a space for research. *Journal of Communication* 42: 5–22.

This article discusses the technological and social background of virtual reality and virtual environments as well as the social implications of their future developments. The article mentions LucasFilm's *Habitat* as one example of an early example of an online community.

Boulos, Maged N. Kamel, Lee Hetherington, and Steve Wheeler. 2007. Second Life: An overview of the potential of 3-D virtual

worlds in medical and health education. *Health Information and Libraries Journal* 24: 233–245.

This article discusses the potential of virtual worlds for medical and health education, describing two virtual facilities in the virtual world *Second Life* as examples of how virtual worlds can be used to deliver information about health and medicine.

Bradley, Caroline, and A. Michael Froomkin. 2003. Virtual worlds, real rules. *New York Law School Review* 49: 103–146.

This article discusses the potential for virtual worlds as an environment in which the effectiveness and consequences of policies might be examined without the risk of negative economic and social consequences that a real-world trial of legal rules would entail.

Bruckman, Amy, and Mitchel Resnick. 1995. The MediaMOO project: Constructionism and professional community. *Convergence* 1(1): 94–109.

This article describes the development and function of Media-MOO, a text-based online community designed for media researchers. "MOO" stands for "MUD, Object Oriented," a term describing text-based online environments that are a variation of MUDs (multi-user dungeons).

Bugeja, Michael. J. 2007. Second thoughts about Second Life. *The Chronicle of Higher Education.* http://chronicle.com/article/Second-Thoughts-About-Second/46636/

In this article, the author urges academic institutions to use caution in implementing official activities in the virtual world *Second Life* because the institutions may be held legally liable for adverse events that may take place in the virtual world due to circumstances beyond the institutions' control.

Bushman, Brad J., and Craig A. Anderson. 2001. Media violence and the American public: Scientific facts versus media misinformation. *American Psychologist* 56: 477–489.

This article argues that news media outlets inaccurately report that the research assessing the effects of media violence on users has not reached a definitive conclusion when the authors believe that the negative effects of media violence have indeed been conclusively demonstrated. Among the media effects that the authors claim are inaccurately reported are the effects of violent video games, though the article does not discuss online video games.

Bushman, Brad J., Hannah R. Rothsetein, and Craig A. Anderson. 2010. Much ado about something: Violent video games and a school of red herring: Reply to Ferguson and Kilburn. *Psychological Bulletin* **136: 182–187.**

This commentary article is a response to another commentary article (see Ferguson and Kilburn 2010, below) that is in turn a response to an article (see Anderson et al. 2010 above) describing a meta-analysis (a study that statistically combines and summarizes the findings from a large group of studies examining the same variables) of the effects of violence in video games on aggression and related outcomes. In this commentary, the authors defend the initial meta-analysis and criticize many of the claims in the initial commentary by Ferguson and Kilburn. The commentary article does not discuss online games specifically.

Byun, Sookeun, Celestino Ruffini, Juline E. Mills, Alecia C. Douglas, Mamadou Niang, Svetlana Stepchenkova, Seul Ki Lee, Jihad Loutfi, Jung-Kook Lee, Mikhail Atallah, and Marina Blanton. 2009. Internet addiction: Metasynthesis of 1996–2006 quantitative research. *CyberPsychology and Behavior* **12: 203–207.**

This article reviews previous research dealing with the disputed phenomenon of Internet addiction conducted during the previous decade, pointing out inconsistencies and flaws in that body of research and making recommendations for future study. The article briefly mentions online game play as one activity indulged in by some so-called addicts and also mentions literature indicating that problematic Internet users tend to perceive the Internet as more entertaining than people not exhibiting problematic Internet use.

Caplan, Scott. 2002. Problematic Internet use and psychosocial well-being: Development of a theory-based cognitive-behavioral measurement instrument. *Computers in Human Behavior* **18: 553–575.**

This article introduces a new questionnaire instrument designed to measure problematic Internet use, the Generalized Problematic Internet Use Scale (GPIUS), and describes research conducted to test its effectiveness. The article does not address games specifically except to mention previous findings that some people prone to problematic Internet use tend to enjoy playing interactive games online.

Caplan, Scott, Dmitri Williams, and Nick Yee. 2009. Problematic Internet use and psychosocial well-being among MMO players. *Computers in Human Behavior* **25: 1312–1319.**

This article describes findings from a study that examined problematic Internet use among users of the online role-playing game *EverQuest 2* by combining a survey of more than 4,000 users with behavioral data from their game use. The study found that more time spent playing the game and the use of voice chat within the game were both linked to higher rates of problematic Internet use among users.

Carnagey, Nicholas L., and Craig A. Anderson. 2004. Violent video game exposure and aggression: A literature review. *Minerva Psichiatrica* **45: 1–18.**

This article reviews existing research dealing with the effects of violence in video games on aggressive thoughts, feelings, and behavior in users. The article mentions that online games, including massively multiplayer online role-playing games, are increasingly popular forms of video games that also frequently contain violence.

Castronova, Edward. 2006. On the research value of large games: Natural experiments in Norrath and Camelot. *Games and Culture* **1: 163–186.**

In this article, the author argues that virtual worlds can serve as environments for natural experiments wherein social phenomena within the virtual worlds are observed in order to gain a better understanding of real-life social phenomena. Two examples from behavior observed in the virtual worlds *EverQuest* and *Dark Age of Camelot* are cited.

Castronova, Edward, Travis Ross, Mark Bell, Matthew Falk, Robert Cornell, and Matt Haselton. 2008. Constructing Arden: Life inside the machine. *Multimedia IEEE* **15(1): 4–8.**

This article describes the authors' efforts to create and develop *Arden*, a virtual world based on the works of William Shakespeare and designed to allow academic research of its users' behavior.

Castronova, Edward, Dmitri Williams, Cuihua Shen, Rabindra Ratan, Li Xiong, Yun Huang, and Brian Keegan. 2009. As real as real? Macroeconomic behavior in a large-scale virtual world. *New Media and Society* 11: 685–707.

This article describes a study examining data from the online role-playing game *EverQuest II* to determine whether large-scale economic patterns in virtual worlds mirror economic patterns observed in the real world. Findings suggest that the virtual economies of online virtual worlds do exhibit patterns similar to real-life economies.

Chappell, Darren, Virginia Eatough, Mark N.O. Davies, and Mark Griffiths. 2006. *EverQuest*—It's just a computer game right? An interpretive phenomenological analysis of online gaming addiction. *International Journal of Mental Health and Addiction* 4: 205–216.

This article reports interpretive analyses of online forum posts from users of the online role-playing game *EverQuest* who reported playing the game excessively. The article indicates that these *EverQuest* users exhibited many symptoms consistent with other addictions such as alcohol or gambling addiction.

Charlton, John P., and Ian D. W. Danforth. 2007. Distinguishing addiction and high engagement in the context of online game playing. *Computers in Human Behavior* 23: 1531–1548.

This article reports a survey exploring the application of criteria previously applied to addiction and to problematic computer use to the specific area of massively multiplayer online role-playing game use. The authors conclude that application of some previously used criteria and measures related to addiction may be inappropriate and could confuse users' high levels of engagement with compulsive use.

Childress, Marcus D., and Ray Braswell. 2006. Using massively multiplayer online role-playing games for online learning. *Distance Education* 27: 187–196.

In this article, the authors provide an overview of the definition and history of virtual worlds, describe their experiences using the virtual world *Second Life* for educational applications, and make recommendations about education use of virtual worlds.

Chin, Bettina M. 2007. Regulating your Second Life: Defamation in virtual worlds. *Brooklyn Law Review* 72: 1303–1349.

This article discusses the application of how existing law regarding defamation might apply to defamatory conduct in virtual worlds, exploring issues with application of law that may be unique to virtual worlds.

Cole, Helena, and Mark D. Griffiths. 2007. Social interactions in massively multiplayer online role-playing gamers. *CyberPsychology and Behavior* 10: 575–583.

This article reports a survey of more than 900 users of online role-playing games. Findings indicated that a large portion of users in the survey formed close interpersonal relationships with other users in the online game environments.

Dill, Karen E., and Jody C. Dill. 1998. Video game violence: A review of the empirical literature. *Aggression and Violent Behavior* 3: 407–428.

This article provides an overview of existing research dealing with the effects of video game violence on users. The authors conclude that there is evidence for negative effects of violence in video games but that more research is needed in the area. The article does not address online games specifically.

Ferguson, Christopher J. 2007. Evidence for publication bias in video game violence effects literature: A meta-analytic review. *Aggression and Violent Behavior* 12: 470–482.

In this article, the author argues that there are flaws in the conclusions drawn from a previous meta-analysis (a study that statistically combines and summarizes the findings from a large group of studies examining the same variables) of the effects of violent video games (see Anderson and Bushman 2001 above). The article includes a new meta-analysis using different methodology and concludes that research may exaggerate effects of violent video games because articles not finding such effects are less likely to be published. Online video games are not addressed specifically.

Ferguson, Christopher J. 2007. The good, the bad, and the ugly: A meta-analytic review of positive and negative effects of violent video games. *Psychiatric Quarterly* **78: 309–316.**

This article describes a meta-analysis (a study that statistically combines and summarizes the findings from a large group of studies examining the same variables) examining both positive and negative effects of violent video games. Based on results, the article concludes that some positive effects of violent video games may be stronger than often-researched negative effects, and that research on violent video games should therefore acknowledge the possible presence of both positive and negative outcomes. Online video games are not addressed specifically.

Ferguson, Christopher J. 2010. Blazing angels or resident evil? Can video games be a force for good? *Review of General Psychology* **14(2): 68–81.**

This article reviews research on the effects of violent video games, arguing that some negative effects of violent video games have been overrepresented by researchers and that some positive effects of violent video games should receive more attention. Social dynamics of games played online are mentioned as potential game elements that may have positive social effects.

Ferguson, Christopher J. 2011. Video games and youth violence: A prospective analysis in adolescents. *Journal of Youth and Adolescence* **40: 377–391.**

This article describes a study of youth conducted over the course of 12 months to examine the effects of violent video games on youth violence over that time period. The study found that exposure to violent video games and violent television content were not significantly related to serious youth violence and aggression, though depression and antisocial traits were related to violent behavior and exposure to video game violence was related to bullying behavior. Online games are not investigated specifically.

Ferguson, Christopher J., and John Kilburn. 2010. Much ado about nothing: The misestimation and overinterpretation of violent video game effects in Eastern and Western nations: Comment on Anderson et al. *Psychological Bulletin* **136: 174–178.**

This commentary article is a response to an article (see Anderson et al. 2010 above) describing a meta-analysis (a study that statistically combines and summarizes the findings from a large group of studies examining the same variables) of the effects of violence in video games on aggression and related outcomes. In this commentary, the authors claim that the meta-analysis includes methodological flaws that lead to overestimation of the negative effects of violent video games. Online games are not addressed specifically.

Gentile, Douglas. 2009. Pathological video-game use among youth ages 8 to 18. *Psychological Science* **20: 594–602.**

This article reports a survey of more than 1,000 American children aged 8 to 18. Based on the study's findings, the author concludes that about 8% of the children in the survey were pathological players with harmful use patterns similar to those exhibited by people with other pathological behavior such as pathological gambling. Online games are not addressed specifically.

Gentile, Douglas A., Hyekyung Choo, Albert Liau, Timothy Sim, Dongdong Li, Daniel Fung, and Angeline Khoo. 2011. Pathological video game use among youths: A two-year longitudinal study. *Pediatrics* **127: e319-e329.**

This article describes a panel study carried out over two years with a group of more than 3,000 elementary and secondary school students in Singapore. Based on the study's findings, the authors conclude that approximately 9% of the study's participants are pathological users of video games. Predictors of pathological game play included more time spent playing video games, lower social competence, and higher levels of impulsivity. Apparent consequences of pathological game play included depression, anxiety, social phobias, and lower performance in school. Online gaming at the beginning of the study did not predict pathological game play later in the study, though participants' time spent playing games online tended to increase over time.

Griffiths, Mark D. 1999. Violent video games and aggression: A review of the literature. *Aggression and Violent Behavior* **4: 203–212.**

This article reviews research examining the effects of violence in video games on aggression, concluding that more research is needed to provide conclusive results about such effects because of the limited number of studies in the area and the lack of diversity in the methods used in those studies.

Griffiths, Mark D., Mark N. O. Davies, and Darren Chappell. 2004. Demographic factors and playing variables in online computer gaming. *CyberPsychology and Behavior* 7: 479–487.

This article reports a survey of users of the online role-playing game *EverQuest*. Among other findings, the article reports that a small minority of players used the game excessively and sacrificed other activities to play the game.

Griffiths, Mark D., Mark N. O. Davies, and Darren Chappell. 2004. Online computer gaming: A comparison of adolescent and adult gamers. *Journal of Adolescence* 27: 87–96.

This article reports a survey of users of the online role-playing game *EverQuest*. Analyses compare responses of adolescent and adult users, finding that users from the two age groups exhibited different behaviors when using the game and had different motivations for playing the game.

Griffiths, Mark D., and Alex Meredith. 2009. Videogame addiction and its treatment. *Journal of Contemporary Psychotherapy* 39: 247–253.

This paper examines developments in the area of video game addiction, acknowledging that the increasing availability of online video games may be increasing the number of people whose video game use is problematic, and reviews options for clinical treatment for those whose video game use is excessive enough to cause problems.

Grimes, Sara M. 2006. Online multiplayer games: A virtual space for intellectual property debates? *New Media and Society* 8: 969–990.

This article discusses issues related to intellectual property rights in online games, focusing particularly on friction between the rights of game providers and game users. The article examines how this topic has been addressed in previous research and popular media, as well as how existing intellectual property law is applied to online games.

Glushko, Bobby. 2007. Tales of the (virtual) city: Governing property disputes in virtual worlds. *Berkeley Technology Law Journal* 22: 507–532.

This article reviews the issue of property disputes in virtual worlds, argues that current end user license agreements (EULAs) for virtual worlds are inadequate for dealing with such disputes, and makes recommendations regarding how EULAs can better govern virtual worlds and resolve disputes within them.

Horowitz, Steven J. 2007. Competing Lockean claims to virtual property. *Harvard Journal of Law and Technology* **20: 443–458.**

This article examines the property rights of virtual world users, arguing that disputes over virtual property between users can be resolved via relatively simple comparisons of the users' rights to that property but that disputes between users and operators of virtual worlds require a more complex conceptual understanding of virtual property.

Huhh, Jun-Sok. 2008. Culture and business of PC bangs in Korea. *Games and Culture* **3: 26–37.**

This article provides an overview of the social and economic function of PC bangs (popular Internet cafés) in South Korea and describes the concurrent success of PC bangs and online computer games in South Korea. The article also speculates on possible future developments for both PC bangs and online games in South Korea.

Hussain, Zaheer, and Mark D. Griffiths. 2009. Excessive use of massively multiplayer online role-playing games: A pilot study. *International Journal of Mental Health and Addiction* **7: 563–571.**

This article describes a small survey investigating problematic use of online role-playing games. The article reports that 41% of online role-playing game users played online games as a form of escape and that 7% of online role-playing game users in the study were at risk for becoming dependent on game-playing.

Lastowka, F. Gregory. 2009. Rules of play. *Games and Culture* **4: 379–395.**

This article discusses application of law to virtual worlds, emphasizing the importance of reconciling legal governance of virtual worlds with the rules and goals already in place in the game atmospheres within virtual worlds. The paper argues that the legal jurisdiction of virtual worlds should be unique in some ways that are analogous to the legal jurisdictions of sporting competitions and other competitive play.

Lastowka, F. Gregory, and Dan Hunter. 2004. The laws of virtual worlds. *California Law Review* 92: 1–73.

This article provides an overview and history of virtual worlds and discusses the application of law to them, exploring whether virtual world users' personal and property rights should be comparable to personal and property rights in the real world.

Lebling, P. David, Marc S. Blank, and Timothy A. Anderson. 1979. Zork: A computerized fantasy simulation game. *IEEE Computers Magazine* 12(4): 51–59.

In this article, the authors describe the development and function of *Zork,* an early text-based game that they cocreated and which would later serve as inspiration for the text-based online games that were ancestors of virtual worlds. The article also provides examples of game content.

Lo, Shao-Kang, Chih-Chien Wang, and Wenchang Fang. 2005. Physical interpersonal relationships and social anxiety among online game players. *CyberPsychology and Behavior* 8: 15–20.

This article reports a survey of college-aged Taiwanese online game players that examined relationships between online game play and social problems. The study found that survey respondents who spent more time playing online games tended to have lower-quality interpersonal relationships and have more social anxiety.

Lofgren, Eric T., and Nina H. Fefferman. 2007. The untapped potential of virtual game worlds to shed light on real world epidemics. *Lancet Infectious Diseases* 7: 625–629.

This article describes the virtual "corrupted blood" epidemic that took place in the online role-playing game *World of Warcraft,* then argues that the incident provides evidence that virtual worlds could be used to examine the function of real-world disease epidemics in ways that might be superior to existing methods of computer-modeled simulations of disease epidemics.

Malaby, Thomas. 2006. Parlaying value: Capital in and beyond virtual worlds. *Games and Culture* 1: 141–162.

This article argues that value in virtual worlds exists in three forms: market capital, social capital, and cultural capital. Applying a broad range of economic and cultural concepts to virtual worlds such as *Second Life,* the article discusses how these forms of value interact within virtual worlds.

Miller, Greg. 2007. The promise of parallel universes. *Science* **317: 1341–1343.**

This article describes several research studies that have used virtual worlds such as *Second Life, World of Warcraft,* and *EverQuest II* to examine phenomena that are either specific to online environments or that are difficult to examine in real-world settings.

Mortensen, Torill Elvira. 2006. WoW is the new MUD: Social gaming from text to video. *Games and Culture* **1: 397–413.**

This article draws connections between the modern online role-playing game *World of Warcraft* and the early text-based online role-playing games known as MUDs (multi-user dungeons), arguing that there are many similarities between the two types of applications despite their pronounced technological differences.

Ng, Brian D., and Peter Wiemer-Hastings. 2005. Addiction to the Internet and online gaming. *CyberPsychology and Behavior* **8: 110–113.**

This article reports results from a survey of questions related to video game addiction that was given a group of online role-playing game users and to a comparison group who used video games not played online. Based on comparisons between the online game players and offline game players, the authors conclude that online game users use the games more and for different reasons compared to uses of other video games, but that the online game users do not exhibit tendencies consistent with addiction.

Ondrejka, Cory. 2004. Escaping the gilded cage: User created content and building the metaverse. *New York Law School Law Review* **49: 81–101.**

This article describes the growing prevalence of content within virtual worlds that has been created by its users, even within virtual worlds that do not encourage content creation by users, and makes recommendations as to how policy can be used to best guide user contributions to virtual worlds in a way that will ensure they are rich environments.

Ritzema, Tim, and Billy Harris. 2008. The use of Second Life for distance education. *Journal of Computing Sciences in Colleges* **23: 110–116.**

This article reports a study investigating the utility of the virtual world *Second Life* as an application for distance education in the field of computer science. Based on data collected from study participants, the authors conclude that *Second Life* can be effective for use in distance education in computer science.

Schiano, Diane J. 1999. Lessons from LambdaMOO: A social, text-based virtual environment. *Presence: Teleoperators and Virtual Environments* **8: 127–139.**

This article describes a series of studies examining users in the text-based online community *LambdaMOO*. "MOO" stands for "MUD, object oriented," a term describing text-based online environments that are a variation of MUDs (multi-user dungeons). The article includes data collected from a survey, interviews, and other methods to provide insight about social interaction among *LambdaMOO* users.

Shapiro, Andrew. 1998. The disappearance of cyberspace and the rise of code. *Seton Hall Constitutional Law Journal* **8: 703–723.**

This article argues that online environments should not be regarded conceptually as distinct places, but as unique interfaces through which people interact with the existing world, and discusses the social and legal implications of this different conceptualization of "cyberspace."

Sherry, John L. 2001. The effects of violent video games on aggression. *Human Communication Research* **27: 409–341.**

This article describes a meta-analysis (a study that statistically combines and summarizes the findings from a large group of studies examining the same variables) investigating the results of research on the effects of violent video games on aggression. Based on the analysis of 25 studies, the author concludes that research has observed a correlation between violent video games and aggression, but that this effect is smaller than has been observed by similar studies on the effects of television violence. The article does not mention online games specifically.

Smahel, David, Lukas Blinka, and Ondrej Ledabyl. 2008. Playing MMORPGS: Connections between addiction and identifying with a character. *CyberPsychology and Behavior* 11: 715–718.

This article reports a survey examining what characteristics might make users of online role-playing games particularly prone to problematic use. Among the survey's results were findings that younger users and users who strongly identified with their game characters were more likely to exhibit problematic use tendencies.

Smythe, Joshua M. 2007. Beyond self-selection in video game play: An experimental examination of the consequences of massively multiplayer online role-playing play. *CyberPsychology and Behavior* 10: 717–721.

This article describes a survey in which a group of 20-year-old participants were randomly assigned to play either arcade games, console video games, computer games not played online, or online role-playing games for one month. After the one-month period, participants assigned to the online role-playing game group reported higher rates of a number of negative health and social effects compared to participants in the other groups, but participants assigned to the online role-playing game group also reported higher rates of a number of positive outcomes as well.

Steinkuehler, Constance. 2007. Massively multiplayer online gaming as a constellation of literacy practices. *E-learning* 4: 297–318.

Based on the author's research in the online role-playing games *Lineage* and *Lineage II*, this article argues that users of virtual worlds engage in a variety of literary practices, both within the virtual world environment and in their related online activities outside of the virtual environment.

Steinkuhler, Constance, and Sean Duncan. 2008. Scientific habits of mind in virtual worlds. *Journal of Science Education and Technology* 17: 530–543.

This article reports an analysis of online discussion forum posts related to the online role-playing game *World of Warcraft* conducted to examine whether discussion of the game included evidence of reasoning and analytical thinking representative of informal science-related thinking. Based on their analyses, the authors conclude that online role-playing games provide an environment that encourages users to exercise reasoning and thinking skills conducive to science education and practice.

Turkle, Sherry. 1994. Constructions and reconstructions of self in virtual reality: Playing in the MUDs. *Mind, Culture, and Activity* **1: 158–167.**

This article describes findings and conclusions from the author's research in the text-based online environments called MUDs (multi-user dungeons). Using a number of anecdotes from users' interactions in the online environments, the author argues that MUDs provide unique opportunities for users to explore and express their identities online.

Van Mierlo, Jan, and Jan Van den Bulck. 2004. Benchmarking the cultivation approach to video game effects: A comparison of the correlates of TV viewing and game play. *Journal of Adolescence* **27: 97–111.**

This article reports results of a survey examining whether video game use might distort players' perceptions of social reality so that their perception of the real world is skewed toward the world portrayed in video games. Results of a survey of Flemish elementary-school students indicated that survey respondents who spent more time playing games reported higher rates of violence and crime in the real world. The article does not address online games specifically.

Williams, Dmitri. 2006. Virtual cultivation: Online worlds, offline perceptions. *Journal of Communication* **56: 69–87.**

This article reports results from an experiment examining whether online role-playing games might distort users' perceptions of reality so that their views of the real world are skewed toward the reality portrayed in the online games. In an experiment, users assigned to play the online role-playing game *Asheron's Call 2* for one month reported higher estimates of some types of crimes compared to a control group not assigned to play the game, but these changes were only observed for types of crimes portrayed within the game.

Williams, Dmitri, Scott Caplan, and Li Xiong. 2007. Can you hear me now? The impact of voice in an online gaming community. *Human Communication Research* 33: 427–449.

This article describes a field experiment examining the effects of voice communication on feelings of community among users of the online role-playing game *World of Warcraft*. Results of the study indicated that the addition of a voice communication feature to the game led to the development of closer and more trusting relationships between users.

Williams, Dmitri, Mia Consalvo, Scott Caplan, and Nick Yee. 2009. Looking for gender: Gender roles and behaviors among online gamers. *Journal of Communication* 59: 700–725.

This article describes a study examining male and female users of the online role-playing game *EverQuest II* through a survey combined with behavioral data collected directly from the game. Results indicated that there were more male users than female users, but that female users tended to spend more time playing the game than male users and tended to underestimate the amount of time they spent playing the game more than male users.

Williams, Dmitri, Nicolas Ducheneaut, Li Xiong, Yuanyuan Zhang, Nick Yee, and Eric Nickell. 2006. From tree house to barracks: The social life of guilds in World of Warcraft. *Games and Culture* 1: 338–361.

This article reports a study using surveys and interviews to examine the social behavior of users of the online role-playing game *World of Warcraft*. Results indicated that the game's players used the game both to continue existing social relationships and to form various types of new social relationships.

Williams, Dmitri, and Marko Skoric. 2005. Internet fantasy violence: A test of aggression in an online game. *Communication Monographs* 72: 217–233.

This article describes an experiment testing the effects of a violent online role-playing game on users' aggressive behavior. In the study, participants assigned to play the online role-playing game *Asheron's Call 2* for one month did not report significantly higher rates of aggressive behavior compared to a comparison group of participants not assigned to play the game. The authors conclude that there is insufficient evidence that violence in online video games causes aggressive behavior in users.

Williams, Dmitri, Nick Yee, and Scott Caplan. 2008. Who plays, how much, and why? Debunking the stereotypical gamer profile. *Journal of Computer-Mediated Communication* 13: 993–1018.

This article reports results of a study examining users of the online role-playing game *EverQuest II* through the combination of a survey of users and direct collection of data about users' behavior within the game. Among results were the finding that users spent an average of more than 25 hours per week playing the game, the finding that users tended to underestimate the time they spent playing the game, and the finding that users had higher rates of substance abuse and depression than the general population.

Wood, Richard T. A. 2008. Problems with the concept of video game "addiction": Some case study examples. *International Journal of Mental Health and Addiction* 6: 169–178.

This article reviews research dealing with the disputed concept of video game addiction and discusses relevant examples of individuals with problematic game use. Based on analysis of previous research and the individual case study examples, the author concludes that cases incorrectly identified as video game addiction are more likely to be cases where individuals play video games too much due to poor time management or as a means to escape from other problems.

Yee, Nick. 2006. Motivations for play in online games. *Cyber-Psychology and Behavior* 9: 772–775.

This article reports results from a survey of more than 3,000 users of online role-playing games that explored the motivations users had for playing the games. The survey's findings indicated that male and female users tended to have different motivations for playing the games and that some motivations were more strongly linked to problematic use of the games than others.

Yee, Nick. 2006. The demographics, motivations, and derived experiences of users of massively multi-user online graphical environments. *Presence: Teleoperators and Virtual Environments* 15: 309–329.

This article describes results from a series of surveys examining the demographics of more than 30,000 users of online role-playing games and their use of these games. Among results of the surveys were the findings that users of many different ages enjoyed the games and that users spent an average of more than 20 hours per week playing the games.

Yee, Nick, Jeremy N. Bailenson, Mark Urbanek, Francis Chang, and Dan Merget. 2007. The unbearable likeness of being digital: The persistence of nonverbal social norms in online virtual environments. *CyberPsychology and Behavior* 10: 115–121.

This article describes a study in which observational data were collected from users in the virtual world *Second Life* to investigate whether users' avatars observed social norms related to eye contact and interpersonal distance in patterns consistent with related research on people's behavior in real life. Results indicated that avatars tended to follow behavioral norms related to interpersonal distance and eye contact, suggesting that the behavior of avatars in virtual worlds follows similar social rules as those followed by people in real life.

Yellowlees, Peter M., and James N. Cook. 2006. Education about hallucinations using an Internet virtual reality system: A qualitative survey. *Academic Psychiatry* 30: 534–539.

This article describes a study examining the effectiveness of a virtual tour created within the virtual world *Second Life* that provided users with a simulation of the auditory and visual hallucinations experienced by a person suffering from schizophrenia. Based on survey responses from *Second Life* users who took part in the tour, the authors conclude that simulations of mental illness can be effectively deployed in virtual worlds to enhance users' understanding of these illnesses.

Young, Kimberly S. 1998. Internet addiction: The emergence of a new clinical disorder. *CyberPsychology and Behavior* 1: 237–244.

This article reports results from surveys investigating the potential phenomenon of Internet addiction among individuals with behaviors indicating problematic Internet use. Based on the data, the author argues that some Internet users may exhibit dependent tendencies in their use of the Internet. The article notes that the text-based online environments known as MUDs (multi-user dungeons) were among the most common applications used by survey respondents with dependent Internet use tendencies.

Zhou, Zhongyun, Xiao-Lin Jin, Douglas R. Vogel, Yulin Fang, and Xiaojian Chen. 2010. Individual motivations and demographic differences in social virtual world uses: An exploratory investigation in Second Life. *International Journal of Information Management* 31: 261–271.

This article describes a survey exploring the motivations and activities of users in the virtual world *Second Life*. The study found that there were a number of motivations behind users' activity in the virtual world and that male and female users tended to engage in different activities when using *Second Life*.

Other Academic Papers

Axelsson, Ann-Sofie, and Tim Regan. 2002. How belonging in an online group affects social behavior—A case study of Asheron's Call. http://research.microsoft.com/pubs/69910/tr-2002-07.pdf.

This technical report from Microsoft Research examined relationships between membership in groups in online games and game users' behavior. The researchers surveyed more than 5,000 users of the online role-playing game *Asheron's Call* and also directly observed the online behavior of 22 users during their game sessions.

Bell, Mark W., Edward Castronova, and Gert G. Wagner. 2009. Surveying the virtual world: A large scale survey in Second Life using the Virtual Data Collection Interface (VDCI). http://papers.ssrn.com/sol3/papers.cfm?abstract_id=1418562.

This research paper describes findings from a survey of more than 2,000 users of the virtual world *Second Life* using a tool called the Virtual Data Collection Interface (VDCI) to automatically collect responses from survey participants within the virtual environment. Findings of the study suggest that the demographic makeup and behavior of *Second Life* users is unique in many ways compared to users of other widely researched virtual worlds.

Bray, David A., and Been R. Konsynski. 2008. Virtual worlds, virtual economies, virtual institutions. In *Proceedings of virtual worlds and new realities conference.* http://ssrn.com/abstract=962501.

This research paper reviews the history and development of virtual worlds and online communities and discusses how the economic and social structures of these environments can be better understood through research.

Castronova, Edward. 2001. *Virtual worlds: A first-hand account of market and society on the cyberian frontier.* CESifo Working Paper No. 618, December. http://ssrn.com/abstract=294828.

This research paper describes research investigating users and economic activity in the online role-playing game *EverQuest.* Surveyed players reported spending an average of 28.9 hours playing the game in a typical week, and 31.5% of adults in the survey reported spending more time in the game's virtual world of Norrath than at their jobs.

Castronova, Edward. 2002. *On virtual economies.* CESifo Working Paper No. 752, July. http://ssrn.com/abstract=338500.

This research paper provides a history of virtual worlds, discusses the function and growing significance of economies in virtual worlds, and speculates on the potential significance of virtual worlds' economies for real-world economies.

Castronova, Edward. 2003. *Theory of the avatar.* CESifo Working Paper No. 863, February. http://papers.ssrn.com/abstract=385103.

This research paper discusses concepts and models related to decisions virtual world users may make when creating and using avatars in virtual worlds and suggests a series of rights that should be maintained for virtual world users as they use their avatars.

Castronova, Edward. 2008. *A test of the law of demand in a virtual world: Exploring the petri dish approach to social science.* CESifo Working Paper No. 2355, July. http://papers.ssrn.com/sol3/papers.cfm?abstract_id=1173642.

This research paper describes an experiment conducted to examine economic behavior within *Arden,* a virtual world designed for academic research dealing with users' behavior. The paper's findings provide evidence that some economic laws that are valid in real life are also valid in virtual worlds, suggesting that economic behavior in virtual worlds might be observed to inform an understanding of real-life economic behavior.

Ondrejka, Cory. 2004. Living on the edge: Digital worlds which embrace the real world. http://ssrn.com/abstract=555661.

This research paper argues that even though many virtual worlds strive to ensure that virtual worlds remain independent from real-world laws and economies, it may be ideal for virtual worlds to develop strong legal and economic connections to the real world in order to be most successful.

Websites

1UP.com
http://1up.com

1UP.com is a site devoted to providing video game news, reviews, and other information as well as community-based content such as game guides from the site's users. The site, which was founded in 1999 by Ziff Davis media, is named for the popular video game term "1UP" that has been used for decades to denote that a player has been awarded an extra life (and previously by pinball machines to indicate the start of a player's turn). *1UP.com* is currently operated by IGN Entertainment, a division of NewsCorp that also operates a number of other sites related to video games and other entertainment.

The Daedalus Project
http://www.nickyee.com/daedalus/

This site includes reports from six years of surveys investigating the users of massively multiplayer online role-playing games conducted by virtual worlds researcher Nick Yee between 2002 and 2009. The project was launched as a successor to Yee's surveys of users of the online role-playing game *EverQuest* conducted in 2000 and 2001. Yee continued the project while a doctoral student at Stanford University in Palo Alto, California. Yee announced that data collection for the project would be temporarily placed in hibernation in 2009, but the existing reports remain available on the site.

Gamer Widow
http://www.gamerwidow.com

This site provides an online community for people in relationships with others who play video games excessively. The "widow" term is used loosely to describe males or females who are in relationships of any kind (e.g., partners, family members, friends) of people who abuse games. Also provided are support and resources for individuals who overuse video games themselves. The site is not operated by mental health professionals, but it provides information on how professional resources can be accessed.

GameRankings
http://www.gamerankings.com

GameRankings is a site owned by CBS Interactive that aggregates reviews for video games from a variety of sources to produce an average rating score for each game listed on the site, then ranks those games using the aggregate ratings. The site was founded in 2000.

GameSpot
http://www.gamespot.com

GameSpot is a video game journalism site that provides news, previews, and reviews about video games. Founded in 1996, the site is currently owned by CBS Interactive. There are also some international versions of the *GameSpot* site, including *GameSpot UK* (United Kingdom), *GameSpot AU* (Australia), and *GameSpot Japan* (Japan).

GameSpy
http://www.gamespy.com

GameSpy is a video game related website operated by IGN Entertainment, a division of NewsCorp that also operates a number of other websites related to video games and other entertainment. *GameSpy* originated in 1996 as *PlanetQuake.com*, a site dedicated to hosting software and news related to the first-person shooter video game *Quake*. After being reorganized and renamed several times, the site eventually became *GameSpy*, which in its current version provides news, reviews, and other information and services related to video games.

GameStats
http://www.gamestats.com

GameStats is a website that is operated by IGN Entertainment, a division of NewsCorp that also manages several other websites related to video games and other entertainment. Founded in 2002, *GameStats* assesses the popularity of video games by tracking data related to ratings from video game reviewers, Web traffic for IGN-hosted pages devoted to specific games, and other measures related to games' popularity.

IGN
http://www.ign.com/

IGN (which originally stood for Imagine Games Network) is a video game journalism site operated by IGN Entertainment, a division of NewsCorp that also operates several other websites related to video games and other entertainment. The site was founded in 1996 and provides news, reviews, and other information about video games, including online games.

Massively
http://massively.joystiq.com

This site is a journalistic site dedicated to providing news and information specifically focused on massively multiplayer online games. Founded in 2007, the site is part of the Joystiq network of video game-related sites, which is owned by AOL. To maintain journalistic standards, the site specifies that *Massively* does not accept remuneration such as stipends or travel expenses.

MMOData.net
http://www.mmodata.net

MMOData.net was created in 2009 by information technology worker Ibe Van Geel to carry on the work begun by *MMOGCHART. COM* creator Bruce Woodcock when Woodcock stopped updating *MMOGCHART.COM* in 2008. Like its predecessor, *MMOData.net* uses a variety of sources to provide regularly updated information about the population of massively multiplayer online games, including virtual worlds.

MMOGCHART.COM
http://www.mmogchart.com

MMOGCHART.COM was launched in 2002 by video game industry analyst Bruce Woodcock to track and document user activity in massively multiplayer online role-playing games, including virtual worlds. Information about the populations of game sites is provided based on a variety of sources ranging from news and press releases to anonymous reports. Woodcock stopped updating the site in 2008, but historical data from before that time are still available at the site.

MMOHut
http://mmohut.com

MMOHut provides news, reviews, ratings, and other information about hundreds of free-to-play MMO (massively multiplayer online) games, excluding online games that require players to pay a fee to play them.

MMORPG.com
http://www.mmorpg.com

MMORPG.com is a site dedicated to news, reviews, community forums, and other information pertaining to MMORPGs (massively multiplayer online role-playing games), including virtual worlds. Founded in 2002 by current president and CEO Craig McGregor, the site boasts more than 1 million registered members.

MMOSite
http://www.mmosite.com

MMOSite, founded by the TM Group in 2005, is a site that provides news, ratings, and other information about MMO (massively multiplayer online) games, including virtual worlds.

MobyGames
http://www.mobygames.com

MobyGames is a website that provides an extensive database of video games that includes information about both games currently available and games that are no longer available. *MobyGames* was launched by Jim Leonard, Brian Hirt, and David Berk in 1999, and it relies on contributions from users of the site who add and edit entries to expand its descriptions of more than 50,000 video games.

The MUD Connector
http://www.mudconnect.com

The Mud Connector is a website that provides news, reviews, links, and other information related to the text-based online virtual environments known as MUDs (multi-user dungeons). The site was founded by Andrew Cowan in 1995.

MudStats
http://www.mudstats.com

MudStats is a site that provides continuously updated data describing activity on hundreds of the text-based online environments known as MUDs (multi-user dungeons). Information provided for each MUD includes connection address, genre, current number of online users, average number of users online in the past 30 days, and maximum number of users online in the past 30 days.

The Norrathian Scrolls: A Study of EverQuest
http://www.nickyee.com/eqt/

This site provides a comprehensive list of findings from a series of surveys examining users of the online role-playing game *EverQuest* conducted by virtual worlds researcher Nick Yee in 2000 and 2001 when he was an undergraduate student at Haverford College in Haverford, Pennsylvania. The report describes data describing users' demographics, activity in the game, social relationships, problematic use, and more.

Second Life Blogs
http://community.secondlife.com

The community section of the companion website for the virtual world *Second Life* provides regular news and information about the virtual world from its creators, Linden Lab. Regular updates provide visitors with information about notable events being held in the virtual world, reports of economic activity, updated features and technological elements in the virtual world, and more.

Second Life Grid Survey
http://gridsurvey.com/

The *Second Life Grid Survey* is a site managed by Tyche Shepherd since 2008 that provides continuously updated information about activity in the virtual world *Second Life,* including information about virtual land ownership, user population size and activity, economic indicators, warnings and disciplinary actions taken against the virtual world's users, and much more. The site is not affiliated with *Second Life* developer Linden Labs.

Second Life Wiki
http://wiki.secondlife.com

The *Second Life Wiki* is a site about the virtual world *Second Life* that is collaboratively developed and maintained by Linden Lab, the creators of *Second Life,* and the virtual world's users. (A "wiki" is a website whose pages can be added and edited quickly by site users, named for a Hawaiian word meaning "fast" or "quick"). The site contains an ever-growing group of thousands of pages with information about using the virtual world.

Terra Nova
http://terranova.blogs.com

Terra Nova describes itself as "an interdisciplinary weblog about the intersection of society, simulation, and play." The site was founded in 2003 by Edward Castronova, Julian Dibbell, Dan Hunter, and Greg Lastowka to provide a venue for discussion and commentary about virtual worlds from prominent scholars and workers in relevant industries. The site has welcomed postings from more than 30 prominent contributors.

Top Mud Sites
http://www.topmudsites.com

Top Mud Sites is a website that ranks thousands of the text-based online environments known as MUDs (multi-user dungeons) based on ratings provided by MUD users.

Virtual Worlds Observatory
http://www.vwobservatory.com/

This site is a repository for academic articles, book chapters, and papers produced by team members working with the Virtual

Worlds Observatory, a series of studies investigating behavior and interactions in virtual worlds and online communities. The Virtual Worlds Observatory's studies involved researchers from several research universities and was supported in part by industry partners and the National Science Foundation, the Army Research Institute, the Air Force Research Laboratory, and the Army Research Laboratory.

Virtual Economy Research Network (VERN)
http://virtual-economy.org/

This site, founded in 2006 by the Helsinki Institute for Information Technology, provides information and discussion about economic issues related to virtual worlds.

The WorldForge Project

This site is the home of a collaborative project to provide the tools needed for developers to create their own virtual worlds free of charge. Founded in 1998 with the original name *Altima*, the project was originally an attempt to create a large-scale virtual world comparable to the online role-playing game *Ultima Online*. Since then, the project has evolved to become a community of volunteer developers working to create tools for virtual world designers that can be freely used and modified in the open-source software tradition.

WoW Insider

This site is dedicated specifically to news and other information about the online role-playing game *World of Warcraft*. Launched in 2005, the site is part of the Joystiq network of video game-related sites, which is owned by AOL. The site is not affiliated with or supported by *World of Warcraft* creators Blizzard Entertainment.

Glossary of Terms

U sers and creators of virtual worlds and related applications rely on a unique lexicon of terms and jargon to describe objects and events that take place in those online environments. Below is a partial glossary of unique terms (or unique usages of common words) that are relevant to virtual worlds, either because they are used in virtual worlds by users or because they are relevant to the industry. Some of these words are used in this book, while other words defined here are commonly used terms and jargon related to virtual worlds that are not used in this book. Many other unique terms exist that are used by certain groups in virtual worlds or in relevant professions, but this glossary includes some of the more common terms used by relatively large numbers of people involved with virtual worlds and related applications.

Adverworld A virtual world operated by a commercial entity, or by an organization funded by a commercial entity, for the purpose of exposing its users to advertising content and product placement from that commercial entity within the virtual world.

AFK Away from keyboard. Used to describe a user who is logged in on a virtual world but is temporarily inactive and not attending to the virtual world. Often used as an announcement signaling that the user is temporarily inactive (e.g., to use the washroom or answer a telephone).

Aggro Short for "aggression," this term describes attacks from computer-controlled nonplayer characters on users' character avatars in online role-playing games. A user's character avatar can generate aggro from enemy nonplayer characters accidentally or purposely by taking actions such as moving within a certain distance of the nonplayer character, moving into the nonplayer character's line of sight, or entering an area in the game environment that otherwise triggers a response from hostile nonplayer characters.

AI   Artificial Intelligence; used to describe the programmed decision making and behavior of computer-controlled nonplayer characters in online role-playing games, virtual worlds, and other video games and simulations.

Alt   An alternate character avatar owned by a virtual world user in addition to the user's primary character avatar. Most virtual worlds allow the creation and operation of one or more alts but do not allow a user to have multiple character avatars logged in on a virtual world simultaneously.

Attribute   Any of several variable traits assigned to characters in an online role-playing game, such as strength or hit points. Users can typically improve their attributes by gaining experience and levels within the game, by obtaining and using certain virtual items, and by temporary modification of attributes through character actions such as magical spells.

Avatar   The graphical character that a virtual world user controls to represent himself or herself within the virtual world. The term is borrowed from the Hindu use of the term to describe a physical incarnation of a Hindi deity. Shortened forms include av, avy, and avie.

Bank   A term used to describe a location within some virtual worlds where a user can store virtual objects when the user cannot or does not want to carry those objects on the character avatar's person.

Bio   A term used in virtual worlds as a euphemism for a visit to the washroom. This term allows the user to quickly indicate away-from-keyboard status to other users.

Buff   Actions taken by a user to prepare for combat or other tasks in an online role-playing game. Usually refers to special actions, such as magic spells, that temporarily enhance a character's abilities, such as hit points. Conversely, a debuff is such an action taken on a character that decreases its abilities, which is usually performed by a user on an enemy character or by an enemy character on a user.

Camp   To occupy a location in an online role-playing game while waiting for another character or event, such as the arrival of another user or a reoccurring nonplayer character. Particularly used in cases where a user character's avatar camps in wait to attack a character.

Class   In online role-playing games, any of a series of thematic character types that define the skills and general attributes of the character. The class of a user's character avatar is typically selected by the user when the user creates the character. Although the specific names of classes in different online role-playing games vary, many games include similar class types, such as a class that is adept at close-quarters combat, a class with unique abilities to heal other characters, or a class skilled at long-range combat. The specific strengths and weaknesses of classes vary, and most games carefully balance classes so that no class tends to have a consistent advantage throughout the game's content over others and so that some game tasks encourage cooperation between users with character avatars of different classes. Some games also feature classes that are better suited for novice users or advanced users based on the amount of difficulty involved in mastering the skills associated with that class.

Crafting   An activity in many online role-playing games that users' character avatars can engage in to convert collected virtual raw materials into usable virtual goods. For example, a character might be able to mine metals in the game and convert them into weapons. Compared to the virtual combat and adventures many people may associate with online role-playing games, crafting might be viewed as a relatively pedestrian activity.

Ding   A one-word announcement often made by users of online role-playing games when their character avatars advance to another level by accumulating a set number of experience points. Derived from the sound some games generate when a character's level increases.

Emotes   Commands in a virtual world that a user can enter to make his or her character avatar execute a gesture or other nonverbal behavior, such as laughing, nodding, waving, and so forth.

Experience Points   A quantity of score points accumulated in online role-playing games by users' character avatars for completing tasks in the game, such as defeating enemy characters or completing assigned quests. A user's character avatar begins the game with no experience points and accumulates them throughout the game. Experience points, like other attributes of the character, are preserved from game session to game session. A user's character avatar increases in level upon reaching a predetermined number of experience points, which typically awards that character with enhanced traits, skills, and access to game features. Experience points systems were also used in earlier computer role-playing games and in the paper-and-pencil games that preceded them. Sometimes abbreviated as "exp" or the approximate abbreviation "XP."

F2P   Free to Play; used to describe online role-playing games, virtual worlds, and other online games and communities that do not charge users a subscription fee. With no income from subscriptions, these applications typically generate revenue through advertising, optional fees for premium virtual goods and services, or transaction fees for users who exchange virtual currency for real money.

Gold   The virtual money in some virtual worlds, whether the unit of currency is formally called gold within the virtual world or not. In some cases, this virtual currency can be exchanged for real-world currency through either an official purchase/exchange mechanism within the virtual world or a black market in virtual worlds that forbid the sale of virtual goods for real currency.

Gold Farmer   A virtual world user who engages in activity in the virtual world for the specific purpose of generating virtual currency and selling that virtual currency to other users for real-world money. The practice, which allows gold farmers to generate income from time spent in the virtual world and allows those who patronize gold farmers to gain virtual assets without spending much time in the virtual world, is frowned upon or forbidden in many virtual worlds. In other virtual worlds, particularly those that encourage real-life economic activity, practices where users invest time in the game to earn money are allowed and even encouraged.

Grid   In the virtual world *Second Life,* the interconnected group of computer network servers that create the virtual environment, services, functions, and features that make up a complete and continuous virtual world. The term can also be used to describe the complete virtual environment that they simulate, which has the virtual geographic shape of a rectangular flat Earth. An avatar can travel to all places in a grid, but not to another grid because each grid is a distinct virtual environment. Most *Second Life* users are on the main grid, but there are also preview and testing grids that staff and some users occupy. The term is also sometimes used in other virtual worlds in a similar fashion to describe the virtual world's entire simulated environment.

Griefer   A virtual world user whose primary purpose in the virtual world is to harass, annoy, or create problems for other users. For a griefer, misbehavior supersedes other goals in the virtual world such as completing goals in a game or earning virtual currency. Penalties applied in the virtual world, such as suspension from the virtual world, are usually not an adequate deterrent to griefing because griefers are not concerned about their performance in the virtual world. Some griefers engage in relatively innocuous pranks, while others perform offensive and abusive stunts.

Grind   The act of completing mundane and repetitive tasks to accomplish an objective in the virtual world, such as killing large groups of unchallenging enemies to earn virtual currency or gain experience levels in an online role-playing game. The term can be used as a verb to describe the act of completing such a series of tasks or as a noun to describe the tasks themselves.

Group   A temporary group of users' character avatars who join together by mutual consent of their users in an online role-playing game in order to complete one or more tasks. Characters in a group can interact in ways that are not possible between characters who are not in a group. For example, they may be able to cast spells to assist one another. Players may form groups to accomplish tasks that are otherwise difficult or impossible, but they may also form groups in order to socialize while playing. A user leaves a group voluntarily or automatically upon ending a game session, and a group is disbanded when all group members leave it. Some games use alternate terms for this type of group. In the online role-playing game *The Lord of the Rings Online*, for example, this type of group is called a fellowship.

Guild A long-term group of users' character avatars who join together by mutual consent of their users in an online role-playing game. Unlike a group, membership in a guild does not end when a player ends a game session. A guild often has a hierarchical organizational structure, either through official positions in the game or unofficial positions defined by guild members. Users in a guild may have long-term responsibilities and may schedule to meet and complete game activities. Some games use alternate terms for this type of group. In the online role-playing game *The Lord of the Rings Online*, for example, this type of group is called a kinship.

Hit Point A unit of a character's health in an online role-playing game. A character has a number value of maximum hit points and a number value of current hit points. When a character is damaged in combat with other characters, the character loses hit points. A character gains hit points by healing over time or through various available treatments until reaching the character's maximum hit points. A character's maximum hit points will usually increase as the character's level increases.

HUD Head Up Display; the display of information and command options shown on a virtual world user's screen as an overlay superimposed on the user's view of the virtual environment.

Instance A location in a virtual world that is generated privately for a user or group of users when entered instead of being shared across all of the virtual world's users. For example, two users of an online role-playing game whose characters can interact in a general region of the virtual environment and who both enter a specific instanced cave would have separate but identical instances of the cave created for them in the virtual world. In the instances, the two users could experience the virtual world, but they would not encounter one another's characters until leaving the separate instances and returning to the shared virtual space.

Interactivity The term used by some researchers to describe one of the three characteristics of a true virtual world. An online environment that has interactivity is one where users can interact with and influence the environment and each other with their actions, as opposed to an environment where users do not interact with each other or where users' actions do not influence the environment and experiences of others in it. Note that this term has other conceptual meanings in research areas not related to virtual worlds.

Inventory   A virtual world character avatar's virtual possessions, carried on the character's person, and the amount of virtual space available to hold them. A character can typically use and trade items in that character's inventory and pick up more items to add them to the inventory. When a character's inventory is full, the character must drop items, trade them, give them away, or locate a bank to store them.

In-World   A term sometimes used, particularly in the virtual world *Second Life,* to describe the state of being logged in on a virtual world, as well as virtual persons, places, objects, and events that take place in a virtual world.

IRL   In Real Life.

Island   In *Second Life,* a piece of virtual land surrounded by virtual water to isolate it from other land masses, just like an island in real life. A user or group of users might choose to lease an entire virtual island to dedicate it to a distinct purpose, such as a virtual business or a real-life university's virtual campus. Other users may lease smaller and less isolated pieces of virtual property or not lease property at all.

Lag   The state that occurs when there are delays in the correspondence between a virtual world's representation and the user's input caused by a slow Internet connection, the user's computer application running slowly, an issue with a virtual world server, or other problems. For the user, lag will create the appearance of jerky or frozen motion in the virtual world and the virtual world will seem unresponsive to the user's commands.

Level   A numerical value assigned to describe the experience and general prowess of a user's character avatar in an online role-playing game. A character gains experience points by accomplishing tasks in the game, and the character's level increases at set intervals of accumulated experience points in the game. For example, a Level 20 character has generally accomplished more in a game than a Level 16 character but less than a Level 37 character. As characters increase in level, their attributes, skills, and access to game features may be enhanced. Levels may also be assigned to specific traits or attributes of the character, as well as to items and other game elements. The term can be used as a noun to describe a character's level status or as a verb to describe the act of increasing a character's level.

Level Cap   The maximum level that an online role-playing game allows a user's character avatar to achieve. A level cap may be the same for all users or may be unique to certain groups of users, such as users who are not paying a subscription fee. Many games slowly increase their level caps over time as new game content is introduced to motivate users to continue playing or return to the game from a period of inactivity.

LFG   Looking For a Group; used in online-role-playing games to announce that a user is seeking other users to form a temporary group to complete a task.

LFM   Looking For More; used in online role-playing games to announce that a partial group of two more users is seeking one or more other users to complete a temporary group to complete a task.

Linden Dollar   In the virtual world *Second Life,* the unit of currency within the virtual world. The unit of currency takes its name from Linden Lab, the company that created *Second Life.* Also referred to as Lindens and L$.

Linden Scripting Language   The specific programming language that *Second Life* users can employ to control the behavior of objects that they create in the virtual world. Named after *Second Life* creators Linden Lab, Linden Scripting Language is similar to some other common computer programming languages, but its specifics are unique to *Second Life.* Although a *Second Life* user does not need to learn or use advanced skills such as the Linden Scripting Language to use the virtual world, it is one of the features of the virtual world that allow users to create a nearly unlimited variety of virtual goods and services within the virtual environment.

Log   To end a session in a virtual world. The term is also sometimes used to describe records of a session in an online community, such as a copy of the text generated in a MUD session.

Loot   In online role-playing games, to take virtual items from a defeated enemy character and add them to the inventory of one's own character avatar. The term is also used to describe the items that are obtained from this activity.

Lore   The source material used to guide the setting, plot, and features of an online role-playing game. For example, the online role-playing game *Star Wars: The Old Republic* uses the *Star Wars* film franchise and associated media such as novels and television series as its lore, while the online role-playing game *World of Warcraft* uses previous video games in the *Warcraft* series as its lore. Games vary in terms of the prominence that their lore has in game play and the extent to which they are faithful to the content of that lore, but in many cases games that use other media as their lore must make some adaptations for the sake of creating an enjoyable game.

MMORPG   Massively Multiplayer Online Role-Playing Game; used to describe online role-playing games, including but not limited to virtual worlds, that allow a large number of users to log on and interact with one another within the game environment. Alternate terms include MMO, MMOG.

Mob A nonplayer character in an online game, including a virtual world or a MUD, who is not motionless in the game environment but instead moves around of its own accord. The term is an abbreviation of "mobile," and was used by *MUD* cocreator Richard Bartle to describe such characters in that early text-based online role-playing game who moved from room to room in the game environment. In more recent online role-playing games, the term is often used to describe generic nonplayer characters that appear in the game environment, are generally indistinguishable from other similar nonplayer characters, and are hostile to users' character avatars.

MUD Multi-User Dungeon; used to describe a genre of text-based online environments, usually online role-playing games, patterned after the original *MUD* text-based online role-playing game created by Roy Trubshaw and Richard Bartle. The original *MUD* and the genre of MUDs that followed it are generally acknowledged as predecessors of graphical online role-playing games and virtual worlds. MUD is also used as a general term encompassing both MUDs and the many variations of the genre, including MOOs (MUD, object-oriented) and MUSHes (multi-user shared hallucination). These MUD-type variations are generally distinguished from MUDs and from one another by trends in the structure of the environments' programmed code and the nature of users' possible interaction with the environment allowed by the code (e.g., whether or not a character is able to create new virtual objects and add them to the games). There are also trends in terms of differences between the types of behavior engaged in by users of different MUD-type genres (e.g., MUSH games typically involve extensive role-playing).

Nerf The practice of reducing the relative advantage of a specific character type, such as a race or class, or an object such as a specific weapon or type of weapon. Nerfing is carried out by a game's staff to remove advantages that may be held by one character type over other, vary the difficulty of game elements, or encourage users to use different virtual items and strategies while using the game. The term references the NERF brand of foam toys, implying that the administrative practice of reducing the effectiveness of virtual characters and items is analogous to the harmlessness of NERF toy weapons. Some nerfing by game staff has relatively minor effects on game dynamics, while nerfing adjustments can influence game dynamics dramatically and elicit impassioned responses from players.

NPC Nonplayer Character; in a virtual world, particularly an online role-playing game, a character that is computer-controlled rather than a user's character avatar.

PC Bang An Internet café in South Korea whose patrons play a small hourly fee to play online games at the PC Bang's high-quality personal computers. PC Bangs also provide services such as food and drink and may allow users to smoke while playing. The social atmosphere, comfort, and high-quality hardware make PC Bangs a popular venue for video game players even though the home broadband Internet penetration rate of South Korea is among the highest in the world. Professional online game competitions in South Korea sometimes host entry-level competitions at PC bangs to identify candidates for careers as professional video game players.

Persistence   The term used by some researchers to describe one of the three characteristics of a true virtual world. An online environment that has persistence is one that continues to exist and respond to the actions of other users whether a user is present or not, as opposed to an online environment that is temporarily created for the exclusive use of one or more users and eliminated or held static when those users end a game session.

Physicality   The term used by some researchers to describe one of the three characteristics of a true virtual world. An online environment that has physicality is a three-dimensional graphical environment that simulates some physical laws of the real world and that can be generally perceived from a first-person perspective, though the first-person perspective in virtual worlds is often actually a view from just behind and above the users' character avatar to aid the user in controlling the character and viewing the character's immediate surroundings. Some conceptualizations of virtual worlds do not consider all of these traits to be necessary for an environment to be called a virtual world. For example, some consider text-based MUDs to be virtual worlds even though they have no graphics at all.

Ping   In virtual worlds, the amount of time needed for data to travel through the online network between a users' computer and the server providing the virtual world. Ping is usually described in milliseconds in this context, with a higher number indicating more delay in communication and a consequently less fluid game experience. High ping may result from issues with the user's computer, the virtual world server, or the network between them, as well as physical distance between the user and the server. For example, a person in Australia using a virtual world server in the United States will likely have higher ping than a user in the United States. Minor differences in ping will not be noticeable to a virtual world user, but higher ping will create lag that may reduce the quality of the user's experience in the virtual world and affect the user's ability to complete tasks and actions effectively in the virtual world.

Power Leveling   The practice of playing online role-playing games for the specific purpose of rapidly increasing a user character's level without regard to other game features and plot elements. This may be accomplished by playing exclusively in an area that provides a character with opportunities to quickly gain experience points and related rewards. Another power-leveling strategy is accompanying more experienced users' characters on tasks that would normally be too challenging for a user's character in order to earn game rewards rapidly. Although these tactics may be frowned upon in some games, other practices described as power leveling, such as paying a service to increase the level of a character by playing the game with the user's character, are viewed even more negatively and are forbidden by some games' providers.

Prim   The simplest virtual object unit in the virtual world *Second Life*. An abbreviation of "primitive," a prim is a simple three-dimensional virtual shape created by a *Second Life* user. A prim can be created in a variety of shapes and sizes, such as a cube or a cylinder, and can also be sculpted into more complex shapes and given textures. These prims are used to create a number of virtual objects in *Second Life*, such as furniture, vehicles, and more. Although some virtual objects in *Second Life* are made from a single prim, many are created by combining several prims to form a complex structure. A *Second Life* user does not need to create or work with prims to use the virtual world, but many users do so in order to create new virtual objects for use by themselves and others.

PVE   Player versus Environment; used to describe an online role-playing game, or an area within such a game, where game users' characters engage exclusively in combat against computer-controlled player characters rather than against other users' characters.

PVP   Player versus Player; used to describe an online role-playing game, or an area within such a game, where game users' characters can engage in combat against other users' characters.

Quest   A task in an online role-playing game that a users' character avatar completes to earn a reward, either alone or in a group with other users' character avatars. Typical rewards for completing a quest include experience points, virtual items such as weapons, virtual currency, and access to new locations, privileges, or challenges in the game. Quests typically involve defeating one or more computer-controlled enemy characters, obtaining or delivering one or more virtual items, or protecting a computer-controlled ally character from harm. Some quests are necessary to the advancement of the game's plot, while others are optional "side quests" that are not central to the game's primary story.

Quest Chain   A group of quests in an online role-playing game that a user completes in sequence, with completion of one quest in the series making the next quest in the series available. A quest chain may be integral to the plot of a game, a prerequisite to a key element of the game, or an optional and peripheral series of tasks not related to the central plot of the game.

Race   Any of a number of mostly fictional species and breeds that characters may represent in an online role-playing game, often including humans but also fantastic races such as elves and orcs. The various races of online role-playing game characters are usually anthropomorphic to some extent. The term is not typically used in this context to refer to ethnic, cultural, and geographical distinctions between humans as it is in other settings.

Raid   A large-scale group event in an online role-playing game that requires cooperation among a group of many users to complete, such as a difficult quest. The number of player characters involved in a raid can number in the dozens, so scheduling and organizing a raid requires some effort on the part of the players.

Resident   The term used by *Second Life* creators Linden Lab to describe the virtual world's users.

Rez   The act of creating a virtual object in the virtual world *Second Life.* The term is borrowed from the science-fiction film *Tron,* where it is used as an abbreviation for "resolution" to describe the appearance of a character or object in the film's virtual environment. The date on which a *Second Life* user's character avatar was created is often called a "rez day" by the virtual world's users, and some users celebrate a character avatar's rez day in *Second Life* each year like a birthday. Alternately, this term is used by online role-playing game users to describe the act of resurrecting a user's defeated character.

RL   Real Life.

Roll   The act of creating a new character avatar by a user in a virtual world, particularly in an online role-playing game. The term references the process of character creation in paper-and-pencil role-playing games such as *Dungeons and Dragons,* which involved a user rolling dice to determine a character's skills and traits. This process is automated in online role-playing games and may not actually involve any random roll decisions by the game at all if characters in a given race and class start with identical traits. The term is also used in some online environments to describe the act of using a random number generator to resolve uncertainties and disputes, such as which member in a group should receive a virtual item earned by the group.

RP   Role Play; used in a variety of online applications ranging from MUDs to online role-playing games to other virtual worlds to describe the practice by some users of taking on a character's role much as one would play a part in a dramatic performance. The practice in online environments emulates role-playing sessions using paper-and pencil role-playing games such as *Dungeons and Dragons,* in which users would assemble to act out their characters' actions "in character." Role players in online environments take turns typing detailed descriptions of their characters' dialogue and actions to accompany their use of the online environment's commands. The result is something of a collaborative scene with each contributor having contributed elements to the narrative. A role-playing session can last for hours to accommodate the time required for users to create the typed poses in sequence. In some online environments, such as certain MUD-type games, role-playing is the norm or even required, while in others, such as online role-playing games, only a minority of characters actually engage in extensive in-character role-playing activity.

RVR   Realm versus Realm; used to describe an online role-playing game, or an area within such a game, where game users' characters can engage in combat against other users' characters only when the combatants are representatives of opposing factions in the game. The "realm" factions in a game are predefined by the game's creators and might be defined by characters' political affiliation, geographic, origin, or species. Players in a game with realm-versus-realm elements choose what predefined faction their character represents when they create a character and choose the character's traits. Some games offer similar guild-versus-guild combat where users can form their own factions by affiliating with other users, then engage in combat with other users' characters who represent opposing user-created factions.

Server   Technically, a piece of computer hardware used to deliver an online application's content and events to an application's connected users and receive input from the users in order to connect them to the application and to each other. In reference to virtual worlds, the term is commonly used more metaphorically to refer to multiple coexisting versions of a virtual world. The multiple iterations of the virtual world are necessary because the group of physical computer servers hosting a virtual world online is limited in terms of how many simultaneous users it can support (often numbering in the thousands). To allow the virtual world to host more players than a server can handle and to ensure that a virtual world's environment is not overcrowded with users' character avatars, multiple servers (each of which is actually provided by multiple physical computer servers in most cases) provide multiple versions of the virtual world. In some virtual worlds, different servers have different features (e.g., one server might allow different forms of combat than another), while some virtual worlds' servers are identical to each other except for the users who populate them.

Shard   A synonym for servers in virtual worlds used to describe the multiple versions of a virtual world that are hosted to accommodate large numbers of users and prevent a virtual world's environment from becoming overcrowded with users' character avatars. The term was used to provide an explanation in the game's plot for the different game servers for the online role-playing game *Ultima Online;* the servers were purported to represent different copies of the game's fictional world that were created when a magical crystal was destroyed during the plot line of an earlier game in the *Ultima* series. The term has since become very common, and "sharding" is even used in contexts unrelated to virtual worlds to describe the practice of sharing information in large databases across multiple computer servers that can be accessed separately.

Solo To complete one or more tasks in an online role-playing game alone without the assistance of other users. This term is often used to describe a user's character avatar completing a task alone when a group of user character avatars is often required. Although online role-playing games allow and encourage interaction and cooperation between users, the majority of many games' content and tasks can be "soloed."

Spawn A character's sudden appearance in a place within a virtual world. For example, some computer-controlled nonplayer characters spawn at random places in areas in the virtual environment to populate the game, and some particular nonplayer characters "re-spawn" in a set location after they have been defeated. This term can also be used to describe the reappearance of a player's character avatar after the character is defeated or otherwise temporarily absent from the virtual environment.

Teleport To instantly move one's character avatar from one place to another in a virtual world. Most virtual worlds have some sort of teleport function to reduce tedious travel, though its use may be limited in online role-playing games to maintain challenge in the game. Sometimes the abbreviation "port" is used.

Text Chat The act of using a chat window to communicate via instant messaging within a virtual world. Many virtual worlds allow users to engage in text chat with groups of varying size, ranging from private messages ("tells") with a single other user to discussions with users in the immediate vicinity, an established group, or all users in a region.

Toad In some MUD-type text-based online communities, this term is used as a verb to describe the complete and permanent removal of a character from the game environment. This effectively bans the user from the online community and "kills" the user's character, as no record of the character remains after the character is toaded. The ability to toad a character is reserved for administrators of a virtual environment, and toading is typically only performed as a disciplinary action for severe offenses against the communities rules or norms. The most well-known use of the term was probably the toading of the "Mr. Bungle" character in the *LambdaMOO* text-based virtual community, which was enacted unilaterally by one of the community's administrators after he was the perpetrator of the infamous "rape in cyberspace" incident in *LambdaMOO*. In some other role-playing games, though, toading merely describes a magical command that turns a user's character into a toad with limited powers, usually temporarily.

Toon A term used by some in virtual worlds to describe an alternate character avatar a user maintains in the same virtual world, particularly an alternate character avatar that is not considered the user's primary character avatar in the virtual world. Most virtual worlds allow multiple character avatars to be created under the same account, though the different characters are usually not allowed to be active in the virtual world at the same time.

UI User Interface; the features that a virtual world (or any computer application) uses to provide information to the user and receive commands from the user. The UI includes the design and content of the graphic display, the control scheme, and other features.

Voice Chat The act of using a microphone and a headset, earpiece, or speakers to communicate with other users via voice telephony within a virtual world. Many virtual worlds allow voice chat between small groups of users, such as users in a voluntarily created temporary group, but in most cases voice chat is not available among large groups or without consent of all involved users in order to prevent abuse and to limit noise in the virtual environment.

Wizard An administrator of an online community, particularly a non-commercial online environment such as a text-based MUD-type game, who has substantial powers to create and control content and events within the online environment. Wizards typically represent a very small portion of an online community's population. Even a large online community may only have a handful of wizards at most who are in charge of the community's administration. The term is a reference to the user's administrative power in the environment and not to any in-character status of the character; even in a fantasy-themed role-playing game, a Wiz character need not have any sort of in-character magical powers or special abilities.

Index

About the Author

JAMES D. IVORY (PhD, University of North Carolina at Chapel Hill, 2005) is an assistant professor in the Department of Communication at Virginia Polytechnic Institute and State University (a.k.a. Virginia Tech). He conducts research dealing with the social and psychological dimensions of new media and communication technologies, particularly the content and effects of interactive communication technologies such as video games, virtual worlds, and simulations.

Dr. Ivory is the founding director of the Virginia Tech Gaming and Media Effects Research Laboratory (VT G. A.M. E. R. Lab), a small research facility hosted by the Virginia Tech Department of Communication. He is currently the vice chair of the International Communication Association's Game Studies special interest group and will serve as chair of the group for two years beginning in 2013. He has also served as head of the Association for Education in Journalism and Mass Communication's Communication Technology division and the Association for Education in Journalism and Mass Communication's Graduate Education interest group. He has taught university courses on communication technology, media effects, mass communication theory, research methods, basic Web production, and public speaking.

Born and raised in Cody, Wyoming, Dr. Ivory lives in Blacksburg, Virginia, with his wife Adrienne Holz Ivory and their two children.